Taking Ideology Seriously

Recent years have witnessed a resurgence of the 'end of ideology' thesis, not as a theoretical stance but as a reaction to what appears to have been the decline of major ideological families, such as socialism, in a changing world order. Globalization, as well as internal national fragmentation of belief systems, have made it difficult to identify ideology in its conventional formats.

This collection of paper challenges the notion that we are living in a post-ideological age. It offers a theoretical framework for exploring some of the new manifestations of ideologies, and combines this with a series of case-studies relating to recent ideational phenomena, such as populism, environmentalism and Islamic fundamentalism. It reassesses some typologies, such as the left-right axis, as an explanatory device.

This collection of papers is unique in using ideology research to bring together different scholarly perspectives including party-political analysis, the history of ideas, postmarxism, and movement politics.

The purpose of the essays is to revitalize the scholarly understanding of ideology as central to the concerns of political science. Recent political movements are reinterpreted through using new approaches to the analysis of ideology. In so doing we seek to bridge the gap between empirical and theoretical research in the field.

This book was previously published as a special issue of *The Critical Review of International Social and Political Philosophy*.

Gayil Talshir is a lecturer and the head of the Graduate Programme in Citizenship and Democracy, in the Department of Political Science, the Hebrew University of Jerusalem, Israel.

Mathew Humphrey is Senior Lecturer in Politics at the University of Nottingham.

Michael Freeden is Professor of Politics and Director of the Centre for Political Ideologies at the University of Oxford, Professorial Fellow at Mansfield College, Oxford, and ESRC Professorial Fellow 2004–2007.

Taking Ideology Seriously

21st Century Reconfigurations

Edited by Gayil Talshir, Mathew Humphrey and Michael Freeden

Routledge
Taylor & Francis Group
New York London

First published 2006 by Routledge
2 Park Square, Milton Park, Abingdon, Oxon, OX14 4RN

Simultaneously published in the USA and Canada by Routledge
270 Madison Ave, New York, NY 10016

Routledge is an imprint of the Taylor & Francis Group

© 2006 Taylor & Francis Group Ltd

All rights reserved. No part of this book may be reprinted or reproduced or utilised in any form or by any electronic, mechanical, or other means, now known or hereafter invented, including photocopying and recording, or in any information storage or retrieval system, without permission in writing from the publishers.

British Library Cataloguing in Publication Data
A catalogue record for this book is available from the British Library

Library of Congress Cataloging in Publication Data
A catalog record for this book has been requested.

ISBN13: 978-0-7146-5080-7

Contents

Notes on Contributors vi

Preface viii

1. The Phoenix of Ideology
   Gayil Talshir 1

2. Visions of Popular Sovereignty: Mapping the Contested Terrain of Contemporary Western Populisms
   David Laycock 19

3. Ideology and Antagonism in Modern Italy: Poststructuralist Reflections
   James Martin 39

4. The Democratic Ideology of Right–Left and Public Reason in Relation to Rawls's Political Liberalism
   Torben Bech Dyrberg 55

5. Al Qaeda: Ideology and Action
   Jeffrey Haynes 71

6. A Globalist Ideology of Post-Marxism? Hardt and Negri's *Empire*
   Gary K. Browning 87

7. The Intellectual as a Political Actor? Four Models of Theory/Praxis
   Gayil Talshir 103

8. (De)Contesting Ideology: The Struggle over the Meaning of the Struggle over Meaning
   Mathew Humphrey 119

9. Confronting the Chimera of a 'Post-ideological' Age
   Michael Freeden 141

Index 157

Notes on Contributors

Gary K. Browning is Professor of Politics at Oxford Brookes University. He is the author of *Plato and Hegel; Two Modes of Philosophising About Politics* (Garland, 1991), *Hegel and the History of Political Philosophy* (Macmillan, 1999), *Lyotard and the End of Grand Narratives* (UWP, 2000) and *Rethinking R.G. Collingwood: Philosophy, Politics and the Unity of Theory and Practice* (Palgrave, 2004). He has co-edited and co-written other works, including *Understanding Contemporary Society: Theories of the Present* (Sage, 2000). He is co-editor of the journal, *Contemporary Political Theory* (Palgrave/Macmillan) and is currently completing a book on political economy.

Torben Bech Dyrberg is Lecturer in the Department of Social Sciences, Roskilde University, Denmark. Recent publications include 'Right/left in the context of new political frontiers: What's radical politics today?', *Journal of Language and Politics*, 2(2), 2003, pp. 333–361; (with Henrik Paul Bang) 'Governing at close range: demo-elites and laypeople', in Henrik Paul Bang (Ed.), *Governance as Social and Political Communication* (Manchester University Press, 2003), pp. 221–240; 'The political and politics in discourse analysis', in Simon Critchley (Ed.), *Laclau: A Critical Reader* (Routledge, 2004), pp. 241–255.

Michael Freeden is Professor of Politics and Director of the Centre for Political Ideologies at the University of Oxford, Professorial Fellow at Mansfield College, Oxford, and ESRC Professorial Fellow 2004–2007. Among his books are *The New Liberalism: An Ideology of Social Reform* (Clarendon Press, 1978); *Liberalism Divided: A Study in British Political Thought 1914–1939* (Clarendon Press, 1986); *Rights* (Open University Press, 1991); *Ideologies and Political Theory: A Conceptual Approach* (Clarendon Press, 1996); *Reassessing Political Ideologies: The Durability of Dissent* (Ed.) (Routledge, 2001); *A Very Short Introduction to Ideology* (Oxford University Press, 2003); *Liberal Languages: Ideological Imaginations and 20th Century Progressive Thought* (Princeton, 2005). He is the founder-editor of the *Journal of Political Ideologies*.

Jeffrey Haynes is Professor of Politics at London Metropolitan University, where he teaches courses on international relations. Recent articles and books include: 'Comparative politics and "globalisation"', *European Political Science*, 2(3), 2003; 'Tracing connections between comparative politics and globalisation', *Third World Quarterly*, 24(6), 2003; 'Religion and international relations: what are the issues?', *International Politics*, 41(3), 2004; *Comparative Politics in a Globalizing World*, 2005; *Palgrave Advances in Development Studies*, 2005.

Mathew Humphrey is Senior Lecturer in Politics at the University of Nottingham. His main area of research is in political theory and its relationship to environmental problems. Publications include *Political Theory and the Environment: a Reassessment* (Ed.) (2001) and *Preservation versus the People? Nature, Ecology, and Political Philosophy* (2002).

David Laycock is a Professor of Political Science at Simon Fraser University in Burnaby, British Columbia. His is author of *Populism and Democratic Thought in the Canadian Prairies* (1990) and *The New Right and Democracy in Canada* (2001), editor of *Representation and Democratic Theory* (2004), and co-editor of *Studies in Comparative Political Economy and Public Policy*, a research series published by the University of Toronto Press.

James Martin is Senior Lecturer in Politics at Goldsmiths College, University of London, UK. He has published research on modern, particularly Italian, political theory and political ideologies. He is author of *Gramsci's Political Analysis* (1998), co-author (with Steve Bastow) of *Third Way Discourse* (2002) and editor of the four-volume *Antonio Gramsci: Critical Assessments* (2001). He has recently co-edited (with Terrell Carver) *Palgrave Advances in Continental Political Thought* (2005).

Gayil Talshir is a Lecturer and the head of the Graduate Programme in Citizenship and Democracy, in the Department of Political Science, the Hebrew University of Jerusalem, Israel. She writes about political ideologies, New Politics, parties and civil society. Among her publications are *The Political Ideology of Green Parties: From Politics of Nature to Redefining the Nature of Politics.* (Palgrave, 2002) and 'The objects of ideology: historical transformations and the changing role of the analyst', *History of Political Thought*, forthcoming.

Preface: Taking Ideology Seriously

The articles in this special issue challenge the notion that the twenty-first century has ushered in a 'post-ideological' age. To the contrary, the 'post-ideological' thesis may itself be seen as an ideological manifestation. It improperly attempts to remove ideas from politics and adopts a minimalist approach towards the public sphere, reducing it to a medley of institutions, leaders and governmental mechanisms whose powers vis-à-vis world forces – such as globalization, social fragmentation and citizens' apathy – appear to be in constant decline.

We maintain, rather, that politics is, and always will be, a contest over views, interests, values and ideas – and we are quite content that this should be the case. In the public sphere perennially competing social groups and collective actors – at local, national and international levels – develop their own shared identity. They define and redefine their needs, interests and norms, and play with, and against, other groups in order to influence, change, preserve or undermine the social order. Such collective associations, far from being artificial constructs or theoretical mirages, are viable inhabitants of the political world, easy to detect if you know where to look. Their ways of defining themselves, arguing their causes, organizing their political aims and values are in permanent, and usually creative, flux.

Ideology, we contend, accompanies that constant ideational struggle between social actors, both as its shaper and its effect. The study of ideology seeks to trace, expose, decipher, decontest and understand that immanent aspect of politics.

Not least, the analysis of ideology has a crucial role within the discipline of political studies, as it serves to connect the two branches of politics – social philosophy and empirical research. Just as there is no politics without a struggle over ideas, so there is no philosophical thinking outside of a political context.

There are, however, many new challenges to the study of ideology in today's world. Novel worldviews contest our traditional sensibilities about ideology. Religious fundamentalisms defy the assumption that ideologies are secular worldviews by nature, while concurrently obfuscating the political boundaries of ideology. Contemporary arguments for a 'global free market', 'global governance', as well as 'global civil society' and 'global social democracy' attempt to depose the nation-state as a privileged locus of ideologies. The emergence of the Greens and of the politics of identity questions the old left/right axis.

This special issue responds to these challenges. The authors proffer suggestions for mapping the new frontiers of studying ideology in the twenty-first century, and for posing new questions, as well as offering ways of analyzing ideology today. Each article pursues further research into ideational formations in society, transcending old methodological assumptions and aspiring to redefine the theory of ideology itself. This collection has grown out of a workshop on 'Working with ideologies in a post-ideological age' convened under the auspices of the European Consortium for Political Research in Uppsala, April 2004. We hope it may contribute to the future study of ideology in politics and build on the recent pace it has gathered.

The Phoenix of Ideology

GAYIL TALSHIR

Karl Dietrich Bracher (1984) titled his book *The Age of Ideology: A History of Political Thought in the Twentieth Century*. Ideology, he contended, is the most distinctive feature of politics since the turn of the last century, characterized by the attempt of groups – nations, states, organizations – to simplify complex realities into one, all-embracing truth in a bipolar framework of foe/friend (Bracher 1984: 5). Yet the major processes of the second half of the twentieth century seem to mark the very demise of the era of ideology. Ideology is at the heart of three different crises that have dramatically changed the way we think about society today: the end of ideology, the end of politics and the end of history. Each concerns a different set of presuppositions, contexts, objects of investigation and 'big questions', yet 'ideology' plays a key role in them all. Thus, the end of ideology mainly addresses the rivalry between totalitarian regimes and democracy. Ideology in this context symbolizes the dominant feature of dictatorships – be they Fascism, Nazism or Communism – in all of which terror and coercion were used alongside means of persuasion and justification to enforce the worldview of the ruling elite. The end of politics refers rather to the diminishing difference between the traditional left and right as constitutive poles of the political axis in democracies. Here again ideology plays a central role by moulding the very matrix on which the major political powers are deciphered. The race to the center – the median voter, media attention, mainstream opinion – has resulted in the transformation of the major competing sides into catch-all and cartel parties, with direct dependency on the state and less and less connection to civil society, or to the people (Kirchheimer 1990; Mair & Katz 1995). The end of history features yet another dimension, which goes beyond Fukuyama's celebration of liberalism: the end of history is in fact the end of progressive history, the sense of purposefulness and improvement in human society that is captured through the rise of cultural relativism, moral scepticism and post-modernism. Here again ideology, as the rational, all-embracing long-term program aimed at changing the world to conform to a master plan, symbolizes the collapse of the project of modernism. Yet at the very moment that the decline of ideology – on all three fronts – becomes apparent, ideology also regains its poignancy. Islamic fundamentalism on the one hand and anti-globalization on the other (or maybe the same?) hand, offer but two examples. The rise of New Politics provides another interesting case in point.

In *Challenging the Political Order* the authors explore the rise of the new social movements, collective actors of civil society in advanced democracies. They argue that, in contrast to other approaches which emphasize the political style, collective action or motivation of extra-parliamentary politics, 'the defining characteristic of new social movements is their advocacy of a new social paradigm which contrasts with the dominant goal structure of Western industrial societies ... The ideology of these movements is the major factor distinguishing them from other traditional European leftists movements and their own historical predecessors' (Dalton & Kuechler, 1990: 10–11). Thus, ideology is being identified as the most distinctive feature of the new collective actors since the 1960s. Curiously, while perceiving ideology to be the key feature of New Politics, they term the worldview of the new social movements 'post-ideological' for they lack a strict doctrine (ibid., p. 281). How can a political phenomenon be at the same time identified primarily as ideological and defined as post-ideological? The centrality of ideological phenomena at the beginning of the twenty-first century, and the difficulty of exploring such ideologies in a seemingly 'post-ideological age', is at the heart of this study. We contend that ideology is at once an immanent part of political life and a phenomenon that needs to be rethought in terms of the concepts, objects and methodologies used to analyze it. The article first examines the three crises of contemporary politics, the role of ideology in each of them and the survival prospects of the concept of 'ideology' in the aftermath of these crises. It then explores five challenges for studying ideology in the twenty-first century. Finally, it introduces the authors of the volume and positions their contributions in light of the challenges of studying ideology in today's world.

The Three 'Ends' of Ideology

Rarely does one phenomenon come to symbolize such distinct areas of study as international relations, democratic politics and grand theory. The role of 'ideology' in all three realms, areas that have undergone major transformations over the last generation, reifies Bracher's thesis concerning the age of ideology. However, in this section I hope to go beyond considering ideology as a thing of the past, as the icon of the previous century. I argue that even with the collapse of totalitarian regimes, the changing role of the political realm vis-à-vis civil society, and the critique of the enlightenment project of human progress, the study of ideology remains vital. In fact, analyzing ideology within these theoretical corpuses and beyond them becomes even more crucial for grasping the nature of politics in a changing world. Ultimately, I contend that ideology is itself part and parcel of politics, and that people, as political animals, always construct their shared identity in terms of a certain historical analysis, a common social vision and a possible political course for materializing this vision, be it within the community, the region, the state or the global village. The nexus of ideas and political action is constitutive to the way we are in this world, to the way we make sense, understand and act in society.

The End of Ideology

Daniel Bell's *End of Ideology* came out in three editions, each of which was received as the most timely addition to contemporary public discourse. The 1960 book captured the aftermath of the Second World War, with the horrors of the most ideological of wars in full view, but with processes of de-Nazification and democratization of Germany, Japan, Italy and Spain well on their way. Moreover, the manuscript was published when the almost-official ideology of anti-communism in the United States was on the wane, after a long decade of McCarthyism; the End of Ideology thesis thus encapsulated a defining moment in American history. However, the book failed to anticipate one of the most significant ideological developments of the twentieth century – the students' revolt, the rise of the civil rights and Black movements, and the emergence of the extra-parliamentary opposition in the West. The withdrawal from Vietnam, the critique of cultural imperialism, and the call for alternative politics escaped the social thinker. Curiously, for the 1988 edition all this was almost forgotten: the students of the 1960s were now well positioned in the knowledge society, and social movements were institutionalized. Bell himself explained this in his 1988 epilogue: 'The event that seemed to contradict the end-of-ideology thesis was the upsurge of radicalism in the mid-sixties and seventies. Its intensity, its anger, its rhetoric, its calls for radical change, all seemed to bespeak a new phase of ideology' (Bell 1988: 425). Nonetheless, Bell argued that these events and social forces may have channeled enthusiastic youth and passions, but they lacked the economic and political dimension which could have made them ideological:

> Did the upsurge of radicalism in the 1960s 'disprove' the thesis of the end of ideology? I think not. What one saw was not a political but cultural (and generational) phenomenon ... It was a utopian dream. But from a dream one awakens, or one continues into a nightmare. In all this turbulence there were no new socialist ideas, no ideologies, no programs. (Bell 1988: 432)

Wait long enough, and the major ideological phenomena will be transformed beyond recognition. Thus, Bell's second edition came out with perfect timing, a year before the Berlin wall fell. The writing on the wall was once again loud and clear: the end of ideology is here. Indeed, on the eastern front history seemed to have joined the global village which was now racing towards democratization under the free market. The fact that one of the most crucial ideological moments of all – the upsurge of neoliberalism and its adoption by the conservative and republican political camps – beset the political scene in the 1980s, and completely contradicted the original thesis of the convergence of the left and right on the welfare state model, advocated by Bell in 1960, was not reflected in any changes in the chapter. And for a good reason: the Clinton administration in the United States, and the Third Way in Europe, swung the pendulum back in the mid-1990s against the harsh individualism of the market place, in time for the third edition of the book. The 2000 edition became one of a genre, joining Fukuyama's End of History thesis and the overall acknowledgement of the globalization thesis.

However, once again the book seemed to miss one of the most important developments of the year following 9/11 and the rise of Islamic fundamentalism. Does al Qaeda represent an ideology? Was Bell's thesis decisively wrong? Following Bell's own definition, seeing ideology as part of the trade of the intellectuals, as a secular worldview which puts ideas into a political action plan in order to rule a state, the thesis may hold water. Fundamentalism – Islamic, Christian or of any other cult – is very different from the classic ideologies. First of all, it is based on a religion. In that respect it violates one of the main features we usually identify with ideology as a secular phenomenon. Second, Islamic fundamentalism has no state it seeks to take over, has no unified political or economic vision, has no one people united behind it, has no geographical center. Rather, it is decentralized and spontaneous. It involves local cells in Muslim, Arab and ethnic diaspora in Western societies organized in a loose network of Internet connections, using the big money of some of the prominent capitalistic families and high technology to fund terror and training camps for its activists and to spread their teaching to new recruits and followers. That is rarely the way we traditionally think about ideology. Still, it is a distinctive ideological phenomenon from a new brand.

Thus, the definition of ideology may change, the type of collective body, the causes, the ends, the means – but ideology is part and parcel of the way people act in the world. Ideology does not end – it transforms itself. And one of the main causes for the transformation of the phenomenon is the transition of post-industrial democracies.

The End of Politics

The second process of change of which ideology is a key player is representative democracy. On the face of it, the institutionalization of liberal democracy in the twentieth century became identified with a procedural mechanism: the competitive struggle among parties for people's votes (Schumpeter 1942: 269). Political parties thus developed as the central actor of the political system; as Schattschneider explained: 'modern democracy is unthinkable save in terms of political parties' (Schattschneider 1942: 1). However, lurking behind this procedure of election among representative bodies is a question about what distinguishes each party, what each party stands for. In party-democracy, the distinctive feature of each party is its political ideology; there is a worldview, a set of values, principles and policies on the basis of which members, activists and voters choose to align themselves with political actors. The party ideology is manifested in election platforms, party programs and policy documents; the party manifesto 'is probably the single most important indicator of party policy, and a pointer to underlying ideology which meshes with membership of a generic "family" and other distinguishing party characteristics' (Budge and Klingemann, 2001: 19). Thus, ideology is a centerpiece of contemporary politics in institutionalized democracies.

The constitutive axis on which the parties are being positioned and compared is the left/right ideological continuum, which gradually evolved since the late seventeenth century, when the distinction between the individual and the state, the private and the public, became central to liberalism. In the eighteenth century, the economic realm became identified with the private sphere, whereas the political realm with the public sphere; the private (economic) and the public (political) were thus separated. This demarcation was strengthened after the French revolution and during the nineteenth century, with the advent of the nation-state and the development of parliamentary democracies. It was crystallized in the structuring of the ideological spectrum around the relations between the state and the individual; put crudely – pro-interventionists to the left, anti-interventionists to the right. In a more sophisticated framework – social cleavages were represented in the major political parties (Lipset and Rokkan 1990). True, over the years the left and right came to represent different issues and policies; however, as a comparative tool the ideological axis remained a good indicator of the political poles. As Gordon Smith observed: 'it is precisely the "plasticity" of left and right which enables them to combine coherence with flexibility, to absorb new issues and ward off challenges, besides maintaining a clear demarcation from other parties on the opposite side of the left/right divide' (Smith 1990: 159). The left/right continuum thus shapes the public realm and makes sense of the main political forces within the public domain.

While the patterns of political alignments persisted throughout much of the twentieth century, over the last generation the party system as the manifestation of collective interests, as well as the legitimacy of the institutional political processes, came under question. Evidence of dealignment – electoral volatility, declining party affiliation, decreasing trust in politicians and the rise of alternative political actors – has been largely persistent in advanced industrial democracies since the 1970s (Dalton & Wattenberg 2000). On the party system level, two concomitant trends were observed. On the one hand, political realignment, the decline of party membership, the rise of new, often anti-party parties and issue-based politics characterize contemporary European polities. On the other hand, these countries have witnessed the institutionalization of parties – the emergence of the cartel party as part of the state apparatus itself (Mair & Katz 1997). Both suggest the weakening of the structural ties between the citizenry and the traditional parties. All accounts point to the apparent crisis of the parties as the key players within representative democracy, a growing threat to party democracy itself. Consequently, persistent trends concerning the key political player in parliamentary systems began to change rapidly. Parties altered their electoral bases and saw an overall decline of their power and weakening relation with their traditional voters. The search for alternative bases of support generated more flexible agenda and ideological change. Moreover, the 'Americanization' of European politics – the growing emphasis on the personality of the leader, on media performance, on themes and issues rather than coherent worldviews, and the need to accommodate diverging audiences and compete not just for votes, but for mobilizing people even to consider voting – allegedly symbolized a decline of ideology. The transition from elite to mass parties, to catch-all and to cartel parties, symbolized the race to the center and the blurring of political ideologies.

Crucially, part of the problem with analyzing ideologies lies in the methodological toolkit of political scientists. Just as survey data and opinion polls opened a new methodological niche to the study of electoral fluctuations, so did the quantitative analysis of policy preferences lend itself to issue analysis much more than to the study of comprehensive ideologies. Thus, Peter Mair argues that the electoral bias in studying party system change amounts to 'the neglect of assessments of change with regard to other aspects, such as, for example, party ideology, organization, or strategy' (Mair & Katz 1997: 71). Indeed, three of the most intriguing ideological developments have taken place since the 1970s: first, the emergence of neoliberalism as the hegemonic paradigm of political economy; second, the emergence of the New Left and identity politics as an alternative; third, and against these two renewed ideological poles, the Third Way positioned itself as the program of social democratic parties.

If Bell's analysis regarding the end of ideology relied on the endorsement of the welfare state by both left and right parties (Bell 1988: 402), the attack launched by the neoliberals on the planned economy and their call to roll back the state and free the market again to act on principles of supply and demand swayed public discourse. Aided by trends of globalization, it became the new hegemony of the 1980s and 1990s. This radical transformation of the conservative right justified its individualistic, interest-based politics by appealing to Christian roots and the work-ethic, as Thatcher passionately argued: 'Our religion teaches us that every human being is unique and must play his part in working out his own salvation.' (Thatcher 1989: 52). That radical transformation of republicans and conservatives led to the erosion of the welfare state and to the diminishing role of the trade unions and was crystallized through the passage from industrial to post-industrial societies. The ideological reaction of the left was quick to follow: notably, it emerged from civil society rather than the established political system. The radical left developed as a new collective actor that rejected the consumer-ethos of the new paradigm and connected it to cultural imperialism and materialism (Inglehart 1990). The new social movements and the extra-parliamentary opposition that developed in civil society since the late 1960s demanded a reconceptualization of what is politics, arguing that the personal, the familial, the community, the region, the international and the global were no less political than national interest. Furthermore, they maintained that the left–right continuum was based on a narrow economic perspective, which failed to see the challenges of sustainable development, of quality of life issues and of identity politics. The New Left thus advocated the politicization of the social realm, active civil society and participatory citizenship, based on grassroots democracy. At the center of its worldview stood the cultural, ethnic, religious, sexual or national community. These groups sought political recognition, and demanded collective social rights. The radical left insisted that distributive justice had to be expanded to include social justice and identity politics, not just the hard currency of economic budgetary.

Between these new poles – the neoliberal Right and the cultural Left – the Third Way emerged in the mid-1990s, hoping to constitute a viable alternative for the social democratic left. The principles of this ideology revolved around changing the role of the state from the main employer, to the coordinator and inspector, of the public sphere. Civil society was to acquire a central role in working with the political institutions to enable better public services, leaving to the government the tasks of setting the standards and inspecting the implementation of its policies (Giddens 1998). The welfare state, which under the conservatives was reduced to a safety net for the most needy groups of society, and was perceived as a burden on the middle class, would be refashioned as the mechanism to endow the whole working population with benefits and training (Labour 2001). The key factor, in accordance with the information society, was the emphasis on education: life-long education, the extension of free public teaching to three year olds and the aspiration to extend university education to 50% of the population in the next 10 years (Blair 2004). Confronted with the decline of party democracy, both the traditional and the new parties have taken up the challenge and tried to update their ideologies. They reacted to changes in the economy and the global setting, attempting to refashion their worldview.

The End of Politics is introduced thus:

> As the twenty-first century dawns, American politics is in an increasingly pathetic condition. Elections have become more meaningless than ever, significant differences between Republicans and Democrats are scarcely discernible despite all the political hue and cry, public discourse is drawn increasingly toward trivial concerns, and legislatures at all levels are in gridlock. (Boggs 2000: 1)

Yet even in the United States the Clinton administration introduced a much clearer social democratic vision, while the second Bush election in 2004 was decided by a markedly ideological crowd of evangelists and value-conservative Republicans. The political alternatives still present and justify themselves in ideological terms, as a choice between political agenda, social principles and moral values. Even though processes of dealignment and realignment are on their way, the parties reacted by refurbishing their worldviews, rather than deserting all attempt at generating a political program. This characterizes both the traditional parties and – even more persuasively – the new social actors in civil society that emphasize values and principles. The fragmentation of the political scene does not mean the end of politics, or that of ideology – it merely means that there are more collective actors, more contextual considerations and more complex public realms in which ideology continues to play a crucial role.

The End of History

The third dimension of the public sphere in the turn of the twentieth century relates to the critique of postmodernism. From this perspective, the End of History, far from symbolizing the moral victory of liberal democracy (Fukuyama 1992) stands rather for the end of our presuppositions about the very nature of history as a meta-narrative, as an unfolding story towards a better world, imbued with a sense of historical progress and a growing ability to advance toward a just society. Modernism, according to this approach, dwelled on the enlightenment ideas of belief in science, technology and moral progress, assuming that human society could always improve itself in the pursuit of wellbeing and happiness (Eagleton 1996). In that sense, ideology epitomized the project of modernism: it presented a coherent and consistent worldview, starting from moral presuppositions about human nature, developing a social vision and seeking political ways to transform society and implement the public ideal. However, modernism – according to this critique – failed to realize there is no one over-arching truth, no grand-theory in light of which all humanity acts, no ever-growing progress toward the good society. Rather, what prevails is moral relativism, many different visions of the good life, and varied narratives of diverse cultures. The end of history, from a postmodern perspective, symbolizes the dissemination of a meta-historical unified plot of the world; rather, there are many different stories, perspectives, ideas, none of which encompasses an Archimedean point of moral superiority or objectivity. The same history can be told from very different points of view, in which the facts of the matter and their interpretation will differ, as will the heroes, the issues and the outcomes.

Thus, the privileged position of ideology in the modern era is over. To take one example, Foucault argued in *Truth and Power* that ideology is no longer a viable term due to two problems. First, ideology presupposed the existence of truth. The obsession with striving to uncover real roots, unmasking appearances and attaining some inner truth that lies beneath the surface was a feature of modernism that post-modern thinkers have challenged (Foucault 1980: 118). Second, Foucault also brought out the emphasis on power as practice, contrary to Marx's notion of possessing power (Barrett 1991: 135). Those two reasons propelled Foucault to replace ideology with what he named discourse: the identification of ideology with the search for deeper truth, characteristic of modernism, and with its underlying assumption that ideology entailed specific authorships of deception.

However, the post-structuralist critique does not mean the end of the study of ideology, as Foucault and others have moved on to the analysis of ideology as discourse:

> An order of discourse constitutes the discoursal/ideological facet of a contradictory and unstable equilibrium ... discoursal practice is a facet of struggle which contributes in varying degrees to the reproduction or transformation of the existing order of discourse, and through that existing social and power relations. (Fairclough 1995: 77)

Thus, the critical perspective strongly relates ideology to power, and discourse studies analyze relations of domination. Crucially, the focus on discourse, socially situated text, still analyzes ideology; far from abandoning ideology, due to the postmodern critique, the analysis now forcefully moves ideological analysis to adopt a critical perspective. The need to decipher the underlying norms, conventions, practices and ways of thinking focuses the critical approach far more on ideas and ideology. Ideology is not obsolete; rather, it becomes the new center for understanding power-relations and different identity constructions in society. Thus, the three dimensions of the public sphere at the turn of the century – the end of ideology, the end of politics and the end of history – have all diagnosed ideology as a cornerstone of the relevant corpus of writing. The breakdown of the unitary framework of analysis – the end of the Cold War, the changing nature of politics in advanced democracies, and the postmodern condition – suggest that rather than a clear ideological pole – totalitarian vs democratic, left vs right, progressive vs reactionary – there exists a much more fragmented public realm with many collective actors, political units and types of discourse. In the next part of the essay, we explore some of the challenges which studying ideology in the twenty-first century presents.

The Challenges Ahead: Studying Ideology in Today's World

Beyond the State

The first challenge has to do with the boundaries of the state. Throughout the twentieth century, realist international theory referred to sovereign states. The way to enter the family of nations was to appeal to self-determination and ultimately to establish an independent state. Ideology, as we have seen, became closely related either to types of regimes or to political systems within states. However, in contemporary politics processes of globalization and those of social fragmentation have taken place side by side, thus generating new collective actors and new frameworks for ideological analysis. In the aftermath of the Cold War and the collapse of the Soviet Union, new state-like entities came into being. The breakdown of the former Czechoslovakia, Yugoslavia and other states saw their disintegration into smaller units, now struggling between their collective identity under Soviet rule, their historical heritage as independent countries, and their possible future as 'pure' ethnic, religious or cultural units. The same process can be seen in places like post-invasion Iraq, with the Shiites, Sunnis and Kurds each organizing as autonomous social units, bringing into being new forms of geographical communities which may not be viable as states. On the other hand, processes of integration – such as the emergence of the European Union as a political union with the signing of the social chapter – have given rise yet again to a political body previously unknown.

In terms of ideology, both localization and globalization produce new challenges. To take but two examples, could we analyze globalization itself as a political ideology? While globalization – as an economic and possibly cultural process – is certainly making its way in the world, there is a question as to whether it is a new macro-ideology; thinking about globalization through the lenses of Fukuyama's End of History, it may indeed suggest itself as the ultimate new ideology of economic and political liberalization. Indeed, the claim was made that globalization is the hegemonic new ideology of our era (Steger 2005). However, if we follow Mannheim (1955) in perceiving ideology as a product of social groups, as a collective good, it becomes less clear who is the group that generates that ideology, whether it is indeed a macro-ideology or an economic process used in public discourse to enforce certain political ideologies, or whether there is intentionality in propagating globalization as a social vision. Can we, for that matter, analyze multinational corporations such as MacDonalds, Intel or Sony, or international bodies as the World Bank or the IMF, as collective actors with political ideologies?

If globalization as a political ideology presents problems for the analyst, it seems that the counter-ideology – anti-globalization – is indeed carried by new collective actors with an international grouping, be they the anti-globalism movement or the world social forum. However, it is no less obvious how to analyze the loosely connected network of al Qaeda and how to make sense of its ideology, than it is to determine whether the anti-globalism movement, made up of grassroots organizations, international activists who can afford to go to global summits such as in Seattle or Porto Alegro, and public intellectuals who write manifestos and theoretical accounts (Held & McGrew 2002; Callinicos 2003) form a viable, identifiable collective group with meaningful shared social experiences and a common political ideology. The charter of principles of the World Social Forum states:

> The World Social Forum is an open meeting place for reflective thinking, democratic debate of ideas, formulation of proposals, free exchange of experiences and interlinking for effective action, by groups and movements of civil society that are opposed to neoliberalism and to domination of the world by capital and any form of imperialism, and are committed to building a planetary society directed towards fruitful relationships among Mankind and between it and the Earth. (WSF 2004)

While they certainly share the rejection of 'world capitalism', 'globalization', and neoliberalism, and object to any form of oppression, it is still hard to discern whether there is a viable social group and an autonomous political ideology behind these new global actors.

Collective Actors

This brings us directly to the second challenge of studying ideology today: the question of the relevant collective bodies which can be identified as professing an ideology. Take for example the emergence of the new social movements in the civil society of advanced democracies. Can we say that the host of women's and feminist movements, the plethora of international, national and local environmental organizations, or associations based on colour, race or ethnicity emerge as new ideologies? Three responses present themselves. One is to follow the collective actors themselves: if feminists perceive their own project as developing a new ideology, if environmentalists believe they have a new, ecological worldview, then the cement of their shared identity can be seen – and analyzed – as a new ideology, regardless of the question whether as a theoretical construct it encompasses the features identified with the traditional ideologies, such as liberalism or fascism. The second response suggests that such collective actors may indeed add a new dimension or a new issue which unites them and which they develop in a unique way, but it does not necessarily mean that a new ideology has evolved. Freeden thus titles such ideational manifestations 'thin ideologies': 'A thin ideology is one that, like mainstream ideologies, has an identifiable morphology but, unlike mainstream ideologies, a restricted one ... It does not embrace the full range of questions that the macro-ideologies do, and is limited in its ambition and scope' (Freeden 2003: 98). Thus, while macro-ideologies like socialism or conservatism are all-embracing, enhancing a distinct view of human nature, of the connections between man and society, the relationships between politics, economics and civil society, and generated a developed political vision of the good society, thin ideologies accept, say, the ethos of liberal democracy but add a new perspective, a set of values or concerns to this or other worldview. In fact, one of the interesting features of thin ideologies is that they can be adapted and adopted to different macro-ideologies: there are conservative and religious environmental organizations, as there are radical and socialist green movements.

The third option attempts to go beyond the traditional view of ideology, but in rather a different direction than the thin-ideology thesis. The contemporaneous emergence of new collective actors in civil societies of advanced democracies – new social movements, protest groups, citizens' organizations and minority associations – as well as their shared experience as the outsiders of the established political system, has created common social experiences and shared sensitivities centered on the injustices produced within advanced capitalist societies. The modular ideology thesis thus argues that these collective actors share a conceptual framework of second order principles: respect for the other, politics of recognition, social inclusion, grassroots democracy, civic activism and political empowerment. Within these shared values, each group promotes its own sub-ideology, be it feminism, ecologism or radical democracy (Talshir 2002). What emerges from all these analytical approaches, is that the traditional institutional approach – even if bringing the state back in – focuses on the established political actors such as parties, governments or countries and has to be complemented with a more pluralistic apprehension of the public sphere. The decision concerning which social groups or political associations encompass a political ideology remains one of the greater challenges of studying ideology today.

Public Discourse

The emergence of the public sphere in contemporary politics cannot be detached from the growing influence of the media, and the evolution of new technologies – primarily the Internet and electronic mail – which enable communication beyond geographical and cultural boundaries. Public discourse becomes instrumental in analyzing politics and arguably an independent sphere of political action. One interesting manifestation of the new role of public discourse arises from the critique of representative democracy by political theorists and social activists. The main bone of contention of deliberative democracy is with the fundamentals of institutional democracy, with its emphasis on universal participation embodied in elections, and its focus on parties as representative political institutions; consequently, liberal democracies have tended to perceive citizenship in terms of the individual right to vote. In contradistinction, contemporary political theorists prefer concrete forms of active participation and deliberative processes. Seyla Benhabib explicates the model of deliberative democracy: 'the procedural specifications of this model privilege a *plurality of modes of association* in which all affected can have the right to articulate their point of view. These can range from political parties to citizens' initiatives, to social movements, to voluntary associations, to consciousness-raising groups, and the like' (Benhabib 1996:73). With the change from the established political realm to an extended social arena, which enhances the public sphere, the centrality of public discourse emerges as the prime locus of interaction, and the transformation from voting as the quintessential feature of citizenship to deliberation. Benhabib continues:

> It is through the interlocking of these multiple forms of associations, networks, and organizations that an anonymous 'public conversation' results. It is central to the model of deliberative democracy that it privileges such a public sphere of mutually interlocking and overlapping networks and associations of deliberation, contestation and argumentation. (Benhabib 1996: 73–74)

Not only does civil society gain primacy as the realm of the public sphere where most of the networks and organizations operate, but the unique feature of this realm is public discourse, argumentation and communication. It calls for active participation, diverse associations and the channel of deliberation as constitutive of the normative model of democracy.

Most theoreticians of deliberative democracy follow Habermas's account of the third normative model of democracy, understanding its main feature as part of communicative action and conveying the role of public discourse as crucial vis-à-vis the state and the economy (Habermas 1996, 1999). Legitimacy, rationality and associations become quintessential to the normative power of deliberative democracy. However, the transformation from fragmented deliberating communities to a single public conversation, from diverse associations of value to a unifying procedure, or in Habermas's case to ideal speech situation is, to say the least, problematic. Some of the deliberative processes in religious, ethnic or racial communities might not be egalitarian, would not aspire to rationality and in fact may well reject some of the pillars of democracy – liberal or deliberative – altogether. The idea of a public conversation, of a public discourse in which different communities in civil society develop their own modes of communication – and ideology – and throw them open to public deliberation is a powerful idea, but exhibits many problems when thinking about political reality. There is an obvious gap between political theory and social practice. In any case, public discourse becomes an autonomous social sphere.

In contradistinction, one can argue that the major problem in today's world is precisely the lack of a universal conversation, even within states. The public sphere may indeed be fragmented rather than universal. For the diversification of the public sphere enables people to watch their own news channel, read the paper which expresses their own political views, and send their children to schools which represent only their own religion or culture or political inclinations. It is a moot point whether there is any public conversation, any shared facts or data that connects people. For different groups can learn, experience and be educated strictly within their own camp, with little exposure and understanding to the other groups in society. But here the nature of the public sphere, as mediated by the media, becomes central. Whether there is one public arena or several biased political communication networks may not be the central issue. There is a viable option according to which the media, television and cinema provide the means for total political apathy altogether. Thus, if the presuppositions of representative democracy were that at least prior to elections each individual considers the party in government or the current administration and, based on its worldview and judgment of policies votes for her own representatives, it is not clear that there is such a shared apprehension of politics, and the decline in electoral turnout and citizens' apathy appear to corroborate that. Public discourse should not be taken for granted. We may be a long way from a universal conversation or a shared political forum. The new technologies and media present both challenges and dangers to political consciousness.

Outside the West

The next challenge that students of ideology in the twenty-first century have to address is the question whether ideology is indeed a *sui generis* phenomenon, closely related to the era of modernism in Western political cultures, or whether it is an aspect of every human society, regardless of historical period and the social order. The two main responses to this question are the contextual and functional approaches; both argue that ideology should be studied in non-Western societies as well as in advanced democracies.

The contextual approach contends that whereas ideology may have evolved as an integral part of Western civilization, in today's world, when economic and cultural globalization is well on its way and the Internet has become a central tool for global communication, ideology has been imported to most other societies, together with other mechanisms, values, procedures and ways of thinking and acting politically. The reaction may be different – some religious fundamentalisms may reject the notion of ideology and construct a theology against it; other indigenous cultures may seek their own philosophical traditions as an alternative to what they perceive as Western values; still other states may endorse the parliamentary system and the left–right ideological axis. All these examples – whether they reject Western notions of ideology or endorse them – may be characterized and analyzed as ideological phenomena. Indeed, the evolution of ideology in the West was in part a conscious rejection of existing ideologies. The best example is of course that of Marxism, which today serves as the *par excellence* case of an ideology, but its own characterization of 'ideology' is deeply connected to false consciousness. Another example is democracy itself: when ideology was associated with totalitarian regimes by the critics, ideology was thought to be a political system and not an ideational construct. As the critique of representative democracy, coming from the 'deliberative' and 'participatory' schools demonstrates, democracy is constituted on shared values that were institutionalized in a certain form in different political cultures and can be scrutinized and improved to become more democratic, or democratic in a different way (Gutmann & Thompson 2004). Both Marxism and democracy could be studied as forms of ideological systems. So could cultures, organizations and states with different roots from the Western ones.

The second, functional approach argues that just as there are different types of leadership – tribal, religious, traditional, constitutional – so are there many manifestations of ideology. Ideology – in the West or elsewhere – does not have to come packaged in a party program or a manifesto. Ideology can be deduced from ways of collective action, norms of behavior, patterns of thinking, rituals and belief systems (Geertz 1973). Thus, the group, society or organization under question does not have to use the term ideology in order to possess one. From this perspective it is much more significant to identify the functions which ideology fulfills, the ways ideas are embedded in and determine political action, then to define the term and look for this usage in different cultures. There is a distinction between the objects – collective actors – of ideology and its analysts. No privileged position of groups and parties exists in the West vis-à-vis other organizations in terms of exploring and exposing the working of their ideologies, as long as the analyst knows what she is looking for and how to adapt its ways of investigation to the society in which she works.

Theory/Ideology

Finally, the range of social groups, geographical localities and the challenges of old, transformed and new ideational systems greatly expand the scope of the study of ideology. One crucial aspect of delimiting the compass of such endeavor is to demarcate the type of relevant scientific pursuit. The main distinction which needs to be made is the one between political philosophy and the study of ideology. Just as philosophy is the queen of sciences, so does political philosophy perceives itself to be the first lady of political science. Political philosophy, arguably, engages with the cream of politics, namely, the good society itself. Its nobility comes from its normative pursuit. One branch of it seeks to delineate the counters – the moral and just principles – of the good society. Analytical philosophy thus deals with refining the concepts, moral principles and clarifying the set of values of the good society, seeking the coherence and consistence of the ideal world. The second branch, critical theory, focuses on scrutinizing political discourse and social phenomena in society, on the basis of principles of justice or moral standards. The former are the architects of the good society; the latter the 'reconstructers' of the existing social order. The scholar of ideology, for that matter, is the archaeologist of modern society: she excavates the political concepts, the belief system, the social values of political actors and communities – either in recent or contemporary history – and explores, compares, maps and analyzes the conceptual and ideational assemblages their social groups have constructed in the real world. While the political philosopher draws the contours of the imagined society, and the critical theorist acts as the organic intellectual, the student of ideology has the rather less prestigious job of conducting research on active political actors in society. She deals with the 'good society' inasmuch as the collective actors she studies design their utopia; she engages in critical theory since she exposes the infrastructures of the normative presuppositions concerning human nature, man–society relations and the power-relations among concepts and values in the worldview of the political actors under question (Freeden 1996). She is a political scientist as she addresses the very matter – of thought and action – that politics is made up from collective knowing of thyself, thinking social ideals into being, understanding and acting in the world.

True, there are many examples of thinkers who began as social scientists and ended up as public intellectuals and political actors; who started as theorists and became ideologists, a subject of the analysis of students of ideology. Marx is the most obvious case of a figure that thought himself to be a positivist scientist, a material historian of social processes, and became the proponent of the socialist revolution. A contemporary example could be Anthony Giddens, the sociologist and head of LSE who was appointed a personal adviser to PM Tony Blair in the UK, the philosophical architect of the Third Way who became the house ideologist of the party, with publications such as 'Where now for New Labour' and 'Did they Foul up my Third Way?' (Giddens 2002, 2004). The boundaries are shifting ones: one can be a social scientist in one's day job and a political activist in one's civic life.

However, the study of ideology is a scientific endeavor whose objects of research are changing social phenomena and collective actors.

The Structure of the Volume: Responding to the Challenge

The analysis of ideology in contemporary society is thus far more complicated and demanding today in terms of methodology, the objects of research and the type of political actors and social phenomena. This volume sets the scene by responding to some of the challenges and opening the way to the study of ideology as part and parcel of the analysis of politics in today's world.

David Laycock attempts to go beyond the traditional left–right axis, taking populism as a case in point. He studies how – far from being exclusively a feature of the far right and the conservatives – populism has manifested itself in Leftist discourse. Deciphering the morphology of populist ideologies, using Freeden's method of conceptual analysis, he exposes the core concepts, the mechanisms of justification and the values at play in populist thinking, thus driving further the role of comparative ideological analysis beyond the traditional left–right categories.

James Martin's chapter addresses the question of public discourse with regard to Italian politics, through the application of post-structuralist theory. He argues that antagonism, perceived as a negative ideology on one level, actually functions as a constructive force when looking at the public sphere, for it facilitates processes of identification and positioning within Italian political culture. The discursive mechanism of disagreement thus enables political identity formation and transformation, as the case of Anti-Fascism in Italy demonstrates.

Torben Bech Dyrberg offers another usage of the left-right continuum, by challenging the assumption of the analysts of ideology in the mid-twentieth century that only totalitarian regimes encompass ideology. Democracy, he argues, is itself an ideology which evolved against religious and cultural orders. Treating the left–right as orienting metaphors for an alternative worldview, he emphasizes the role of public reason, as manifested in Rawls's theory, in providing the justification for democracy as a rival ideology to its predecessors. This essay thus stretches further the main concepts with which we think about ideology, stressing the symbolic order and the affective outcomes of political life.

Jeffrey Haynes picks up the formidable challenge of exploring the ideology of al Qaeda, as an alternative collective actor, outside the West, yet with inherent – antagonist – connections to it. Providing a contextual approach based on the study of the movement in the Middle East, he argues that the prime target of the organization was to replace the leaders of Arab and Muslim countries; upon the failure of this end, al Qaeda turned to a global struggle against the West, transforming its methods, aims and ideas accordingly. The changing contours of al Qaeda's ideology, and its key tenets, are thus analyzed.

Gary Browning also engages with analyzing ideology beyond state boundaries. He contends that 'post-Marxist' arguments against globalism and the hegemony of (the Western) empire display many a feature of Marxist ideology, despite the claim of the authors to theoretical novelty. He examines Hardt and Negri's *Empire* as an ideology, thus exploring also the boundaries between political theory and ideology.

Gayil Talshir also addresses the post-Marxist tradition, but from the perspective of the role of the intellectual, outlining four models: (a) theorists should leave their cathedra and join social activists; (b) critical theory is itself a form of social activism; (c) the organic intellectual has a social role in refining and scrutinizing his society; (d) the intellectual as possessor of knowledge-as-power, serving to preserve the status quo. The question remains whether it is possible to see the study of ideology as a scientific endeavor with no clear normative role.

Mathew Humphrey takes issue with this question, examining the boundary between political philosophy and ideology from the other end: does the theory of ideology itself manifest ideological features? Can we expose the worldview of the analyst, merely by examining his methodology of studying ideology? Can the scholar of ideology escape the gilded cage of projecting his own ideological inclinations through his scientific endeavor? Offering a productive analysis of the evolution of the theory of ideology in view of the 'restrictive–inclusive' distinction, Humphrey poses serious questions about the supposed neutrality of the student of ideology: as is the case with liberalism, the professed neutrality masks an inclination to endorse pluralism. This is radically different from the project of studying ideology as a social critique. Both approaches are legitimate as long as they are reflective about their goals, methods and objects of analysis.

Michael Freeden engages with the problem of the ideology behind the analytical methodology, by examining the contribution of liberalism to the study of ideology. He argues that it is important to distinguish between the epistemology that liberalism has imparted to scholarly research and the micro-values that liberalism promotes, claiming that the study of ideology has benefited from the first, but doesn't have to reflect the second. However, there is still a battle over liberalism going on, one which mutates between pluralism and fragmentation, given the ethos of consumerism and mass democratization processes. Not only do traditional ideologies transform and develop new faces, new forms of ideology emerge. One particularly interesting one, is the thesis of the 'post-ideological' age itself, which Freeden decontests and challenges. He then sets the scene for the future study of ideology, asking where we find ideologies in today's world, and what we do when we meet them. The volume concludes that ideologies contain the codes that organize political practice, diversified and heterogenous as politics may be, claiming that the analysis of ideologies is therefore part of the study of mainstream politics.

References

Barrett M. (1991) *The Politics of Truth* (Oxford: Polity Press).
Bell, D. (1960) *The End of Ideology* (Cambridge, MA: Harvard University Press).
Bell, D. (1988) *The End of Ideology* (Cambridge, MA: Harvard University Press).
Bell, D. (2000) *The End of Ideology*. (Cambridge, MA: Harvard University Press).
Benhabib, S. (1996) Towards a deliberative model of democratic legitimacy. In *Democracy and Difference* (Princeton, NJ: Princeton University Press).

Bhagwati, J. (2004) *In Defense of Globalization* (Oxford: Oxford University Press).
Blair, T. (2004) The opportunity society. *The Labour Party Conference, Brighton*.
Boggs, C. (2000) *The End of Politics* (New York: Guilford Press).
Bracher, K. (1984) *The Age of Ideologies* (London: Methuen).
Budge, I. et al. (Eds) (2001). *Mapping Policy Preferences: Estimates for Parties, Electors and Governments 1945–1998* (Oxford: Oxford University Press).
Callinicos, A. (2003). *An Anti-Capitalist Manifesto* (Oxford: Blackwell).
Dalton, R. & Kuechler, M. (Eds) (1990) *Challenging the Political Order* (Cambridge: Polity Press).
Dalton, R. & Wattenberg, M. (Eds) (2000) *Parties without Partisans: Political Change in Advanced Industrial Democracies* (Oxford: Oxford University Press).
Eagleton, T. (1996) *The Illusions of Postmodernism* (Oxford, Blackwell).
Fairclough, N. (1995) *Critical Discourse Analysis* (London: Longman).
Fairclough, N. (1989) *Language and Power* (London: Longman).
Foucault, M. (1980) Truth and power, in: C. Gordon, (Ed.), *Power/knowledge: Selected Interviews and Other Writings, 1972–1977)* (Brighton: Harvest).
Freeden, M. (1996) *Ideologies and Political Theory: A Conceptual Approach* (Oxford: Clarendon Press).
Freeden, M. (2003) *Ideology: A Very Short Introduction* (Oxford: Oxford University Press).
Fukuyama, F. (1992) *The End of History and the Last Man* (New York: Free Press).
Geertz, C. (1973) *The Interpretation of Cultures: Selected Essays* (New York, Basic Books).
Giddens, A. (1998) *The Third Way* (Cambridge, Polity Press).
Giddens, A. (2002) *Where Now for New Labour* (Cambridge: Polity Press).
Giddens, A. (2004) Did they foul up my Third Way? *New Statesman*, pp. 24–25.
Gutmann, A. & Thompson, D. (2004) *Why Deliberative Democracy?* (Princeton, NJ: Princeton University Press).
Habermas, J. (1996) Three normative models of democracy, in: Benhabib, S., *Democracy and Difference* (Princeton, NJ: Princeton University Press).
Habermas, J. (1999) *The Structural Transformation of the Public Sphere* (Cambridge, MA: MIT Press).
Held, D. & McGrew, A. (2002) *Globalization/Anti-Globalization* (Cambridge, Polity Press).
Inglehart, R. (1990) Values, ideology and cognitive mobilization, in: R.D.M. Kuechler (Ed.), *Challenging the Political Order* (Cambridge, Polity Press), pp. 43–66.
Kirchheimer, O. (1990) The catch-all party, in: P. Mair (Ed.), *The West European Party System* (Oxford: Oxford University Press), pp. 50–61.
Labour (2001). *Ambition for Britain, Labour's Manifesto 2001* (London, Labour Party).
Peter, M. & Katz, R. (1997) *Party System Change* (Oxford: Clarendon Press).
Mannheim, K. (1955). *Ideology and Utopia* (New York: Harcourt).
Schattscheneider, E.E. (1942) *Party Government* (New York, Reinhart).
Scumpeter, J.A. (1942) *Capitalism, Socialism and Democracy* (New York: Harper & Row).
Smith, G. (1990) Core persistence, system change and the 'People's Party', in: P. Mair & G. Smith (Eds), *Understanding Party System Change in Western Europe* (London: Frank Cass), pp. 157–168.
Steger, M.B. (2005) Ideologies of globalization. *Journal of Political Ideologies*, 10(1), pp. 11–30.
Talshir, G. (2002) *The Political Ideology of Green Parties: From Politics of Nature to Redefining the Nature of Politics* (London, Palgrave).
Talshir, G. (forthcoming).The objects of ideology: Historical transformations and the changing role of the analyst. *History of Political Thought*.
Thatcher, M. (1989) *The Revival of Britain: Speeches on Home and European Affairs 1975–1988* (London, Aurum Press).
WSF, <http://www.wsfindia.org/charter.php>.

Visions of Popular Sovereignty: Mapping the Contested Terrain of Contemporary Western Populisms

DAVID LAYCOCK

Introduction

Since the early 1970s, new parties with populist credentials have helped to reconfigure competitive politics and policy debates in North America, much of Europe, New Zealand and Australia. Major party leaders have used populist appeals to connect with cynical publics, to displace old party establishments or to set them up for 'hostile takeovers',[1] and to create ideological maneuvering room for major policy change. We have witnessed heightened interaction between political entrepreneurs on the 'new right', nationalist xenophobia and cultural insecurity, increasing anxiety about the national sovereignty-limiting effects of 'globalization', and a deep sense of democratic malaise and disenchantment with established political elites.

However, populist themes have also been important to the left in Western societies for many years,[2] and are likely to remain so in the future. Over the past century, much of the public support for extensions of popular sovereignty has been developed and harnessed by parties and movements with important populist dimensions. It would thus be analytically short sighted to reserve the term 'populism' for the politics and ideology of xenophobic parties and movements of the far right. We need an analytical approach that clarifies similarities and differences in hybrid-populist ideologies' use of key terms connected to central problems of democratic politics. A better conceptual grasp of populist visions of popular sovereignty is needed to help us to see that although populism is not a holistic ideology, populist ideological elements possess great flexibility in relations with fuller ideologies.

In this essay I investigate several conceptual foundations of populist ideological attempts to decontest the language, symbols and ambitions of popular sovereignty. I argue that unpacking the conceptual basis of populist incursions into left- and right-wing political narratives sheds important light on left–right cleavages and contests over the nature of democracy in Anglo-American and many European polities. Employing Michael Freeden's morphological approach to understanding the conceptual structure of modern ideologies (Freeden 1996), I treat populist discourses on popular sovereignty as key dimensions of the interpenetration of populism with contemporary ideologies. I follow Margaret Canovan in rejecting the search for a 'general theory' of populism (Canovan 1980, 1982, 2004), and accept Paul Taggart's contention that there are no 'core values' binding all expressions of populism (Taggart 2004). But populist sharing of core concepts need not imply shared values; as I show, competing populisms employ a shared set of basic democratic concepts while contesting their normative and policy implications.

Every account of ideologies is a view from somewhere, which highlights some features and accords less prominence to others. Some contemporary commentators on populism see it through the lens of responses to 'globalization' (Betz 2004) or in terms of the revival of cultural nationalisms in Western polities (Ignazi 2003; Schain et al. 2002). In focusing on populist visions of popular sovereignty, I am concerned with identifying populist responses to what Norberto Bobbio calls the 'broken promises' of democracy (Bobbio 1987a: ch. 1 & 4), and interested in how populist discourses critical of diminished popular sovereignty conceptually anchor their appeals in many Western polities. My attention is directed primarily to the ways in which these discourses overlap with left–right cleavages over the welfare state and its regulatory role within capitalist economies.

Mapping Populist Morphologies: Populism's Flexible Democratic 'Core'

To fully convey the interpenetration of populist ideological elements and fuller ideologies of the left, centre and right, one would have to map these elements as influential but dependent parts of broader ideological frameworks. Yet, in a brief discussion, highlighting the democratic significance of populist elements within contemporary ideological competitions requires us to isolate the democratic conceptual foundations of populist appeals, operating almost as if populisms can be understood as 'thick-centred' or 'holistic' ideologies. I attempt to make up for this distortion by identifying conceptual bridges to the broader ideological homes of particular visions of popular sovereignty.

With this important caveat, then, we can say that the populist democratic component of western political ideologies has a flexible normative morphological core with three elements:

1) a 'problematicization' of the relationship between popular sovereignty and representation;
2) an understanding of equality; and
3) a normative political economy of the conflict between 'the people' and elites.

Each of these core elements within any specific populist ideology is decisively shaped by the others, and by key features – adjacent and perimeter concepts, to use Freeden's language – of nationally specific liberal, neo-conservative, and social-democratic ideologies. Interaction between core, adjacent and perimeter concepts links broad political and normative orientations (conveyed by core and major adjacent concepts) to specific institutional and policy agendas (minor adjacent and perimeter concepts). In this essay, space constraints require me to focus on contending constructions of the same core concepts by two general populist families, and offer only passing reference to their adjacent and perimeter conceptual morphologies.

Popular Sovereignty and Representation

When conceived as rule by citizens over as much of their collective public life as possible, popular sovereignty's desirability is seldom openly questioned.[3] The real debate concerns how citizens can engage in collective decision making in how much of public life and civil society. Like other key terms in democratic ideologies, popular sovereignty is an essentially contested concept.

Toqueville contended that following the American Revolution, 'the doctrine of the sovereignty of the people ... took possession of the state: every class was enlisted in its cause ... until it became the law of laws' (de Toqueville 1961: vol. 1, 49). However, since Rousseau popular sovereignty has often been contrasted with not just elite rule, but also with democratic decision making by representatives. As Sheldon Wolin has recently suggested, for over two centuries in Western political cultures, popular sovereignty has been 'the ultimate, all-powerful master whose secret, which the world knows, is that it cannot act' (Wolin 2001: 349).

For Norberto Bobbio, the idea that 'true' popular sovereignty would eschew representation was both central to early democratic theory, and its first 'broken promise' (Bobbio 1987a: 28).[4] All six broken promises in modern democratic rule ultimately transgress the principle of unmediated popular sovereignty, even when they are broken in the name of democracy. Still, the idea that true democracy entails sovereign individuals directly extending their wills into binding pubic decisions has never died for a broad swath of the left, including many Marxists (Bobbio 1987a: chs 3 & 4). It has also appealed to parties, movements and some theorists on the right over the past century – including various European fascisms between the world wars, and parties of the 'radical populist right' over the past generation. A broad public recognition of the depth of democratic broken promises creates an ideological environment within which populist discourses on the left and the right find popular resonance.

Several recent commentators on populism have highlighted modern populists' antagonism towards representative institutions and processes.[5] Nadia Urbinati contends that European populist support for 'direct relationships between people and leaders' is implacably opposed to the 'principle of representation' upon which liberal constitutionalists must ground pluralistic and representative democracy. The populist 'distrust in the forms and institutions of representation', leads to a 'despotic' faith in the will of the people as against the deliberations of representative legislatures and the rule of law, 'empty and ritualistic' elections, demagogic leadership and attacks on pluralistic debate in legislative assemblies and civil society (Urbinati 1998: 116–122). This portrait raises appropriate concerns about the anti-democratic tendencies of some populisms, but mistakenly attributes a single democratic logic to all expressions of populist concern for popular sovereignty.

Hans-Georg Betz's recent account of parties of the 'radical populist right' in Europe emphasizes their attack on the unrepresentativeness of centrist or social democratic political elites. He argues that the combination of socio-economic and political globalization, threatened national identities, and already declining public trust in political parties, has allowed new parties of the radical populist right to pose as the champions of true democracy and offer facile remedies to contemporary 'representational failure'. (Betz 2004: chs 2 & 3).

Paul Taggart stresses how variations among representative (and other) institutions produce differing populist responses. In most European Union member states, adding representative institutions with new and broad policy scope, institutional scale and complexity has produced an upsurge in populist politics. As the scale and impacts of representative politics increases in Europe, with a strengthening of EU representative institutions and weakening of national representative institutions, so will the range of 'ideological partners' with which populism can operate (Taggart 2000, 2004).

Taggart argues that 'populism has the task of constructing itself as an entity out of reaction to representative politics' (2000: 116). Nonetheless, his analysis points in the direction of an expanding continuum of relations between representative practices and the quest for popular sovereignty, in which the latter does not necessarily entail rejection of all aspects of the former. Given the impact that particular regimes of representation may have on political cultures and political opportunity structures, this continuum will include everything from complex blends of representation, deliberation, direct and participatory democracy, to a stark rejection of all institutional mediation between citizens and the state.[6]

Right-populism and Representational Failure

The practical question for those advancing populist agendas, then, is not just how popular sovereignty can be extended, but also how representative institutions and processes might be altered, augmented or circumvented to make this possible.[7] In most recent populisms on the political right, altering representative institutions means curtailing them, through the trumping mechanisms of direct democracy, and/ or by reducing the scope of the business to which representative institutions attend.

Promotion of direct democratic remedies to representational failures has been a common feature of new right populisms in North America and Europe. Canada's Reform party (1986–2000) was typical in this regard. It advocated citizens' initiatives on everything from capital punishment to balanced budgets to native self-government agreements. Proposals for particular referenda were accompanied by accusations that corrupt old party legislators had failed to represent their constituents' preferences. The party promoted recall provisions as ways of forcing elected officials to heed the people's voice and stop pandering to the special interests that held old-line parties hostage (Laycock 2001, 2004).

At the heart of these calls for direct democracy is the allegation that 'representational failure' has been systematically generated by the proliferation of mediating forces between citizens' preferences and policy development or implementation. Parties and organized interests supportive of extensive and expensive social programs and business regulation have perverted natural translation, through market transactions, of individual preferences into social results. Representational failure is thus equated with a statist, party-manipulated, socially engineered blockage of consumer/taxpayer sovereignty. Exercises in popular sovereignty via direct democracy were to play an important role in producing a low-tax, minimally interventionist state, an unshackled marketplace, and a substantial boost to law and order (Laycock 2001, 2005).

Advocacy of direct democracy by new parties of the populist right has been far from ideologically innocent. The 'direct democracy industry' in Western states within the United States has produced serious problems for public education and other public services while offering a bonanza for many large business interests (Shrag 1998; Broder 2000) We can also be properly skeptical of parties in Western Europe, North America and Australia whose leaders portray their personalistic political vehicles as 'anti-parties'.[8] Nonetheless, direct democracy need not operate in the interests of the privileged. Many early twentieth-century American populists pushed state legislatures to legislatively enable direct democracy to counteract the control that railroad, banking, and grain trade interests had over the two party competition in regional and national legislatures (Beard & Schultz 1912; Goodwyn 1976). As Jack Hayward reminds us, referenda can strengthen the electorate against representatives who may, like all elites, misrepresent the electorate's views (Hayward 1996: 17).

Another important right-populist perspective on representational failure has adapted the arguments of conservative economists (e.g. Hayek 1979) and conservative political scientists' arguments on 'demand overload' (Huntington et al. 1975).

These perspectives locate representational failure in the interventionist activities of modern welfare states, contending that representational mechanisms are over-responding to illegitimate demands from artificially empowered actors in civil society. For right-populists attracted to such analyses, the appropriate response to distorted over-representation involves removing current group representatives from the policy process in advanced welfare states. Shrinking the public sector and welfare state is crucial, as the public goods delivered through statist social programs distort supply, demand and incentives in the labour market. The public sector and social program matrix also generates strong constituencies of support for extensive public services, and expensive redistributive programmes. So reducing program expenditures and hence taxes becomes much more politically difficult when these programs have their own self-perpetuating representatives built right into their design.

On this account, de-regulating business is desirable partly because it prevents anti-market representatives from meddling in natural market decisions. Similarly, reducing rights-based protections for ethnic minorities will reduce the artificially inflated power of special-interest representatives in labour, educational, cultural and media markets. Cutting subsidies to non-business advocacy groups (women's groups, ethnic minorities, the disabled, the poor, environmentalists) will stop their over-representation in public forums and legislative hearings. All of this will move more social decisions to the level playing field of what Robert Nozick called 'capitalist acts between consenting adults.'

At first blush, reducing the overall number of players in the pluralist competition would seem to be at odds with demands for enhanced popular sovereignty. The populist/new right argues, however, that because these groups' current forms and levels of participation in public life are artificially sustained by state funding rather than market-derived income, such moves will not curtail popular sovereignty. To the contrary: real popular sovereignty is expressed in the same way as consumer sovereignty: consumer–citizens act privately and voluntarily. When the political market is internally corrupted, and registers illegitimate demands more than legitimate demands, the former can be safely undercut without any loss to virtuous consumer–citizens or democracy. Once legitimate voices are represented in the policy process in proportion to their support by citizens voting with their pocketbooks, representational failure will be dramatically reduced, and popular sovereignty seriously enhanced.

So this proposed reduction in the scope and impact of representation is closely tied to promotion of an overwhelmingly market-dominant political economy. If parties and legislatures are corrupt agents of the people's will, the complex representational structures and group advocacy opportunities embedded in the welfare and regulatory state are key sites of representational failure. In such a context, legislative decisions can be legitimately over-ridden via direct democracy. Parties with strong right-populist elements in Canada, the United States, Australia and Europe have linked their critique of representation to an attack on parties complicit in the expansion of the 'special interest state' that is characterized by so many points of access for representatives (or advocates) for self-described disadvantaged groups.

Not all populist discourses contend that popular sovereignty is enhanced if the substantive and institutional scope of representative decision making is reduced. As Bobbio puts it, 'not every criticism of representative democracy leads automatically to the advocacy of direct democracy' (Bobbio 1987a: 46). Their substantially different take on the political economy and power relations within contemporary capitalism means that for left-populists, market relations are not seen as a solution to unbalanced power between formally equal citizens, but rather as the source of unbalanced power, diminished freedom and a gap between formal and substantive equality. To the extent that representative institutions facilitate and disguise this unequal political economy, they are serious obstacles to expansion of popular sovereignty.

Left-populists since the nineteenth century have promoted a more inclusive, broader and deeper extension of representative bodies, linking formal political institutions with organizations and processes in civil society.[9] Popular sovereignty in this view is enhanced when advocates for citizens from non-dominant socio-economic groups have meaningful roles and voices in representative bodies. Left populists have generally accepted the substance of Bobbio's claim that 'the advance of democracy will in future be measured in terms of the infiltration of spaces still occupied by non-democratic centres of power' in big business and public administration (Bobbio 1987a: 57). And for left-populists, this advance has not entailed a substantive diminution of pluralistic representation, suggesting that we need not accept Urbinati's claim that populists, as populists, are anti-pluralist and opposed to representation.

Much of what I refer to in this essay under the heading 'left-populism' is often described with reference to 'social democracy'. Why not just accept that left-populism is simply social democracy? With our focus on the use of political symbols and the construction of ideological appeals, two considerations are germane. First, the 'materialist' redistributive and market-regulatory emphases in social democratic governance have tended to overshadow the often innovative democratic representational content in social democratic movement activities, meant to respond to concerns about democratic deficits in public life as well as distributive deficits. Second, most social democratic leaders and activists from the 1880s onwards have been acutely aware of the importance of engaging existing and potential supporters' 'democratic imaginary'. Political contests could not be won on the back of material promises alone; party/movement activists have needed to see themselves building a basis for expanded popular sovereignty. Re-labeling social democrats as left-populists in this context thus serves the purpose of emphasizing the 'popular democratic' dimensions of social democratic politics.

Left-populism is not the predominant populist perspective on representative institutions and practices today; it is not even a strong force in many social democratic parties. But we should not overlook its historical importance, especially in relation to the growth and defence of the welfare state. Nor should we assume that it has reached the end of its history. A close examination of the anti-globalization movements in OECD countries might well uncover a critique of representation echoing important elements of left-populism of the early to mid-twentieth century. Recent work on 'democratic transformation' since the 1960s suggests that there are important populist elements interwoven in the surge of 'advocacy democracy', where citizens and various groups participate in public forums, legislative committee hearings and other highly public means of influencing decision making by elected representatives. These blend some direct with mostly mediated efforts at broadening the range of voices setting and deciding policy agendas (Cain et al. 2003, chs 1 & 11).

Noberto Bobbio contends that 'the fifth promise unfulfilled by the reality of democracy when compared to the ideal is the elimination of invisible power', a promise based on the notion that 'democratic government could finally bring about the transparency of power, 'power without masks' (Bobbio 1987a: 33). Popular sovereignty was thus to contrast with autocratic and unaccountable power, much of which was exercised by self-selected elites operating outside of public view. Almost all populisms, whatever their other ideological signs, allude to the exercise of 'invisible power' within and behind representative institutions. Richard Hofstader influentially pioneered dismissal of such claims as the conspiracy theory of manipulative leaders and their poorly educated, scapegoat-seeking followers (Hofstader 1955). But as Bobbio reminds us, invisible power has proliferated in government and corporate circles over the past century, as technologies of surveillance and increasing complexity of governance systems annually create more democratic accountability problems than they solve. Calls for more 'visible' power in such an environment should be seen as quite consistent with the legitimizing principles of popular sovereignty, not necessarily the product of conspiratorial imaginations.

Still, the populist case against 'invisible power', and proposals to remedy some of its elements, can be made in very different ways. A citizen who sees increasing corporate power as the major source and beneficiary of invisible power will be attracted to one type of populist message. Her neighbour will prefer another when she looks at the same newscasts and sees increased state power over actors in markets as the key source factor in invisible power. These differing approaches are linked to views on which forms of coercion 'the people' most need protection from, and hence the aspects of freedom that are most politically salient. Popular understandings of the modern political economy, which structure practices of freedom, thus shape perspectives on invisible power, and on the obstacles to popular sovereignty presented by it. These perspectives on political economy also do much to shape criticism of existing representative institutions, and what kinds (and combinations) of direct or 'participatory' democratic remedies are preferred to representational failures.

Equality

All politically relevant populisms make their case for greater popular power with reference to some highly resonant public understanding of equality, which is closely linked to ideas about popular sovereignty and representation.

Between the two world wars, left-liberals and social democrats successfully constructed an influential conception of substantive equality in North America, much of western Europe, and Australia (Sawer 2003). This idea was egalitarian in social class terms, and opposed to landed and corporate wealth as the basis of political power. It rejected the earlier liberal idea that universal voting rights plus equal civil rights would ensure sufficient social or economic welfare for 'ordinary people'. This approach to substantive equality was instrumental in the expansion of social rights, social programs, state-provided public goods, and public sectors between the early 1930s and the 1980s. This expansion was linked to the forward march of popular sovereignty, in so far as these rights, services and public goods were seen as necessary conditions of efficacious citizenship for non-privileged citizens. Expanding the conceptual and material meaning of equality was crucial to the legitimation of representative institutions in evolving social welfare regimes.

Over the past several decades, a powerful assault on the welfare state by the new right has been crucially facilitated by the right's realization that such an assault can only appear legitimate to a large public constituency when grounded in a conception of equality. Perhaps the most striking thing about the ideological structure of new right ideologies is how aggressively they have contested the conceptual field of equality, on to which conservatives had seldom ventured before the 1970s. Earlier conservatives had not seen that to compete successfully against liberal and social democratic rivals, they need to openly and innovatively – if somewhat derivatively (Freeden 1996: chs 7 & 10) – decontest equality. It was not enough to argue that liberal or social democratic governance justified with reference to equality was undermining freedom. By the 1970s, British and American conservative party strategists realized that to make inroads within democratic political cultures, the right cannot afford to cede the ground of equality claims to the heirs of those who had extended the franchise and built the welfare state.

Recognizing that middle-income citizens had become increasingly alienated from representative structures, processes and officials, perceptive new right strategists and theorists have suggested that these citizens see themselves as the objects of unequal treatment by the deficiently representative state. Responsibility for the state's representative failings, in turn, is laid at the feet of distorted representational networks within overdeveloped welfare regimes. The new right's case against redistributive policies, progressive income taxes, state regulation of corporate power, and multicultural inclusion was woven together with a pre-First World War conception of equality of opportunity. In the new right's effective re-definition, equality of opportunity has been undermined because 'special interests' – women, and non-dominant ethnic and social groups – are benefiting from 'special rights'. State economic activity and redistributive programs are portrayed as offences against the equality under the law that governs freely chosen market relations (Sawer 2004; Laycock 2001). According to the new right, 'special interests' aim at 'equality of outcome', to be achieved through egregious coercion, bureaucratic over-employment, and confiscatory taxation, not a defensible or desirable equality of opportunity.

Why is this re-definition of equality of opportunity pertinent to a discussion of contemporary populism? The New Right allegation that representative institutions have been distorted or virtually captured by 'special interests' suggests that the equal right of all citizens to participate in ruling themselves, and to enjoy equal political standing, has thus been diminished. Special interests dependent on the welfare state have become the new elites or 'the new class' (Sawer & Hindess 2004) intent on stifling the promises of popular sovereignty. For citizens who are economically insecure, and feel culturally insecure – despite their being squarely within the cultural mainstream – this kind of elite-labeling can be very persuasive when it is made in terms of offences against equality.

Once the language of equality has been successfully linked to corrupted systems of representation and state provision, it is far easier to make the case that a high-tax welfare state is sustained by self-serving special interests and their benefiting sponsors in the 'political class'. These activities can thus be presented as more than costly (pace fiscal conservatism), or intrusive (pace right-wing libertarianism); they also offend against basic principles of equal opportunity. And since the political order cannot be counted on for equal opportunity treatment, people are encouraged to turn to the market order, with its formal equality of rights among buyers and sellers.

Something like this argument has been made by many populist parties of the new right, in Australia (One Nation), New Zealand (ACT), Austria (FPÖ), Canada (Reform/Alliance) and Scandinavia (Progress parties). What is perhaps even more striking, however, is how successfully this re-definition of equality of opportunity has been deployed by parties of privilege: the British Conservative party, under Margaret Thatcher, and American Republicans, most notably Ronald Reagan, Newt Gingrich and George W. Bush.[10]

After the mid-1970s, equality also became the privileged ideological mainstay of many new right populist cases for direct democracy. Party-mediated decision making in legislatures, and state agencies that report to them, are portrayed as grave instances of political inequality, because elected and appointed officials are all part of the elite. Letting the people decide on selected policy questions means allowing sovereign individuals to choose among policy options, in the way that markets channel 'consumer sovereignty'.

The new populist right has constructed another kind of egalitarianism with clear populist appeal, in which the onus for justifying difference in cultural practices is placed on those who do not wish to assimilate entirely into the values of the majority culture. Cultural difference (or difference in sexual preference) is thus made equivalent to an insistence on inequality. The real inegalitarians, following this logic, are those who insist on 'special treatment', while those who are comfortable with dominant cultural norms and practices are champions of equality. This inverted egalitarianism intersects with experiences of status and economic insecurity to fuel hostility towards non-majority group immigration, towards programs that support multiculturalism, and, as we saw in the 2004 American election, towards gays and lesbians.

Many on the left who dislike the markedly anti-pluralist and illiberal practical policy consequences of these positions deny that they have anything to do with equality. Yet these right-populist equality claims have cultural and democratic legitimacy because they incorporate a specific and powerful conception of equality, which speaks to the broad desire for equal rights among citizens and against elites. Among other things, this desire can tilt referendum results against the interests of cultural and other minorities (Eisenberg 2004).[11]

Populisms of the left have also decontested equality to obtain democratic legitimacy for their visions of popular sovereignty. As Ernesto Laclau argues, practical socialist politics have often been populist in an important sense. Socialist and social democratic articulation of a 'people/power bloc' antagonism has roots in, but extends beyond, social class conflict (Laclau 1977: ch. 4). Hence we see many cases of 'social democratic populism,' especially in societies where large agricultural populations have faced the same political and economic antagonists as organized urban labour.[12] The equality sought by left-populists entails a reduction in corporate power within the economy and within prevailing systems of representation, whether in party competition or the back rooms of state policy development.

The contrast between left- and right-populist approaches to equality can be summarized with reference to the former's idea of equality of opportunity, and its view of representation as a vehicle of, not obstacle to, popular sovereignty. As with right-populist perspectives, left-populist understandings of equality of opportunity and democratic representation hinge on a broad view of the prevailing political economy. Left-populists believe that capitalist market economies produce a high level of material inequality among citizens, and a highly skewed set of political, social and economic opportunity structures. Formally equal civil and political rights are insufficient to redress these related inequalities; distribution of opportunities among citizens will still be badly skewed in favour of those lucky to be skilled or powerful in market transactions. Like Michael Walzer, left populists do not believe that transference of advantage between spheres of social life – especially from the economic to the political – is consistent with a defensible idea of justice (Walzer 1983). So because justice requires meaningful equality of opportunity, reducing the extent to which such transference occurs is equivalent to increasing equality of opportunity.

Left-populists thus believe the state is obligated to intervene in the operation of the economy, and in the representation of citizens' interests within policy processes in state structures, to give material and legal expression to the idea of equality. Left-populists are typically wary of party, organized interest and bureaucratic elites that mediate between citizen preferences and state decisions. But they are on balance warier of corporate power exercised in the economy and through the state. So they see limits to this power as crucial to achievement of an equality of opportunity that gives citizens at least a taste of popular sovereignty. Complex mechanisms for representing diverse popular wills, including forms of 'democratic corporatism', are promoted to ensure that corporate power does not completely undermine popular sovereignty.

Over the past 30 years, the central divide between left and right populisms on the question of equality has been over the extent and future of the welfare state. For right-populists, the welfare state and its representational supports ('left-leaning' party systems, and the intrusion of many social programme-supporting advocates and organizations into the policy process) have exacerbated inequality among citizens by favouring beneficiaries of wrong-headed programmes over hard-working, independent citizens and entrepreneurs. Special rights for various minority groups have introduced new inequalities and hobbled the market, the only social choice mechanism truly capable of treating people equally. This integrated system of corrupted parties and interests, over-taxed citizens and bloated bureaucracies needs to be dismantled and rebuilt, with inspiration from a proper understanding of equality.

Left populists take a broadly social democratic view of the welfare state, seeing it as an instrument of enlarged equality of opportunity and hence more effective popular rule. Over the past two generations they have proposed expanding the welfare state and its representational policy communities, first with universalistic programmes and more recently, with targeted programs justified in terms of 'group-differentiated rights' (Kymlicka 1995) that address inequalities with non-class origins (e.g. gender, ethnicity, sexual preference). Inter-war left-populisms seldom endorsed group-differentiated rights, and envisaged a less complex welfare state than their heirs have developed. But the logic of the earlier and current left-populist positions is largely shared.

It is easy to under-appreciate how equality's extraordinary ideological range has played a major role in the construction and impact of modern populist ideologies. When exploring the concept of 'the people' within populism, Margaret Canovan suggests that for concepts to be central to populism, or any other ideology, they must be central only to that one ideology (Canovan 1984: 312–14). This would seem to disqualify equality from playing a key role within populisms on the political right, given its already prominent place in the socialist core. Yet as we have seen, these populisms have required some compelling version of equality to obtain democratic plausibility and hence political appeal.

Michael Freeden's account of the interaction of concepts within ideologies points a way around this problem. Freeden demonstrates that it is the set of mutual influences and relations among ideologically distinctive concepts – within the core, and between core and adjacent concepts – that makes ideologies distinctive, not their deployment of individual broad conceptual labels. When these interaction effects are carefully examined, we find that left- and right-populist conceptions of equality are unambiguously distinctive.

The People vs Elites

However else they diverge, academic commentators tend to agree that populist ideologies have a people–elites antagonism at their normative and descriptive centres.[13] Populist deployment of this antagonism is as old as the English Civil War.

While discussing how Levellers challenged the Royalist insistence on defining citizenship in aristocratic and exclusionary terms, Sheldon Wolin provides a passage that nicely links our core concepts.

> 'the people', as a distinct entity, was extricated from the corporate hierarchical community of medieval theory and asserted as the sole source of legitimate power and an actor in its own right. The political stake of ordinary beings was argued at length, and as a result a crucial awareness developed of a built-in conflict between the people and any system that claimed to represent and act for them. (Wolin 2001: 67)

Democracy has since then been, among other things, a movement against 'exclusionary politics' (Wolin 2001: 381–382). Populisms of the left or the right virtually always speak of and to a sense of exclusion from power, but employ distinctive definitions of 'the people' along with distinctive political economies to explain the people's exclusion from effective popular sovereignty. In reviewing the broad differences between left and right political economies' relations to their accounts of representation and equality, we have noted numerous references to alleged conflicts between 'the people' and elites.

For right-populists, re-drawing the 'people'–elites tensions begins with a reversal of the long-standing distrust of corporate elites. Earlier right-populists had often vilified at least some element of the corporate elite – typically bankers – as 'special interest' enemies of the people (Laycock 1990: ch. 5). But an effective attack on the welfare state requires an elimination of this residual complaint with the 'business class'. Any hint that the market is other than a field of virtue and freedom-enhancing behaviour must be removed. The source of relevant political inequality, and manifest coercion, is re-located firmly in the complex of state institutions and practices that constrain free market behaviour. The market provides a template of meaningful popular sovereignty in 'consumer sovereignty', where citizens vote freely with their wallets.

Special interests are thus re-defined to include bureaucrats who regulate business and deliver social programmes, and advocates of social programme expenditure or business regulation. Special interests also include the social constituencies that directly benefit from regulation and social programme expenditure, as well as elected officials (and their parties), who legislatively enable confiscatory taxation, bureaucratic expansion, welfare state growth and business regulation. To put it succinctly, special interests become any group facilitating or benefiting from state intervention in consensual market relations.

Once elites are defined so broadly in right-populist discourse, who are the people? They are, by a process of elimination, hard-working citizens and entrepreneurs who do not seek state assistance in distorting the workings of the labour market in particular and the market order generally. Business groups and think tanks that advocate reduction in the scope and intervention of the state are part of the people because of their efforts to secure the people's freedom from a coercive, high-taxing state. Rewards received in market relations are both deserved and natural, while the rewards secured from the state by the special interests are undeserved and artificial.

Another aspect of the new right populist re-definition of 'the people' has no necessary connection to the promotion of a natural market order, though one often finds it made by allies of the anti-statists. This is the often xenophobic drawing of people–elite boundaries on the ground of maintaining cultural homogeneity by either rejecting culturally distinct immigrants, or insisting on their complete assimilation into the dominant national culture. The people are members of the cultural majority in 'the heartland' (Taggart 2004) and their political defenders; elites are promoters of non-discriminatory immigration and state-sponsored 'multiculturalism.' In this way, right-populism makes contact with long traditions of illiberal nationalism and even civic republicanism. What this perspective on the elites–people tension shares with that of the anti-statists is a rejection of state assistance to cultural minority groups and other social categories that benefit from state redistribution of social resources. But while the anti-statists are concerned with such assistance because it adds to tax burdens, and can help legitimize market intervention, anti-multiculturalists see such assistance as undermining a distinctive national culture, or – at the extreme – accommodating inferior and thus undesirable peoples.

This last way of articulating the 'people'–elite antagonism has done more than anything else recently to give populism a bad name among academics, journalists and tolerant citizens in Europe, North America and Australia. When extreme-right populists portray 'the people' as members of the same long-standing national–cultural community, and elites as anyone promoting inclusion of supra-national 'others' into a more diverse national community, the opportunities for racism and intolerance are boosted dramatically. Yet while this is a very worrisome development, it is just one way of harnessing the language of 'the people' in modern populism. This perspective does not even obviously represent the most influential position among right-wing populisms.

The left's way of decontesting 'the people' has helped to drive a great many populisms for the last 150 years. Left-populisms standardly contend that while dominant state elites are the enemies of the people, it is because corporate elites indirectly hold the reins of political power. Because business elites exploit urban workers and farmers, they are the core 'special interests' whose power in the market economy must be subject to some kind of democratic accountability. Otherwise any reforms of state structures, or of parties and other potential instruments of popular will representation, will not have a real effect.

Left-populists construct corporate elites as the people's enemies, and because they are 'anti-big business' rather than strictly anti-capitalist, have always managed to find common ground with left-liberals. Both organized labour and left-liberals speak the language of 'the people' against unaccountable corporate elites. So have leaders and activists in the extensive cooperative movement in most western countries,[14] and promoters of "community economic development" practices in North

America (Boyte et al. 1986). The language of 'the people' vs elites has also been common in recent environmental and anti-globalization movement discourses.

Populist conceptualizations of social and political conflict have been influentially articulated through all of these organizational vehicles. Their talk of the people vs elites has been linked to diverse cases for broader and more inclusive social representation through partisan channels, in accessible and widely observed public forums, in the popular media, in legislative committee hearings, and as parts of quasi-corporatist policy development processes within the modern welfare state. Left-populist references to people–elites tensions are also more or less tightly bound up with arguments about equality of opportunity and less unequal distributions of resources. These connections are drawn more tightly with partisan social democrats and left-liberals, and less tightly but still influentially by activists in cooperatives, environmental organizations and the anti-globalization movement. In the latter two cases, arguments about inter-generational justice mean that 'the people' with claims to welfare and some popular sovereignty are in the future as well as the present.

A Word on Adjacent Concepts

Here we can only note in passing several adjacent concepts' linkages to broader populist ideological morphologies, starting with ideas about *freedom*. Left-populists' beliefs about the necessity of distributive and regulatory functions in welfare states to compensate for capitalist economies' inequalities lead them to adopt a 'positive' view of freedom. They conceive of coercion and obstacles to personal autonomy in terms of the absence of basic developmental resources rather than the presence of constraints on capitalist acts between consenting adults. The right-populist language of the people, by contrast, draws our attention to the pervasive sense in which the interventionist, redistributive, "nanny" state constrains and blocks our simplest desires and legitimate choices. This deployment of a negative conception of freedom allows right-populists to re-connect with some of the earliest anti-statist impulses in the populist traditions of popular sovereignty.

For the New Right and right-populists, an artificial and overly pluralized politicization of civil society has threatened individual autonomy, and generated a state structure of self-augmenting power over the people. Right-populisms, and ideologies of the new right generally, aim to dramatically shrink a destructively large political sphere. Some exhort us to chip away at the state Leviathan which maintains this large political sphere by designing direct-democratic end-runs around corrupted representative structures. Citizens' initiatives are promoted to selectively offset specific 'political market failures'. On a related front, group rights are attacked because they undermine individual autonomy and real equality, since 'special rights' are unequal and hence corrosive to the common rights of the people. And presenting parties of the right as 'anti-party' is intended to help to delegitimize party systems in which mutually supportive activities of state bureaucrats and special interest advocates are now endemic. In sum, right populists seek to convince citizens in various ways that they will not find their interests met in a tax-supported, state-empowered public realm, but rather in the market order's realm of freedom.

Orientations to pluralism and related views of legitimate *rights claims* and the proper reach of the *political sphere* also figure as important adjacent concepts in contemporary populisms. Insofar as left-populists wish to broaden rather than narrow the range of groups which have 'voice' in politics and civil society, they tend to support a more inclusive and broadly defined conception of 'the political'. This contrasts sharply with right-populist arguments about 'demand overload' caused by taking pluralism at its word. Left-populists have been sympathetic to experimentation with 'participatory democracy', and to accommodating group-differentiated rights claims alongside the equal–rights agenda that justified extension of the franchise and the 'civil rights' movement. They contend that 'the people' are necessarily plural and cannot speak with one voice in modern societies. It should be acknowledged, however, that some left-populists are still nostalgic about the days when social rights based on 'solidarity' (Esping-Andersen 1985) and 'fraternity' (Crick 1987) were simpler, because less inclusive and therefore less challenging on matters of tolerance.[15]

Left-populists join social democrats in strenuously contesting the new right's association of *'the political'* and 'the public realm' with venality, corruption, coercion, and unnatural patterns of power. Defending the welfare state requires valorizing the political realm as potentially productive of virtuous behaviour, just distributions, and meaningful self-government. Left-populists thus reject the new right's attempt to divert all populist impulses into anti-political avenues. They reject right-populists' reduction of social obligations to individual responsibilities, and use of market relations as a template for the bonds of citizenship. In the left-populist dimensions of anti-globalization and cooperative movement ideologies, one finds less willingness to deny that politics is corrupt almost by definition, even though these groups are far from embracing the market as an alternative realm of virtuous social choice.

Much more could be said about populist constructions of these and other adjacent concepts, such as insecurity, multiculturalism, market regulation and globalization. American and Australian experiences with 'the culture wars' are worth separate attention, as they show that the new right has found ways of portraying tensions between 'the people' and elites/special interests, and making contact with popular attitudes towards equality.[16] Identifying how this factors into populist visions of democracy would thus be an important part of mapping visions of popular sovereignty in these polities.

There is also much to be said about the interaction between ideas of popular sovereignty and nationalism (Yack 2001), which has been important to the growth of right-wing populisms and the recent anti-globalization movement. Understanding this ideological relationship is crucial to our appreciation of how the discourses of specific parties, movements, think tanks and media have re-shaped national political competitions. Nationalism is itself so varied an ideological construction, with such divergent implications for specific orientations to popular sovereignty, that there are many relevant intersections of nationalism with both left- and right-populism.[17] Such detailed work is crucial to revealing how populist discourses have adapted elements from, and contributed conceptual depth and political reach to, ideologies of the left and the right.

Conclusion

Many tasks remain in making analytical sense of populist ideologies, including showing more directly and systematically why populism does not qualify as a 'holistic ideological contender', given its inability to provide independent and therefore 'satisfying answers to the basic political questions' (Freeden 2003: 8, 13). Here all I have been able to do is scratch the surface, by indicating that right and left-populisms have attempted to provide satisfying answers to basic questions regarding democracy, which on their terms is at the centre of ideological competition. I hope to have shown that two broad tendencies within current populisms each offer a coherent account of why the political establishments they challenge are democratically deficient. I have argued that the cores of these indictments revolve around decontestations of tensions between popular sovereignty and representation, ideas about equality appropriate to modern welfare states, and perceptions of basic social and political conflicts between 'the people' and powerful elites. In this account I hope to have provided some additional tools with which to appreciate the interaction between populisms and other forces on the contemporary landscape of political ideologies.

Notes

1. This has happened with the Canadian Alliance party merger with the older Progressive Conservative party in the autumn of 2003, with Haider's effective hijacking of the FPÖ in Austria, and Chistoph Blocher's success in becoming leader of the SVP in Switzerland. On the latter two cases, see Betz (2004).
2. See Laycock (1990), Goodwynn (1976), Kazin (1998), Boyte et al. (1986), Trautman (1997), Gerring (1998: ch. 6)), Tilton (1990), Clogg (1993), Laclau (1977), Goot (2001), Sawer (2004) and Johnson (2004).
3. Canovan (1999) makes this point in her discussion of populism as the 'redemptive face' of modern democracy.
4. See also Canovan (2004: 245): 'democratic ideology, which is centred on the notion of the sovereign people, generates expectations that are inevitably disappointed'.
5. There are too many to note here, though beyond the authors discussed in this essay, special mention should be made of Mény and Surel (2002), and Panizza, Mouffe and Arditi in Panizza (2005).
6. See Barney and Laycock (1999: 318–321), for a brief discussion of this 'representational space'.
7. As Bobbio points out, there is no practical either/or option here; all modern, large-scale democratic governance requires at least some representation, so the question is which aspects of decision-making can involve the people directly, and under what conditions, not whether direct democracy can supplant representative democracy (Bobbio 1987b: ch. 2, esp. 46–55).
8. See Betz (2004) for the most recent summary of these claims by Austria's FPÖ, the Swiss SWP, Progress Parties in Norway and Denmark, and the Northern League and Forza Italia in Italy. For Canada, see Laycock (2001); for the United States, see Trautman (1997), and for Australia, see Sawer (2003) and Goot and Watson (2001).

9. In this sense, they have indirectly endorsed what Nadia Urbinati argues is J.S. Mill's claim that it is inclusive debate and judgement that give representative democracy its moral legitimacy, not the fact of a majority legislative vote (Urbinati 2000: 770–771)
10. One could also point to the successful deployment of such arguments by John Howard's Liberal Party in Australia, and a variety of Canadian provincial Progressive Conservative and Liberal Parties since the middle 1990s.
11. Also noteworthy here are the 11 overwhelming 2004 American state referendum victories for groups opposing marriage rights for gays and lesbians.
12. See, for example, Laycock (1990: ch. 4)), Goodwynn (1976), Kazin (1998), Olsen (1983) and Esping-Andersen (1985).
13. See, for example, Canovan (1981, 1984), Laclau (1977: ch. 4), Mény (1997), Betz (2004), Gellner and Ionescu (1969), Laycock (1990) and Taggart (2000).
14. For a statement of principles by the International Cooperative Alliance that demonstrates this, see <http://www.wisc.edu/uwcc/icic/def-hist/gen-info/1995-Revision-of-Co-operative-Principles1/Cooperative-Principles-for-the-21st-Cent1/index.html>.
15. For evidence of such nostalgia within Canada's older social democratic activists, see Erickson and Laycock (2002: 313–318).
16. On the Australian case, see Hindess and Sawer (2004) For a sampling of a large American literature, see Lasch (1995), Scatamburlo (1998) Smelser and Alexander (1999), and White (2003). An entertaining and perceptive review of Lasch is Lehman (1996).
17. See Ignazi (2003), Betz (2004), Hainsworth (2000) and Schain et al. (2002), See Betz and Immerfall (1998) and Kitschelt (1995) for a sample of just the comparative European literature on this phenomenon.

References

Arditi, B. (2005) Populism as an internal periphery of democratic politics, in: F. Panizza (Ed.), *Populism and the Mirror of Democracy* (Verso: London), ch. 3.
Barney, D.D. & Laycock, D. (1999) Right-populists and plebiscitary politics in Canada. *Party Politics*, 5(3), pp. 317–339.
Beard, C.A. & B.E. Shultz (Eds) (1912) *Documents on the State-Wide Initiative, Referendum and Recall* (New York: Macmillan).
Betz, H.-G. (2004) *La droite populiste en Europe: Extrémiste et démocrate?* (Paris: Autrement).
Betz, H.-G. & Immerfall, S. (Eds) (1998) *The New Politics of the Right: Neo-Populist Parties and Movements in Established Democracies* (New York: St Martin's Press).
Bobbio, N. (1987a) *The Future of Democracy*. Trans. Roger Griffin, ed. Richard Bellamy (Minneapolis, MN: University of Minnesota Press).
Bobbio, N. (1987b) *Which Socialism?* Trans. Roger Griffin, ed. Richard Bellamy (Minneapolis, MN: University of Minnesota Press).
Boyte, H. et al. (Eds) (1986) *The New Populism: The Politics of Empowerment* (Philadelphia: Temple University Press).
Broder, D. (2000) *Democracy Derailed: Initiative Campaigns and the Power of Money* (New York: Harcourt).
Cain, B., Dalton, R.J. & Scarrow, S.E. (Eds) (2003) *Democracy Transformed? Expanding Political Opportunities in Advanced Industrial Democracies* (New York: Oxford University Press).
Canovan, M. (1981) *Populism* (New York: Harcourt Brace Jovanovich).
Canovan, M. (1982) Two strategies for the study of populism. *Political Studies*, 30(4), pp. 544–552.
Canovan, M. (1984) 'People', politicians and populism. *Government and Opposition*, 19, pp. 312–327.
Canovan, M. (1999) Trust the people! Populism and the two faces of democracy. *Political Studies*, 47, pp. 2–16.
Canovan, M. (2002) The people, the masses and the mobilization of power: the paradox of Hannah Arendt's 'Populism'. *Social Research*, 69(2), pp. 403–422.

Canovan, M. (2004) Populism for political theorists? *Journal of Political Ideologies,* 9(3), 241–252.
Crick, B. (1987) *Socialism* (Milton Keynes: Open University Press, 1987).
Eisenberg, A. (2004) When – if Ever – Are Referendums on Minority Rights Fair?, in: D. Laycock (Ed.) (2004) *Representation and Democratic Theory* (Vancouver, BC: University of British Columbia Press), pp. 3–22.
Esping-Andersen, G. (1985) *Politics against Markets: The Social Democratic Road to Power* (Princeton, NJ: Princeton University Press).
Erickson, L. & Laycock, D. (2002) Post-materialism versus the welfare state? Opinion among English Canadian Social Democrats. *Party Politics,* 8(3), pp. 301–325.
Freeden, M. (1996) *Ideologies and Political Theory* (Oxford: Oxford University Press).
Freeden, M. (2003) Editorial: ideological boundaries and ideological systems. *Journal of Political Ideologies,* 8(1), pp. 3–12.
Gellner, E. & Ionescu, G. (Eds) (1969) *Populism: Its Meaning and National Characteristics* (London: Macmillan).
Gerring, J. (1998) *Party Ideologies in America, 1828–1996* (New York: Cambridge University Press).
Goodwynn, L. (1976) *Democratic Promise: The Populist Movement in America* (New York: Oxford University Press).
Goodwynn, L. (1991) Rethinking 'populism': paradoxes of historiography and democracy. *Telos,* 88, pp. 37–56.
Goot, M. & Watson, I. (2001) One nation's electoral support: where does it come from, what makes it different and how does it fit? *Australian Journal of Politics and History,* 47(2), pp. 159–191.
Hainsworth, P. (Ed.) (2002) *The Politics of the Extreme Right: From the Margins to the Mainstream* (London: Pinter).
Hayek, F. (1979) *Law, Legislation and Liberty, Vol. III: The Political Order of a Free People* (Chicago, IL: University of Chicago Press).
Hayward, J. (Ed.) (1996) *Élitism, Populism and European Politics* (Oxford: Oxford University Press).
Hofstader, R. (1955) *The Age of Reform* (New York: Vintage Books).
Huntington, S. et al. (1975) *The Crisis of Democracy* (New York: New York University Press).
Ignazi, P. (2003) *Extreme Right Parties in Western Europe* (Oxford: Oxford University Press).
Johnson, C. (2003) Anti-elitist discourse in Australia: International influences and comparisons, in: M. Sawer & and B. Hindess (Eds), *Us and Them: Anti-Elitism in Australia* (Perth: API Network), pp. 117–136.
Kazin, M. (1998) *The Populist Persuasion: An American History* (New York: Basic Books).
Kitschelt, H. (1995) *The Radical Right in Western Europe: A Comparative Analysis* (Ann Arbor, MI: University of Michigan Press).
Kymlicka, W. (1996) *Multicultural Citizenship* (Oxford: Oxford University Press).
Laclau, E. (1977) *Politics and Ideology in Marxist Theory* (London: New Left Books).
Lasch, C. (1995) *The Revolt of the Elites: And the Betrayal of Democracy* (New York: W.W. Norton).
Laycock, D. (1990) *Populism and Democratic Thought in the Canadian Prairies, 1910–45* (Toronto, ON: University of Toronto Press).
Laycock, D. (2001) *The New Right and Democracy in Canada: Understanding Reform and the Canadian Alliance* (Toronto, ON: Oxford University Press).
Laycock, D. (2005) Populism and the New Right in English Canada, in: F. Panizza (Ed.), *Populism and the Mirror of Democracy* (Verso: London), pp. 188–218.
Lehman, N. (1996) Cartoon populism. *Atlantic Monthly,* November, pp. 109–116.
Mény, Y. (1997) The people, the elites and the populist challenge, keynote address to the German Political Science Association meetings, Bamberg, October 1997, accessed 26 February 2004 at <http://wwwiue.it/ERPA/Mainfiles/../../RSCAS/WP-Texts/JM98_47.html>.
Mény, Y. & Surel, Y. (Eds) (2002) *Democracies and the Populist Challenge* (New York: Palgrave).
Mouffe, C. (2005) The 'end of politics' and the challenge of right-wing populism, in: F. Panizza (Ed.), *Populism and the Mirror of Democracy* (Verso: London), ch. 2.

Olsen, J. (1983) *Organized Democracy: Political Institutions in a Welfare State, the Case of Norway* (Oslo: Universitetsforlaget).

Panizza, F. (Ed.) (2005a) *Populism and the Mirror of Democracy* (Verso: London).

Panizza, F. (2005b) Introduction, in: F. Panizza (Ed.), *Populism and the Mirror of Democracy* (Verso: London).

Rousseau, J.-J. (1973) *The Social Contract and Discourses*. Ed. G.D.H. Cole (London: J.M. Dent and Sons).

Sawer, M. (2003) *The Ethical State? Social Liberalism in Australia* (Melbourne: Melbourne University Press).

Sawer, M. (2004) Populism and public choice in Australia and Canada: Converting equality seekers into special interests, in: M. Sawer & B. Hindess (Eds), *Us and Them: Anti-Elitism in Australia* (Perth: API Network), pp. 33–57.

Sawer, M. & Hindess, B. (Eds) (2004) *Us and Them: Anti-Elitism in Australia* (Perth: API Network).

Scatamburlo, V. (1998) *Soldiers of Misfortune: The New Right's Culture War and the Politics of Political Correctness* (New York: Peter Lang).

Schain, M. et al. (Eds) (2002) *Shadows over Europe: The Development and Impact of the Extreme Right in Western Europe* (New York: Palgrave Macmillan).

Shrag, P. (1998) *Paradise Lost: California's Experience, America's Future* (New York: New Press).

Smelser, N. & Alexander, J.C. (Eds) (1999) *Diversity and its Discontents: Cultural Conflict and Common Ground in Contemporary American Society* (Princeton, NJ: Princeton University Press).

de Toqueville, A. (1961) *Democracy in America*. Trans. H. Reeve (New York: Shocken).

Taggart, P. (2000) *Populism* (Philadelphia, PA: Open University Press).

Taggart, P. (2004) Populism and representative politics in contemporary Europe. *Journal of Political Ideologies*, 9(3), pp. 269–288.

Tilton, T.A. (1990) *The Political Theory of Swedish Social Democracy: Through the Welfare State to Socialism* (Oxford: Clarendon Press).

Trautman, K. (Ed.) (1997) *The New Populist Reader* (Westport, CT: Praeger).

Urbinati, N. (1998) Democracy and populism. *Constellations* 5(1), pp. 110–124.

Urbinati, N. (2000) Representation as advocacy. *Political Theory* 28(6), pp. 758–786.

Walzer, M. (1983) *Spheres of Justice* (New York: Basic Books).

White, J. (2003) *The Values Divide: American Politics and Culture in Transition* (New York: Chatham House).

Wolin, S. (2001) *Toqueville Between Two Worlds* (Princeton, NJ: Princeton University Press).

Yack, B. (2001) Popular sovereignty and nationalism. *Political Theory* 29(4), pp. 517–536.

Ideology and Antagonism in Modern Italy: Poststructuralist Reflections

JAMES MARTIN

Introduction

Can we live without antagonism? Arguably, in a 'post-ideological' age it is precisely this prospect that we face. The declining salience of class conflict, the end of the Cold War and the proliferation of issue-based politics has re-activated the desire to look 'beyond ideological antagonism', particularly that of the traditional division between 'Left' and 'Right' (see Mouffe 2000, Bastow and Martin 2003). However unrealised such efforts may prove to be in practice, there is little doubt that we continue to live with a sense of exhaustion with received ideological 'grand narratives'. But what might this mean for the experience of conflict and opposition staged by our grand ideological narratives?

This article approaches the question of antagonism as it applies in the context of modern Italy. As we shall see, Italian political life has been widely understood to have suffered from 'too much' ideological antagonism, that is, from a debilitating lack of agreement about the parameters of the state and its political culture. After considering some aspects of this 'problem' of ideology in Italy, I discuss the contribution of poststructuralist ideas to the debate. The importance of poststructuralism lies in the view, common to many of its otherwise contrasting variants, that a 'surplus' always remains in any social or symbolic field, one that is impossible to domesticate within the confines of a foundational logic. This is what Michael Dillon calls a 'radical non-relationality' whose intractable nature 'continuously prevents the full realization or final closure or relationality, and thus the misfire that continuously precipitates new life and new meaning' (Dillon 2000: 5). In the political theory of Ernesto Laclau and Chantal Mouffe, this surplus is understood as antagonism. For them, antagonism is not merely a difference of opinion that can be entirely neutralised within some higher-level rationality. Rather, antagonism has an *ontological* dimension: it imposes a limit on intrinsically polysemic social identities, furnishing them, however temporarily, with a sense of objectivity and potential coherence.

After reviewing key aspects of the debates about ideology in modern Italy, I outline the central elements of Laclau and Mouffe's work. I then set out an agenda for thinking through the fundamental ideological role of antagonism and its application to the Italian context. Finally, I consider briefly the recent debate concerning the decline of Anti-Fascism in Italy. In this debate, the enduring importance of antagonism, but also the perceived dangers of its loss, are usefully exemplified.

The 'Problem' of Ideology in Modern Italy

In his comprehensive study of modern Italian political thought in the twentieth century, Giuseppe Bedeschi (2002: v) begins by noting how Italian thought 'is profoundly saturated by political myths and therefore by ideologies'. By 'myth' Bedeschi (following Cassirer 1946) understands emotive expressions which are then formulated as powerful visions of society and history able to mobilise social groups. It is for this reason, he suggests, that liberal democracy, with its sober and realistic examination of society, has 'always led a wretched life in our country'. As the title of his book indicates, for him political theorising in Italy has been a 'factory of ideologies' producing myths for mass consumption and not, presumably, a source of nuanced, rational dialogue.

Leaving aside for now the issue of how ideology is defined here, we should note that Bedeschi's point is a common one. For many commentators, Italy's failings as a modern democratic state stem from the preponderance of opposed ideological systems that dominate its political culture and hinder the development of sober, reasoned dialogue. Too often, reasonable communication has been sacrificed on the alter of ideological allegiances that command popular and political respect over and above the commitment to moderate and gradual reform (see Bobbio 1955). Moreover, these ideologies have been deeply antagonistic, invoking visions of social order that are radically incommensurable: revolutionary socialism, Catholic social doctrines, Fascism, regionalist secession, to name just a few.

Whilst it might be said that Italy has had, and continues to have, a generous helping of competing political ideologies, the 'problem' of ideology in Italy testifies to the absence of a stable *ground* for political ideology as such. This problem – which elsewhere might be called a problem of 'legitimacy' – means the parameters of ideological contest have not been embedded effectively in a stable institutional order. As a consequence, ideological antagonisms have been free to expand into highly emotive grand narratives – which Bedeschi calls myths – aimed at reconstituting the society and the state as a whole.

There are three, related aspects of this problem worth noting here. Let us briefly consider each of them in turn.

The Incomplete National Subject

Historical and political commentary in modern Italy has been informed by an acute awareness of the incompleteness of the nation-state (see Haddock 2000). The many failings of the post-Risorgimento regime – its lack of popular legitimation, its heavy-handed use of force against its citizens, and so on – are frequently traced back to an original failure of the polity to be constituted on the basis of a unified national subject. In the ideals of the Risorgimento, particularly those of Giuseppe Mazzini, a unified Italy was imagined as a moral unification of its peoples. In the aftermath of unification, however, the evident hostility of the majority of Italy's new citizens towards the state engendered a profound sense of disappointment that fed back into intellectual and political culture as a lingering aspiration to fully complete the national project by, in Massimo D'Azeglio's celebrated phrase, 'making Italians' (see Bellamy 1987: 1–11; Asor Rosa 1975).

Of course, the ideologies competing to define the unfinished national project differed radically. Yet liberals, socialists, syndicalists, anarchists, Fascists, communists, liberal-socialists etc, commonly recognised that the Italian state had failed to fulfil its mission and the opportunity for political reconstitution remained open. As Emilio Gentile (1996: 3–14) argues in his study of Fascism, post-Risorgimento disappointment bequeathed a distinctive language of politics oriented towards producing a 'civil religion', that is, a secular moral framework to unify its diverse citizenry. Liberals and Fascists alike conceptualised their projects as the formation of a certain religiosity, a sacred bond to grip its adherents not purely (sometimes not at all) as 'rational' subjects but as believers in a new 'faith' that would disseminate as a form of 'common sense'. Perhaps the most widely recognised example can be found in Antonio Gramsci's concept of a 'national-popular hegemony' (see Gramsci 1971). For all their influence on post-war Marxism, Gramsci's writings resonate with an idiom that can clearly be traced back through a variety of radical humanist thinkers such as Benedetto Croce, Bertrando Spaventa and others for whom political unification needed to be extended into full cultural unification (Bellamy & Schecter 1993; Martin 1998; Jacobitti 1981).

Likewise, the lingering fascination amongst scholars of history and ideology for Fascism derives in good part from its relative success in undertaking systematically the quest for spiritual unification where liberalism and socialism so clearly failed. Whilst the nature of this success is disputed, increasingly it has become difficult to argue that Fascism constituted an exception, discontinuity or rupture in Italian history. Rather, it emerged precisely from the failings of the antecedant liberal order and, in its own distinctive ways, also sought to provide an ideological horizon against which a unified national culture might be conceived (see Corner 1986; Gentile 1982; Vivarelli 1981). Of course, as Gentile points out, this was more than a civil religion. It was a 'political religion', a bellicose 'sacralization of politics', desiring a *total* identification between the national public and its state. Fascism's answer to domestic social antagonisms was, for the most part, to eliminate them altogether and affirm by brute imposition the unity of the national culture.

From Antagonism to Crisis

Problems of ideology and antagonism emerged again in the wake of Fascism's defeat. The dominance of political parties, in particular the Christian Democrat (DC) and Communist (PCI) parties, in organising post-war democratic politics has been widely noted. As Aurelio Lepre clarifies, however, the parties effectively stepped in to take over the 'total' ideological role previously assumed by the Fascists (Lepre 1993: 52–57). Each with their own 'subcultural' networks (of churches and trades unions) and each identifying in broad terms with the ideological oppositions in play at an international level, the parties returned antagonism to domestic politics, though in a more evenly balanced way. For Pietro Scoppla, instead of merely competing party programmes, both the DC and the PCI mobilised powerfully 'utopian' visions. For the DC, a Christian civilisation was to be built upon an 'objective order of Truth' possessed by the Catholic Church; for the PCI, a revolutionary refoundation of the state would install an organic, classless society (Scoppola 1997: 21–22, 65–77).

These opposed ideological visions continued afresh the problem of antagonism in modern Italy, extending what Salvadori (1996) identifies as the country's recurrent practice whereby governing groups entirely reject the legitimacy of their major opponent and hence block it from power. Thus the PCI was permanently excluded by the DC from holding office. Crucially, however, the dynamic of their opposition was ultimately directed at the defence of the post-war institutions. One paradox of Italian democracy is that for all its undoubted failings in channelling popular choices into programmatic outputs, it remained relatively stable, often in the face of violent popular hostility to its 'blocked' system. The short-term answer to the stalemate of ideological antagonism was elite compromise, a miserable situation of almost continual governmental crisis, collapse and rebuilding that reached its apotheosis in the governments of 'national unity' in the late 1970s.

The end of this last 'consociational' approach to politics in Italy was finally announced with the profound political crisis that followed the Tangentopoli scandals and 'clean hands' investigations between 1992 and 1994 (see McCarthy 1995). The political antagonism that characterised post-war democracy ended, then, not in the success of one side over another but in the dissolution of the party system as a whole. No longer, in the wake of the end of the Cold War, the defenders of 'the faith', neither communists nor Christian Democrats could justify their continued presence.

As elsewhere, the demise of East European communism forced Italy into an ideological malaise, of sorts. The old antagonisms receded into the horizon but the new party system was more fragmented than ever before, with no single, dominant antagonism. Whilst most did not seek to entirely reconstitute the Italian state as a whole, the parameters of the 'Second Republic' were, and to some extent remain, uncertain (see Gundle & Parker 1996).

Which Left and Right?

The end of the Cold War produced in Italy, as it did elsewhere, much reflection on what ought to be understood as the proper boundaries between ideological formations. In Italy, however, there was a particular awareness that the distinction between the polarities of Left and Right had never been firmly established. For many, Left and Right serve as the natural modern parameters of a democratic political culture, the one balancing the other in a stable antagonism that is reflected in a broadly even distribution of values across the electorate and within parliament. Where there is a coherent Left and Right, it is assumed, policy choices alternate with governments consisting of different parties (or coalitions of parties) that self-identify as alternatives to each other. However, where the antagonism is raised to the level of alternative forms of state and society, the boundaries of political ideology do not fit into a clear classification. As Giampiero Carocci (2002) has argued, in Italy the left–right antagonism has been weak and often ideologies 'overlap'. Whilst it is expected that ideologies have an 'internal' spectrum, in Italy the tendency to ambiguity has been especially marked. Mussolini, for instance, was adept at drawing support from both left (e.g. reactionary syndicalists) and right wings (e.g. reactionary landowners, nationalists). Later, under the First Republic, the DC's 40-year dominance in office was achieved, in part, by ruling from the ideological 'centre' and shifting coalition composition to the Left and Right as circumstances required (see Leonardi & Wertman 1989).

Despite a powerful defence of the distinction by one of Italy's leading political philosophers (see Bobbio 1994), ideological conflicts in Italy continue to operate within a party system that does not lend itself easily to a clear left–right spectrum. The spectacular rise of populist movements and parties in recent decades testifies to this. The three current governing parties – Forza Italia!, Lega Nord, and the Allianza Nazionale – each display typical populist features that prevent their simple allocation on the side of the ideological Right (see Canovan 1999). In different ways, each mobilises 'the people' against an established power-bloc and its elites – communists, southern politicians, immigrants, the European Union etc. In the case of Silvio Berlusconi and Umberto Bossi, particularly, we can see a common populist emphasis on charismatic leadership and an enthusiastic 'revivalism' aimed at redeeming national (or regional, in the case of Bossi) virtues sullied by years of corrupt government (Tarchi 2003). Berlusconi, of course, has been outstandingly successful at projecting himself through his own, vast media empire (Ginsborg 2003). Nevertheless, by definition, this populist orientation speaks to a people presumed already constituted and in need of emancipating, rather than to sectoral needs whose interests must be balanced. The left–right distinction continues to be deliberately evaded in an appeal 'over the heads' of such interests.

From Ideology to Antagonism

It would be easy, on the basis of the three issues sketched above, to argue that Italy suffers from some intrinsic cultural malady that prevents it from developing a 'proper', balanced ideological system. A good part of post-war political science has tended to lean this way (see, for instance, Banfield 1958; Almond & Verba 1965). Even when Italy's specific historical conditions are taken into account, many commentators assume that an absent national identity is the underlying cause of its ideological pathology. Salvadori, for instance, suggests the absence of 'national spirit' as the basis of both incessant cultural particularisms and, equally, projects of total refoundation of the society. This spirit, he suggests – echoing Gramsci and plenty others – is missing because there was no hegemonic ruling class (Salvadori 1996: 158–159).

My intention here is not to dwell on the validity of these claims but, rather, to shift attention from the question of ideology to that of antagonism. Trying to specify the 'proper' ideological, or meta-ideological framework within which specific political ideologies might be regulated – be it national identity or some renewed civil religion – often just returns to the very source of dispute. Ultimately, it implies a circular argument, suggesting that the problem of ideological unity can only be solved once we have agreed a unifying ideology! Instead, I want to suggest that the question of ideology be approached from the perspective of antagonism.

Accentuate the Negative? Theorising Antagonism

Rather than treat antagonism as a pathological characteristic of political life, Ernesto Laclau and Chantal Mouffe defend it, and other forms of 'negative' exclusion, in so far as these constitute an ineliminable dimension of 'the political' as such (Laclau & Mouffe 1985, 1990; Laclau 1996; Mouffe, 1993, 2000). Conceiving antagonism as an ontological condition of identity formation, they challenge the view that power and conflict can ever be fully erased from social orders. In whatever guise it comes, they argue, such an aspiration leads inescapably towards authoritarianism and the forced subsumption of difference under appeals to 'consensus' or 'rational' accord. Instead, they promote a theoretical rehabilitation of negativity, in the form of a 'radical democratic' politics. Let us unpack some the arguments in their work before considering its relevance to the Italian case.

Taking their cue from Marxist debates on the relationship between class and ideology, Laclau and Mouffe set out to dispense, once and for all, with the 'essentialism' that seeks out core economic identities beneath a 'superstructural' guise. The result is an expansion of the concept of 'discourse' to denote not merely ideas and speech but the way that political identities are constituted through open-ended chains of signification. Rather than separating out ideology (the 'symbolic' world) from, and subordinating it to, socio-economic structure (the 'material' world), Laclau and Mouffe employ discourse to denote the interdependence of thought and action. Discourses are not merely the linguistic 'frames' through which 'pre-discursive' or 'material' entities (e.g. class interests) are viewed; they are partially constitutive of materiality itself (Laclau & Mouffe 1985: 108–109; 1990). Material practices, then, are themselves discursively organised in so far as they are inserted within a meaningful frame (e.g. the unspoken rules of game).

But, importantly, this discursive organisation is intrinsically open to alteration. Laclau and Mouffe underscore the fluidity by which 'structural' identities are formed, highlighting the essential unfixity, overlapping and mutually modifying character of discursive formations. Naturalised identities such as those of gender, 'race' or nationality are revealed as fundamentally malleable by virtue of their discursive constitution. Drawing upon and extending Saussure's idea of the arbitrary nature of the sign, according to which meaning is produced through the correspondence of 'signifier' and 'signified' rather than through an 'external' reference, they understand social identities as contingent *identifications*. To 'have' any identity is a momentary act, conscious or not, of taking up 'subject positions' (man, woman, property owner, French, etc) within a semi-structured symbolic field of differences. Thus identity is a form of differentiation, ascribing to oneself (or others) a set of attachments and associations whose meaning derives from their simultaneous difference from other elements. However, because identities are conventions with no ultimately 'necessary' foundation (e.g. in nature), they may exhibit an infinite number of permutations, each element changing its meaning as it combines with others. Thus for Laclau and Mouffe social identity has an intrinsically 'ambiguous, incomplete and polysemical character' (1985: 121).

This eminently 'poststructuralist' reading of identity firmly renounces the rationalist 'topography' (as they call it, referring to the base and superstructure metaphor) by which politics is referred back to a foundational instance of whose internal logic it is merely an internal moment: '"Society" is not a valid object of discourse. There is no single underlying principle fixing – and hence constituting – the whole field of differences' (Laclau & Mouffe 1985: 111). In place of 'social' explanation, Laclau and Mouffe argue that political conflicts temporarily cement social formations into relatively unified ensembles of diverse, often contradictory social practices, institutional forms and social identities. This, of course, was one of the meanings of Gramsci's concept of hegemony: the ongoing assemblage, dissolution and reassemblage of social groups and classes around a common project. Politics, according to Laclau and Mouffe, is to be read in terms of 'hegemonic' struggles over meaning and identity, not in the trivial sense of competing lifestyle choices and aesthetic preferences, but as efforts to inscribe diverse social practices and competing, contradictory demands within stable symbolic horizons: as Anna Marie Smith puts it, 'political struggles are primarily struggles to produce subjects' (Smith 1998: 68). Conceiving politics as struggles for hegemony at various levels rather than as reflexes of fixed, paradigmatic interests, they argue, permits us to expand the field of the political to include not only class struggles but also those of other, non-class social movements and identities.

It is within this 'post-Marxist' theoretical framework that Laclau and Mouffe highlight the experience of antagonism: that is, 'the presence of the "Other" [that] prevents me from being totally myself' (Laclau & Mouffe 1985: 125). Antagonisms – the ideological and material conflicts between social groups and against phenomena that prevent subjects from freely being 'themselves' – have a fundamental semantic function in structuring our experience of the objective world. By setting a limit to the discursive elements through which identities are constructed, antagonisms mark off what we identify as part of 'us' from what is 'other' to us. Thus antagonisms delineate identities by asserting global principles of difference (e.g. not British, not White, not civilized, etc) that brings coherence and unity to who we think 'we' are.

But in marking off identity through difference, antagonisms also reveal social identities as themselves 'partial and precarious' objectifications, that is, as social constructions dependent for coherence and unity upon the 'exclusionary limit' of an Other(s). This limit assigns an enemy that threatens 'us' and in so doing it supplies the 'us' with an illusory sense of unity; 'illusory' because it invokes an identity as already and spontaneously present, but this identity exists only by virtue of the hostile Other that threatens it. This 'logic of equivalence' aligns various discursive elements against the enemy. At its most extreme, social space divides according to a simple 'Us–Them' antinomy and subjects are compelled to disregard their differences in favour of an underlying unity.

The Other, or enemy, may be a person (the boss), a country (imperialists), an idea (slavery), or an object (disease). What is fundamental is that we identify it as a threat to destroy or undermine us, perhaps to 'steal' from us our integral identity and undermine the very basis of social order. Hence we find antagonisms producing in their wake a whole variety of mythical associations with excess: evil, impurity, uncontrollable desire and so on. As Laclau points out, it is because antagonism is the 'limit of all objectivity' that it cannot be conceived simply as another difference and represented neutrally. As a universal and total threat, the enemy is likely to take on a caricatured representation, symbolising as it does the total annihilation of meaning and order. In religious discourses the Other is represented as demonic; in more modern incarnations it has included 'foreigners', disease or even 'global terrorism'.

However, a problem arises here, one that a number of critics have taken up (see for instance Žižek 1990). If antagonism supplies coherence to an identity by enacting a discursive closure, then must not all social identities be locked within a permanent condition of opposition? Evidence would suggest that this scenario does not occur; conflicts may be more or less 'on the surface' of society, but many people are not routinely engaged in *any* form of antagonistic opposition. Does this mean they have no coherent identities at all?

Laclau and Mouffe have responded to their critics by weakening their reliance on antagonism as the exclusive key to identity formation. In later and separate work, both have in different ways emphasised a more complex scale of opposition through the wider concept of 'negativity'. This way, the symbolic exclusion denoted by antagonism has been more plausibly displaced onto a variety of different kinds of experience.

Thus Laclau has emphasised the condition of 'dislocation' in which subjects remain at odds with their own incomplete identities, only more or less filling out what he calls (following Lacan) a 'constitutive lack' (see Robinson 2004 for a critique). His recent work has explored the hegemonic function of 'empty signifiers', that is, concepts such as 'freedom' or 'justice' that promise to 'fill the gap' between subjective dislocation and the desire for a unified and fulfilled identity (see Laclau 1996). Mouffe, on the other hand, has developed a political philosophy that promotes an 'agonistic' democracy, one in which potentially dangerous antagonists are transformed into more friendly 'adversaries' (see Mouffe 1993, 2000). Without wishing to overstate the similarities between the two (on this topic, see Wenman 2003), in the recent work of both there is a pulling back from the original emphasis on the moment of extreme antagonism and an effort to envisage subjects in more complex conditions of partial rather than total exclusion. Antagonism remains a limit experience of hostility through which subjects define themselves against Others, but this is now supplemented with a wider range of less intense degrees of hostility and disassociation.

In orienting their work towards a general theme of negativity, Laclau and Mouffe develop upon a wider tradition in Continental European philosophy. This tradition – exemplified in Hegel, Heidegger and others – conceives negativity as an ontological condition, signifying a limit to selfhood and knowledge. Yet, as Coole (2000) indicates, this limit is also *generative* of new possibilities precisely because it cannot be absorbed into any 'positive' conception of 'what is'. 'Positive' is here understood as being a fully formed, self-identical entity; a concept understood by this tradition to ignore the relational context in which identity is formed. Unlike contemporary epistemologies that draw upon empiricism and positivism, this continental tradition declaims efforts to draw conclusions simply from positively identified sources. In its more radical political versions, negativity resists reconciliation with the status quo and functions as the spark for new ways of thinking and being.

Laclau and Mouffe follow this latter route, rejecting the subsumption of negativity within a 'higher', positive sense of historical rationality (a fault they associate with a Hegelian inspiration in Marxism). Embracing the negative as the condition for the positive, and not vice versa, illuminates the ineradicable contingency and hence permanent alterability of social formations. Antagonism, now conceived as one of several possibilities within the overall theme of negativity, compels us to inquire not so much into what social entities *are* but, rather, as Laclau intriguingly asserts, what they *fail to be* (Laclau 1990: 38). For it is in the signification of failure, of limits or obstacles to the full achievement of an identity that negativity – in the form of dislocated subjects, adversaries or full-scale enemies – generates the hallucinating promise of a positive identity. The discursive presence of this failure, I will suggest, provides an alternative perspective on the character of contemporary political ideologies, one that might help us rethink the status of antagonism and ideology in modern Italy.

Rethinking Ideology in Modern Italy

Political ideologies are manifestly discursive formations, typically presenting themselves as complex chains of principles, values, social identities and images of social organisation, all articulated in relatively open-ended structures that can be assembled, disassembled and reassembled in a variety of ways (see Freeden 1996). What our discussion of antagonism demands is that we pay close attention to the presence of negativity and exclusion in the semantic structuring and operation of ideologies. For it is these, in addition to their positive content, that, it is suggested here, accounts for much of both their analytical and, especially, their *affective* force.

Of course, all ideologies indicate generic antagonists: socialists oppose forms of private property, conservatives oppose radical change, liberals oppose restrictions on individual liberty, and so on. What Laclau and Mouffe's work suggests is that these antagonisms help structure the internal coherence and stability of ideologies, articulating their various elements around common markers of exclusion. Without any exclusionary limit to discriminate a common purpose for its policies, principles and values, a political ideology will lack coherence; its 'core', 'peripheral' and 'adjacent' concepts (see Freeden 1996) will remain uncertain and open to endless substitution. As such, it will fail to provide coherent points of identification for subjects to invest themselves and their shared and personal aspirations.

Antagonism, then, can be concieved as enabling a hegemonic closure on political ideologies. Paradoxically, we might say that it is this antagonistic contestation that enables what Michael Freeden identifies as the 'decontestation' of meanings that ideologies function to achieve (Freeden 1996: 76–79). That is, the stability of specific concepts, their taken-for-granted acceptance and usage, is achieved by their positioning in open opposition to other concepts.

Importantly, however, any specific ideological formation will contain a variety of local and particular antagonisms and conflicts amongst its various proponents. A hegemonic antagonism cannot eradicate *all* other points of internal conflict: for example, a principled objection to the market as a provider of public services cannot eliminate disagreements over the ways public control might be exercised. Nor can it solve more 'distant' issues such as those of sexism or racism within public service provision. Hegemonic principles are only ever a temporary point of coalscence amongst a variety of potentially conflictual groups and values. At best they can displace other antagonisms into less severe 'adversarial' conflicts or disperse them into localised disagreements.

How, then, might this poststructuralist approach to antagonism inform an approach to modern Italian political ideologies? Three issues are worth emphasising in particular: First, we should regard antagonism not as pathological but as *productive* of specific ideological formations. Second, what gives character or identity to an ideology is as much the way antagonisms articulate its positive content as the content itself, setting up complex structures and varying degrees of opposition and association between various concepts and principles. Third, antagonisms give rise to a distinctive vocabulary of 'failure' or 'blockage' that invokes certain identities over others. The test of a politically successful ideology can be conceived as the degree to which its 'enemies' become the enemies of other ideologies and their component concepts.

With these points in mind, let us briefly reconsider the three areas of so-called ideological pathology discussed earlier:

The Incomplete National Subject

Although the absence of a spontaneous national subject has been widely recognised in Italian political life, there has nevertheless remained a strong aspiration to link 'making Italians' to an agency that itself incarnated a certain historical objectivity (e.g. the Communist Party, the Catholic Church, etc). Our emphasis on antagonism, however, rejects the aspiration to find some positive (whether rational or divine) basis for this approach. Instead the national subject is understood as *necessarily incomplete*, a project whose realisation could *never* be achieved because its non-achievement is precisely what makes it compelling as an ideal. Efforts to actually realise national unity in any literal way, as Fascism demonstrated, will likely lead to authoritarian imposition. A more democratic approach might best pose the question, not what must Italians be to realise their national subjectivity but, rather, how can Italians' failure to be a unified national subject best be institutionally and ideologically conceived? The virtue of this approach is that it pulls away from asserting an identity whose 'blockage' requires ever more robust assertion and points instead to a collective identity as being constantly renegotiated.

Crisis and Regime Change

There is no doubt that post-war democracy in Italy has been singularly unsuccessful in channelling public demands into policy outputs. However, a more generous view would be one that understood the deep ideological divisions upon which this democratic order was established. What is remarkable about post-war democracy in Italy was the ability of its leaders, for the most part, to avoid violent social breakdown. Where institutional stability is prized over efficiency, however, it is no surprise that corruption is the outcome. This is not to suggest, as some do, that there is merely an 'Italian style' of democracy that works well enough (see LaPalombara 1987). Rather, it is to underline that, if ideological antagonisms are viewed as an unexceptional part of politics, regime crisis in some form will be an ever-present possibility. Given the presence of populist parties in the current Italian government, it is evident that once the status of the regime is itself no longer so intensely in question, the desire for 'something beyond' the current state readily transmutes into something else. The issue is no longer how crisis can be averted by consensus but how can potentially destructive antagonisms be managed as conflicts between 'adversaries' and not sworn enemies?

Left and Right

Finally, the 'slippage' and ambiguity of Left and Right identified in Italy underlines Mouffe's point that one of the primary political distinctions is that of 'Friend/ Enemy' (see Mouffe 2000: ch. 2). In the modern age, this agonistic dimension may well turn to a great part on questions of material equality, but where questions of equality are also bound up with those of immigration, state corruption and regional secession, the primary signifiers in politics are those that succeed in articulating a range of separate demands and local antagonisms around inclusive images of the community as a whole. Whilst Left and Right remain key signifiers in contemporary Italian politics, a poststructuralist approach underlines their unavoidable fluidity. The issue here, then, is less how can Left and Right be defended as the primary structure of political antagonism but, rather, how successfully can political organisations reinscribe current political issues and conflicts within that distinction (rather than outside of it, as 'Third Way' ideologies claim to do: see Bastow & Martin 2003)?

The Loss of the Loss: the Decline of Anti-Fascism

Whilst debate continues in contemporary Italy as to the exact dividing line between Left and Right and the degree to which the Second Republic has stabilized or remains 'in transition', here I want to consider briefly the question of the national subject which has been vigorously discussed in recent years. In many ways, Anti-Fascism and the debates that ensued in the 1990s over its continued relevance exemplify the discursive presence of antagonism and negativity in structuring the field of political ideologies.

By its very nature Anti-Fascism signifies antagonism: its declared enemy is, of course, Fascism. The simplicity of this opposition, however, belies the complex hegemonic function it has sought. Anti-Fascism did not indicate a common goal or a stable set of values; rather, it established a frontier against which a number of different, sometimes contradictory aspirations could be projected at different times and places. As Lepre (1997) demonstrates, Anti-Fascism began with forms of opposition not to the dictatorship but to the presence of the Fascists in government from 1922 onwards when they still operated, broadly, within the parliamentary system. Whilst liberals, socialists and others opposed the presence of Mussolini's party, they did not all do so for the same reasons. For some, opposition was directed merely at a return to liberal institutions, for others it involved looking forward to a new order altogether. These differences had no small part to play in the failure of the parties opposed to early Fascism to agree a unified strategy. During the period of the dictatorship, however, when it became clear that any opposition to Fascism was opposition to a totalitarian regime with an accompanying ideology, Anti-Fascism remained a distant band of exiles and intellectuals unable significantly to expand their opposition into a systematic worldview (Ganapini 2000).

It was only with the initial collapse of the dictatorship in 1943 – a profound and widespread dislocation of the Italian state, in response to which the Resistance movement proper began to organise – that a widespread Anti-Fascist organisation came into effect. Anti-Fascism then expanded into a symbolic frontier behind which a variety of demands and groups could identify. This included the various liberal opponents of the regime, the Resistance movement (including its different parties, the Communists, Liberal-Socialists, etc), the Church and its lay members, monarchists and elements of the military. None of these groups shared exactly the same ideals, organisations or objectives. Because of the division of the country into a half occupied by Nazis and Fascists and another half occupied by the Allies, the south of Italy remained largely outside the Anti-Fascist experience and its discourses of mobilisation and renewal. Nevertheless, for the first time in Italy, a vast section of the population were actively involved in a common project to reconstitute the state (see Battaglia 1970). Through the Committees for National liberation, the Anti-Fascist parties coordinated their efforts with those of the Allies. Though not well organised nor particularly experienced (unlike other Resistance movements, that in Italy existed for only two years), the period of resistance involved many and various acts of courage and sacrifice (see Bocca 1995).

The experience of the Resistance and the complicated set of ideals articulated within the discourse of Anti-Fascism were, and remain, viewed by many as the legitimating ideology of the post-war regime. Within Anti-Fascism, it is believed, lies the ideal of an order yet-to-come, a space within which Italy's diverse communities can identify a common hostility to a totalitarian state and authoritarian system of government. It is, as some have tellingly put it, 'another Italy', one of equality and liberty that is yet to be fully realised but which marks the distance between the present and future (e.g. De Luna & Revelli 1995).

However, in recent years the limitations of Anti-Fascism as a legitimating ideology have been asserted from a number of quarters. As Gundle (2000) argues, although Anti-Fascism served as a set of general ideals against which the mass parties of the First Republic might, in its early years, mobilise their constituencies, the Resistance failed to form into a 'civil religion' or hegemonic worldview. Anti-Fascism was less successful an ideology than Anti-Communism, the discourse that unified Christian Democrat ideology and which achieved a virtual hegemonic position throughout the administrative apparatus they virtually 'occupied'. In the face of this antagonism, which pitted an aggressive, foreign-based communism against the virtuous Christian nation, alternative discourses could not effectively compete. Whilst various groups sought to embody the ideals of the Resistance (the PCI, for instance) they never succeeded fully in shedding their own particular identity nor embedding Anti-Fascism within the institutional order. Anti-Fascism remained primarily an ideology of the Left and associated with the radical institutional reforms it sought. In the South, and increasingly amongst new generations all over Italy, the ideals of the Resistance and opposition to Fascism were not immediate or salient concerns. Moreover, a great deal of historical research has begun to open up Anti-Fascism and the Resistance as partial, contingent phenomena (on which, see Peli 2004). As Franco De Felice (1995) argues, on examination there were evidently different Anti-Fascisms and different Resistances depending on geographical location. Likewise, Claudio Pavone's powerful analysis of the Resistance period in Italy (1943–45), *Una guerra civile* (Pavone 1991), further opened up the idea of the Resistance as a complex, overlapping set of conflicts irreducible to a single Anti-Fascist struggle: it was, he argues, simultaneously a civil war (between Italians), a class war and an Anti-Fascist war.

This gradual deconstruction of Anti-Fascist discourse into competing debates over the relative partiality and contingency of its component ideals and activities marks its dissolution as a potentially hegemonic discourse. Whilst some continue to defend its status as a legitimating ideology (see, for example, De Luna & Revelli 1995), it seems increasingly evident that the Second Republic is being formed within a post-Anti-Fascist context, where those ideals no longer spontaneously or sufficiently inspire the public and its leaders (Rusconi 1995, Rapone 1996, Luzzatto 2004). For some commentators, the time is ripe to find an alternative set of identifications, a new civil religion to regulate social and political differences within a common framework (Rusconi 1999). However, the lesson we take from these developments ought perhaps to be a different one, namely that the problem of post-Anti-Fascism lies not exclusively in the loss of its anti-authoritarian *content* but in the 'loss of the loss', that is, the deprivation of antagonistic horizons against which universal ideals might be projected and contested.

Conclusion

I have argued that the negative function of antagonism illuminates the problem of political ideology in modern Italy. Rather than a pathological condition, antagonism serves an important function of delimiting ideological formations and providing points of identification for subjects. Without discursive mechanisms of disagreement, political life would lack coherence and 'the political' itself would lose its capacity to regulate societal demands. Concieved this way, Italy's purported 'excess' of ideological conflict implies neither its failure to meet some superior standard of liberal reason nor the absence of some necessary national identity. Rather, the historical presence of profound ideological antagonism testifies to the absence, not of any positive identity as such, but of a way to embody the essential *impossibility* of fully achieving such an identity. From a poststructuralist perspective, the political value of ideologies might be said to lie not in their specified goals so much as in their assertion of some principle of an alternative social order. Antagonisms can be more or less disabling, of course, but their negative role in asserting limits to public reason is a vital ingredient in doing any kind of politics. As the example of Italian Anti-Fascism demonstrates, however, just as political ideologies have to be periodically renewed, so too do the antagonisms that structure political life.

References

Almond, G.A. & Verba, S. (1965) *The Civic Culture. Political Attitudes and Democracy in Five Nations* (Boston: Little, Brown and Co.).
Asor Rosa, A. (1975) La Cultura. *Storia d'Italia 4, Dall'Unitá a oggi,* vol 2 (Turin: Einaudi).
Banfield, E.C. (1958) *The Moral Basis of a Backward Society* (New York: The Fee Press).
Bastow, S. & Martin, J. (2003) *Third Way Discourse: European Ideologies in the Twentieth Century* (Edinburgh: Edinburgh University Press).
Battaglia, R. (1970) *Storia della Resistenza italiana* (Turin: Einaudi).
Bedeschi, G. (2002) *La fabbrica delle ideologie: Il pensiero politico nell'Italia del Novecento* (Rome-Bari: Laterza).
Bellamy, R. (1987) *Modern Italian Social Theory: Ideology and Politics from Pareto to the Present* (Cambridge: Polity).
Bellamy, R. & Schechter, D. (1993) *Gramsci and the Italian State* (Manchester: Manchester University Press).
Bobbio, N. (1955) *Politica e cultura* (Turin: Einaudi).
Bobbio, N. (1994) *Destra e sinistra. Ragione e significati di una distinzione politica* (Rome: Donzelli).
Bocca, G. (1995) *Storia dell'Italia partigiana: settembre 1943 – maggio 1945* (Milan: Mondadori).
Canovan, M. (1999) Trust the people! Populism and the two faces of democracy. *Political Studies,* 47(1), 2–16.
Carocci, G. (2002) *Destra e sinistra nella storia d'Italia* (Rome-Bari: Laterza).
Cassirer, E. (1946) *The Myth of the State* (New Haven, CT and London: Yale University Press).
Coole, D. (2000) *Negativity and Politics. Dionysus and Dialectics from Kant to Poststructuralism* (London and New York: Routledge).
Corner, P. (1986) Liberalism, Pre-Fascism, Facsism, in: D. Forgacs (Ed.), *Rethinking Italian Fascism: Capitalism, Populism and Culture* (London: Lawrence and Wishart), pp. 11–20.
De Felice, F. (1995) Antifascismi e Resistenze. *Studi storici,* 36(3), pp. 597–623.
De Luna, G. & Revelli, M. (1995) *Fascismo/antifascismo: Le idee, le identità* (Florence: La Nuova Italia).
Dillon, M. (2000) Poststructuralism, complexity and poetics. *Theory, Culture & Society,* 17(5), 1–26.
Freeden, M. (1996) *Ideologies and Political Theory. A Conceptual Approach* (Oxford: Oxford University Press).
Ganapini, L. (2000) Antifascismo, in: E. Collotti, R. Sandri & F. Sessi (Eds), *Dizionario della Resistenza. Volumo primo, Storia e geografia della Liberazione* (Turin: Einaudi), pp. 5–19.
Gentile, E. (1982) *Il mito dello Stato nuovo dall'antigiolittismo al Fascismo* (Rome-Bari: Laterza).
Gentile, E. (1996) *The Sacralization of Politics in Fascist Italy* (Cambridge, MA & London: Harvard University Press).
Ginsborg, P. (2003) *Berlusconi. Ambizioni patrimoniali in una democrazia mediatica* (Turin: Einaudi).
Gramsci, A. (1971) *Selections from the Prison Notebooks* (London: Lawrence & Wishart).
Gundle, S. (2000) The 'civic religion' of the Resistance in post-war Italy. *Modern Italy,* 5(2), pp. 113–132.
Gundle, S. & Parker, S. (Eds) (1996) *The New Italian Republic: From the Fall of the Berlin Wall to Berlusconi* (London: Routledge).
Haddock. B. (2000) State, nation and Risorgimento, in: G. Bedani & B. Haddock (Eds), *The Politcs of Italian National Identity* (Cardiff: University of Wales Press), pp. 11–49.
Jacobitti, E.E. (1981) *Revolutionary Humanism and Historicism in Modern Italy* (New Haven, CT and London: Yale University Press).
Laclau, E. (1990) *New Reflections on the Revolution of Our Time* (London: Verso).
Laclau, E. (1996) *Emancipation(s)* (London: Verso).
Laclau, E. & Mouffe, C. (1985) *Hegemony and Socialist Strategy: Towards a Radical Democratic Politics* (London: Verso).
Laclau, E. & Mouffe, C. (1990) Post-Marxism without apologies, in: E. Laclau, *New Reflections on the Revolution of Our Time* (London: Verso), pp. 97–132.
LaPalombara, J. (1987) *Democracy, Italian Style* (New Haven, CT and London: Yale University Press).

Leonardi, R. & Wertman, D.A. (1989) *Italian Christian Democracy: the Politics of Dominance* (Basingstoke: Macmillan).
Lepre, A. (1993) *Storia dell prima Repubblica. L'Italia dal 1942 al 1992* (Bologna: Il Mulino).
Lepre, A. (1997) *L'anticomunismo e l'antifascismo in Italia* (Bologna: il Mulino).
Luzzato, S. (2004) *La crisi dell'antifascismo* (Turin: Einaudi).
Martin, J. (1998) *Gramsci's Political Analysis. A Critical Introduction* (Basingstoke and New York: Macmillan).
McCarthy, P. (1995) *The Crisis of the Italian State: From the Origins of the Cold War to the Fall of Berlusconi* (New York: St Martin's).
Mouffe, C. (1993) *The Return of the Political* (London: Verso).
Mouffe, C. (2000) *The Democratic Paradox* (London: Verso).
Pavone, C. (1991) *Una guerra civile. Saggio storico sulla moralità nella Resistenza* (Turin: Bollati Boringhieri).
Peli, S. (2004) *La Resistenza in Italia. Storia e critica* (Turin: Einaudi).
Putnam, R.D. (1993) *Making Democracy Work: Civic Traditions in Modern Italy* (Princeton, NJ: Princeton University Press).
Rapone, L. (1996) L'antifascismo nella società italiana, *Studi storici*, 37(3), pp. 959–968.
Robinson, A. (2004) The politics of lack. *The British Journal of Politics and International Relations*, 6(2), pp. 259–269.
Rusconi, G.-E. (1995) *Resistenza e postfascismo* (Bolgna: il Mulino).
Rusconi, G.-E. (1999) *Possiamo fare a meno di una religione civile?* (Rome-Bari: Laterza).
Salvadori, M.L. (1996) *Storia d'Italia e crisi di regime* (Bologna: Il Mulino).
Scoppola, P. (1997) *La Repubblica dei partiti. Evoluzione e crisi di un sistema politico 1945–96.* (Bologna: Il Mulino).
Smith, A.-M. (1998) *Laclau and Mouffe: The Radical Democratic Imaginary* (London and New York: Routledge).
Tarchi, M. (2003) *L'Italia populista. Dal qualunquismo ai girotondi* (Bologna: Il Mulino).
Vivarelli, R. (1981) *Il fallimento de liberalismo: Studi sulle origini del fascismo* (Bologna: Il Mulino).
Wenman, M. (2003) Laclau or Mouffe? Splitting the difference. *Philosophy and Social Criticism*, 29(5), pp. 581–606.
Žižek, S. (1990) Beyond discourse analysis, in: E. Laclau, *New Reflections on the Revolution of Our Time* (London: Verso), pp. 249–260.

The Democratic Ideology of Right–Left and Public Reason in Relation to Rawls's Political Liberalism

TORBEN BECH DYRBERG

Introduction

In this article I will outline a perspective on democratic ideology centred on what I consider the two basic axes of every ideology: orientation and justification. I will argue that the right–left dyad and public reason are closely related and that they play a vital role for democracy. Modern democracy is based on right–left orientation, which sustains the autonomy of the political symbolic order vis-à-vis cultural and religious orders, and public reason is a distinctively political justification of the priority of right–left in matters of common concern. Democratic orientation and justification outline the skeleton of democratic ideology, which is prior to particular democratic ideologies such as liberalism and socialism, and which is conditioned by the political reversal and re-appropriation of cultural and religious codes (Laponce

1972a: 472, 1981: 41–46). The political reversal states two fundamental demands basic for modern democracy: political equality according to which, say, social, economic and religious differences must be irrelevant with regard to political status, that matters of common concern must be dealt with politically and that political orientation and justification have to be based on the right–left dyad.

In the modern era – symbolized by the American and French revolutions which marked a refusal to accept the inevitability of the hierarchical ordering of politics (monarchical or colonial) – the structuring principle, operational matrix and political value of democratic ideology have been premised on the autonomy of the political symbolic order and centred on right–left political orientation and public reason as political justification. These two aspects of modern democratic ideology are necessary for a political order based on equal political status and equal liberty of its members; pluralism as opposed to monism; and the contingency of identity and signification as opposed to objectivism and fundamentalism. To be able to deal with unity and division and to buttress even-handed judgement, public reason has to be based on a political as opposed to a cultural or religious ground; otherwise it cannot be freestanding in relation to comprehensive reasons.

With respect to *political orientation*, ideology is viewed in terms of the orientational structuring of identification processes. This will be discussed in relation to the articulation between four pairs of orientational metaphors, which demarcate political frontiers and map the political terrain: up–down, in–out, front–back and right–left, each of which is a cluster of oppositions. In–out, for example, includes among other things central–peripheral, near–far, us–them and power–powerless. I will argue that right–left has to play a hegemonic role in democratic ideology. In so doing it will be necessary to distinguish between the 'prototype' and the function of right–left. Whereas the former refers to historical generalisations of what right and left mean and hence how we identify them, the latter attends to the function of this political orientation. The orientational structuring of ideology is, when studied in relation to *political justification*, viewed in terms of public reason. Its democratic structuring is based on the autonomy of the political symbolic order which is centred on political equality, pluralism and contingency as opposed to hierarchy, monism and objectivism. These issues will be discussed in relation to Rawls's public reason where I will look at how it is related to comprehensive views. The argument is that Rawls's political liberalism is central for outlining not simply a liberal ideology but the contours of democratic ideology articulating political orientation and justification. Table 1 illustrates how the two main entries of political orientation and justification are related to the structuring principle, the operational matrix and the political values of democratic ideology, which I will discuss after a brief outline of how ideology can be conceived in relation to the articulation among orientational metaphors.

The Ideological Significance of Orientational Metaphors

I will discuss the significance of right–left for democracy in relation to the three other pairs of orientational metaphors. The aim is to see how the articulations

Table 1. Democratic ideology of the political symbolic order in relation to right/left and public reason

	Political orientation	Political justification
Structuring principle	Right/left	Public reason
Operational matrix	Frame, centre and difference	Anti-perfectionism and recognition/acceptance
Political value	Pluralism, moderatism and agonistic conflict	Freestanding and even-handed judgement

among the four pairs structure the political terrain and political identification processes (Dyrberg 2003: 339–342; Laponce 1975: 11–13; 1981: ch. 3). Orientational metaphors operate at basic levels of understanding and practice and in minute detail by working simultaneously on the individual body and on the body politics (Eliade 1978: 3; Lakoff & Johnson 1980: Ch. 4). This is important for discussing ideology because it indicates that it operates not only strategically and programmatically but also and fundamentally by structuring commonsense. Identification is structured orientationally, which means that it takes form in the articulations between the four dyads, which channel identification processes and shape political lines of contestation (Dyrberg 2003: 340–342):

1. *In–out* concerns issues such as member–non-member and inclusion–exclusion of, for example, a political society or associations; collective self-description and identification in terms of us–them or friend–enemy oppositions; and terms such as here–there and important–marginal measure position in relation to a centre, which again point at belonging and presence.
2. *Up–down* indicates hierarchical positions in terms of high–low status, upper–lower classes, elites–people, patron–client, etc., which are associated with more–less power. Hence it is also related to being in control vs being controlled, domination–subordination, active–passive and life–death.
3. *Front–back* measures position in relation to time and direction as in modern–traditional, progressive–reactionary and development–stagnation, and it measures state of mind or political climate as in open-minded–narrow-minded, honest–dishonest and clear–opaque.
4. *Right–left* is the modern democratic polarity measuring the positions among equal opposites and balances them against each other. It is a governing principle based on the mutual recognition and acceptance of agents having equal political status. Right–left is a specific orientation pertaining to the political symbolic order as well as a medium for expressing the other polarities such as inequality–equality.

Orientational metaphors are universal in the sense that they structure identification and that they are invested with dense symbolic significance in every culture

(Hertz 1973; Laponce 1975, 1981; McManus 2002; Needham 1973; Parkin 1996). They play an active role in structuring political identification both at the level of how people orientate themselves politically, and at the societal level where orientation and justification are ingrained in social interaction. The four dyads perform different functions and have different effects. In–out, for example, is more easily associated with something existential and uncompromising than right–left, because it concerns membership, belonging, commitments, etc. Right–left, on the other hand, not only thrives on taking side, but also on balancing opposites and conducting fair judgements. It is an organising principle of pluralism and an insistence on political authority being exercised democratically. This suggests a close link between right–left and public reason, both of which are based on the premise of equal political standing as the democratic means to regulate the four pairs of orientational metaphors mapping the political terrain. As such they form a battleground structuring democratic political orientation and justification. I will return to this after having illustrated the orientational structuring of identity and political frontiers.

The words listed in Table 2 are extracted from Euro-sceptic arguments by both Right and Left in Denmark in campaign material (primarily posters) on the referendums on EC membership in 1972, the Amsterdam Treaty in 1998 and the single currency in 2000. The point is not to analyse Euro-scepticism but to illustrate how ideological mechanisms establish positive self-description, which makes identification possible, through the discursive structuring of orientation, that is, through associations which coalesce in chains of equivalence. This implies that the structuring of self-description and identification is simultaneous with discursive ordering and thus with forging a 'reading principle' to make sense of things. When translation (Laponce) and substitution (Laclau) are more pronounced within the positive and negative descriptions, respectively, it is because the terms have been discursively systematised in these two camps vis-à-vis exclusionary limits. The ideological fix points instigate directions ranging from vague forms of orientation to concerted action and further to submission to a course and ultimately to sacrificing oneself for this course (Žižek 1994: 13–14).

Read *horizontally* within each pair, the opposite terms complement each other as in small–big, near–far and equality–hierarchy. When read *vertically* in each column the terms can be associated with one another and have some degree of consistency as in the case of laypeople-rooted-identity, on the one hand, and system-rootless-anonymity, on the other. When read both *horizontally and vertically*, a given term such as identity is opposed to not only anonymity but also to hierarchy-power-rootless-centralisation, among others, due to the equivalential structuring of these terms.

The positive–negative categorisation of opposites provides a basic level of consistency with regard to self- and other-description and implies that translations or substitutions among the terms primarily occur within the same cluster of polar opposites. The proliferation and clustering of terms make up a reservoir of signification which can be drawn on by otherwise very different positions. For those who opposed EC membership in 1972 it was the in–out orientation of nation, and not

Table 2. Euro-sceptic orientation of us/them

	Horizontal: relation of opposition: us vs them	
	Positive: self-description + identification	Negative: other-description ÷ identification
Vertical: Equivalent relation – systematising diffeences: us and them respectively	Small	Big
	Vulnerable	Powerful
	Near	Far
	Presence	Absence
	Decentralisation	Centralisation
	Rooted	Rootless
	Identity	Anonymity
	Community	Elites
	National	International
	Solidarity	Indifference
	Caring	Cynicism
	Laypeople	The System
	Informal	Formal
	Equality	Hierarchy
	Openness	Secretive
	Honest	Manipulative
	Dialogue	Dictates
	Consensus	Force
	Democracy	Bureaucracy

that of Right–Left, that caught the political imagination, although it was primarily the Left that played the nationalist card in a way similar to the Left in the UK (Nairn 1973). Nation became the ideological fix point for various political and cultural identities, and would appear in a continuum from loosely structured forms of identification, which were ordinary, tacit, volatile, ad hoc, evasive and so on, to more established and institutionalised forms in which associations operating at the level of orientation were formed as equivalential links structuring discourses (Laclau & Mouffe 1985: ch. 3; Laponce 1981: 73f). The positive pole is more elaborated and more tightly structured in equivalential links than the negative one (Laponce 1972a: 472f; 1972b: 53; 1975: 18f). Although the positive 'us' cannot be thought without the negative 'them', they are asymmetrical because the latter is defined solely for the purpose of boosting the former and cannot function as a vehicle of self-description.

Two Aspects of Right–Left Orientation in Politics

Right–left has been an organising political orientation and has proved particularly suitable for parliamentary democracy, stretching from its origin as a seating principle in parliament to becoming a matrix of political identification and democratic politics. It has managed to link political elites and people through political representation, and has provided a workable frame for governing under conditions of pluralism in which opposition is legitimate in the political regime and differences are recognised and accepted in the political culture.

It is because right–left has been closely related to issues such as class–elite (up–down) and citizenship (in–out) that it is able to voice a democratic concern for the creation of a political environment in which difference and opposition are cherished as political facts that enhance democracy. Seen in this light, right–left is imperative for democracy as a hegemonic device that structures other forms of orientation. Right–left maps a political scenario that polarises political orientation while maintaining the poles as symmetrical opposites. The articulation between the horizontal (right–left), the vertical (up–down), the frame (in–out) and direction (front–back) creates a centre that balances opposites and evokes a distance to a periphery.

To assess the significance of right–left for democratic politics, a distinction could be made between its prototype and its function, which will make it possible to ascertain the importance of right–left and be able to maintain a critical distance to its particular structuring. The prototype concerns the general and identifiable attitudes of right–left, which have typically been measured in relation to economic issues, class conflicts and the nation-state (Schwartzmantel 1998: 5f). Within this perspective, right has often been identified with individualism and the market while left has been identified with collectivism and state intervention. This differentiation captures some of the significant attitudes of right and left, and it shows how they are bound up with the other orientational metaphors:

1 *Right–left is articulated with up–down* because, historically, right has been linked to the defence of high status, privileges and inequality, whilst left has pushed for more equality in its defence of those with low status and few or no privileges (Bobbio 1996: 39, 51, 58, ch. 6). Traditionally there has been a close link between right–up and left–down, evidenced by the industrial age of class politics where mass movements and organisations coupled political elites with ordinary people (Laponce 1975: 17–19).
2 *Right–left is articulated with in–out* as in struggles for women's right to vote and universal suffrage in general as well as citizenship rights for minorities, which deal with restrictive vs inclusive views of citizenship and, more generally, with recognising and accepting differences. Whether citizenship is viewed restrictively or inclusively is, again, related to the issue of inequality and equality. The distinction is thus between right–up–in and left–down–out
3 *Right–left is articulated with front–back* when left is identified with youth, change and progress and right with seniority, stability and reaction. As front–back

gives direction it becomes associated with imperatives such as nation, people, rationalism, historical necessity or the necessary politics, which right–left has to temper.

Political frontiers are shaped vis-à-vis the articulations among the four pairs of orientational metaphors. This is an ideological structuring of orientation which provides a perceptual and interpretative perspective operating at the threshold between awareness and unawareness, and what is contestable and what is taken for granted. Translations or substitutions between terms show an equivalential logic that sutures political identities, positions them in relation to each other and aims at becoming hegemonic poles of identification and self-description. It is not possible to identify with polar opposites such as right–left, but it is possible to identify democratic politics in this way. There is, accordingly, a difference between (1) people identifying with either right or left and (2) people identifying democratic politics in terms of right–left. This brings us to the function of the right–left dyad.

For a democratic ideology it is vital to distinguish between cultural–religious and political ways of coding orientational metaphors. This is so because it is a near universal pattern that the former views up–front–in–right as positive and down–back–out–left as negative (Hertz 1973: 11–14, 22; Laponce 1981: 29, 67, 73–74, 100, 136; McManus 2002: 39–42). The latter, in contrast, short-circuits the domination of these codes in politics by granting parity between right and left (Laponce 1972b: 472–473; 1975: 17–19; 1981: 13, 41–46, 90–92; Lukes 1992). As a symbol of parity, right–left clears a space in which opposition and disagreement are legitimate and where contending forces are on equal political footing and can be balanced against each other. This assigns right–left with the overarching function of instituting the autonomy of the political symbolic order, and it points at that right–left is related to public reason as balancing different and conflicting claims. Three assertions can be made concerning right–left at this level (Laponce 1981: 27f; see also Table 1):

1   *Frame*: as symmetrical opposites, right–left stands for reciprocal recognition and acceptance of differences (everyone has equal political status), coupled with the categorical proposition of equal liberty.
2   *Difference*: right–left is a vehicle of division for the purpose of opposition and conflict, which entails the acceptance of political opposition, disagreement, conflict, and so on within explicit and negotiable limits.
3   *Centre*: right–left serves the function of setting apart for the purpose of cooperation and exchange, and is geared to strike a balance between contending forces by reaching out for even-handed judgements and reasonable decisions.

The articulation between frame, difference and centre defines the function of right–left by orientating political identification to common concerns, and by linking a political regime marked by competition for power and political culture marked by differences. As democracy is conditioned by the autonomy of the political symbolic order, it has to assert the primacy of political orientation and justification in matters of common concerns, which is the function of right–left. So even though right–left has an anachronistic touch to it in today's political climate as it is bound up with the cleavages structuring politics in the last century such as national–international, state–market, public–private and collectivism–individualism, it cannot be replaced by any of the three other pairs of orientational metaphors as this would destroy the autonomy of the political symbolic order. To get rid of right–left would invalidate the modern democratic principle that societal unity is constituted in the face of division (Lefort 1988: 18, 34–35, 39, 41) and that unity should be political, which means that it is illegitimate from a democratic point of view to base political values on a pre-political or primordial unity such as nation or people. Thus conceived pluralism and equal liberty are all-important for democratic politics (Laponce 1972a: 472f, 1972b: 53, 1975: 16–20, 1981: 41–46).

One should therefore be careful not to mix up the prototype of right–left and its democratic function as the latter cannot be exhausted by the contingent configuration of the right–left polarity. The gap between the historical and functional aspects of right–left makes it possible to assert the primacy of this distinction for democratic politics while upholding a critical stance towards its historical manifestations.

Rawls's Contribution to Democratic Ideology

I see Rawls's account of public reason as a crucial dimension of democratic ideology, which can be related to the fours pairs of orientational metaphors. *In–out* concerns membership of political society governed by mutual recognition and acceptance of differences; *front–back* is about lineage, development, direction, rupture and hence 'readings of history' in the light of the future; *up–down* focuses on relations between political authorities and people, those who are well-off, influential, successful, etc. and those who are not; and *right–left* deals with governing fairly under conditions of pluralism, that is, opposition among equal opposites.

The first two pairs of orientational metaphors organise what in lack of a better term could be called the exterior limits of political society and its political capital: the spatial limits settling who–what can be included and the temporal limits delineating the political capital of a tradition and the directions it can take. The last two are interior limits dealing with power and fairness of where to draw the line between using and abusing power or between power and domination (Foucault 1988: 8, 11–13, 18–19), and how to position and orientate oneself politically and how to govern given the premise of equal liberty.

The autonomy of the political symbolic order vis-à-vis the cultural–religious symbolic order parallels Rawls's discussion of public reason and comprehensive reasons. To speak of public reason as freestanding relies on distinguishing political from non-political concerns, and to assert the distinctively political rules governing common concerns. A democratic structuring of these rules – which finds expression in both constitution and tradition – is only possible if the political symbolic order asserts a hegemonic reading principle, one which is able to incorporate and organise other orientations while remaining distinct. This has been the task of right–left, which is the only type of orientation that is able to support the autonomy of the political symbolic order and the freestanding status of public reason. The hegemonic role of right–left vis-à-vis the other orientations implies that it stands for a specific orientation whilst at the same time being the medium for expressing the others. This is the case, for instance, when issues relating to economic redistribution (up–down), citizenship rights (in–out) or tradition–renewal (front–back) are voiced in terms of right–left. It is the overdetermined status of right–left which makes it crucial for a democratic imaginary. In addition, by locating ideological mechanisms in relations between orientation and justification provides a link between the programmatic aspects of ideology where it is discursively systematised both theoretically and strategically, and the practical or ordinary aspects where it has become commonsense.

A democratic ideology would be one based on the political symbolic order and concerned with asserting the primacy of public political reasoning when addressing common concerns. Democracy has priority to philosophy and is not concerned with solving disagreement among comprehensive reasons or asserting truth claims or claims to morality (Rawls 1997: 771, 799). It is geared to make it possible to agree–disagree in the fist place by creating a political field of interaction in which members treat each other as political equals. This is what the political conception of justice focuses on. 'The dualism in political liberalism', says Rawls (1993a: xxi), 'between the point of view of the political conception and the many points of view of comprehensive doctrines is not a dualism originating in philosophy. Rather, it originates in the special nature of democratic political culture as marked by reasonable pluralism.'

Whereas the philosophical Rawls viewed public reason as an Archimedean point capable of removing irrationalities and particularities from an underlying universal order, the political Rawls considers public reason as a transformative capacity that brings about a contingent democratic order, moves the boundaries of what is political beyond constitutional essentials and pushes for more political equality and liberty (Rawls 1993a: 347). His discussion of public reason can be seen as a democratic way to engage in politics, which is based on political criteria of inclusion-exclusion and open to everyone accepting these criteria. This is the reason Rawls's argument is conducive for democratic ideology. The public–private distinction is inadequate here because it makes the scope of politics – what falls under common concerns – depend on a juridical distinction, which moreover functions so as to keep divisive issues out of politics by confining them to the private sphere, for example, conflicts of class, religion, gender, sex and race.

If the basic distinction for public reason is instead public–nonpublic it will be possible to voice these conflicts politically as the criteria regulating recognition and acceptance will be common political concerns. This makes the principle of public reason suitable in nonpublic contexts as well, which are governed by comprehensive reasons. Public reason thus links political authorities and laypeople as well as public political culture and background culture, tailors comprehensive views to the political conception of justice (Rawls 1993a: 203, 247) and pushes in the direction of fair terms of social cooperation. Thus reasonableness is neither concerned with constitutional essentials only nor is it a mode of conduct designed by and for 'philosophical experts' (Rawls 1995a: 174). It is ingrained in social relations as political capital, which operates in the political culture as well as in the political regime. Justice as fairness is political by being connected with 'the common sense of everyday life' (Rawls 2001: 5).

Political liberalism thus aims to work out 'a conception of political justice for a constitutional democratic regime that the plurality of reasonable doctrines ... might endorse' (Rawls 1993a: xviii). As the former is shared by everybody in a way the latter is not, Rawls distinguishes between 'a public basis of justification generally acceptable to citizens on fundamental political questions and the many nonpublic bases of justification belonging to the many comprehensive doctrines and acceptable only to those who affirm them' (Rawls 1993a: xix). His argument is, in other words, that public reason operates outside the state as sound judgements that draws on and reflects the political capital of democratic traditions. Public virtues can only be cultivated in a society governed by the democratic value of equal liberty, which connects the institutional and the personal dimensions of politics and systematises our intuitions about fairness. He is in this respect outlining a democratic ideology, centred on political orientation and political justification, whose task is to create a workable coupling between democratic regime and public culture so 'that deeply opposed though reasonable comprehensive doctrines may live together and all affirm the political conception of a constitutional regime' (Rawls 1993a: xviii).

Public Reason in Relation to the Political System and Parapolitical Systems

Rawls's distinction between public and nonpublic uses of reason indicates that whilst the former is geared towards the basic structure of society and upheld by free and equal citizens in political society, the latter is applied to what Easton (1965: 50–56) calls the parapolitical systems of associations in which comprehensive views play a governing role. Public reason is in varying degrees built into the structure of subsystems and hence, in part, defined in relation to them. 'To act reasonably and responsibly corporate bodies, as well as individuals, need a way of reasoning about what is to be done. This way of reasoning is public with respect to their members, but nonpublic with respect to political society and to citizens generally' (Rawls 1993a: 220; see also 2001: 92). Public reason is reflected in the various comprehensive views governing these corporate bodies; and opposite, these views partake in shaping public reason (Rawls 1993a: 247–254). This interconnectedness makes it necessary to differentiate between 'freestanding' and 'independent' (Rawls 1995b: 7). The former is a moral category worked out for the political symbolic order, a democratic value, and the latter is a causal category explaining, for example, the nature and degree of the relative autonomy of political agents. Public reason is freestanding by being based on the ethico-political value of democracy, which I have referred to as the political symbolic order. It is neither independent nor dependent on comprehensive views, but is more likely engaged in relations of autonomy–dependence with other values.

Politics is conducted in each subsystem when collectively binding decisions are made and implemented on its behalf. The principle of public reason applies in varying degrees to parapolitical systems, because 'public' refers to the quality of reason and not to its institutional location. If this were not the case public reason would not be able to frame justice as fairness (Rawls 1997: 788ff). The more parapolitical systems interact, the more the resulting overarching system will have to abstract from the conflicting views governing each of them, which is why public reason has to be freestanding in relation to the norms and values ingrained in subsystems (Dyrberg 1995: 20). Two principles are important here. First, that the rules and values governing political society as an all-inclusive aspect of political life are different from those governing the politics in associations. Second, that the symbolic order governing political society has to be freestanding in relation to the political dimension of these contexts and the norms, values and interests they express. Otherwise, the political concept of justice as well as pluralism would be endangered (Rawls 1993a: 42n; see also 146n).

The limits constituting specific contexts might be characterised by a high degree of perfectionism. This does not weaken the principle of public reason, but only affects its scope of application. The relation between the political system and parapolitical systems, and hence the levels in public reason, is spatial, but it also has temporal aspects. Relations between parapolitical systems, and the comprehensive schemes with which they are articulated, take place over time with the result that they become part of the political capital of democratic orientation and justification. Different values, norms and interests constitute a diversified ensemble of ways of living together which over time coalesce into more or less persistent patterns and become common heritage. The liberty of equal citizenship is a focal point of this heritage which is cultivated in civic traditions revolving around common political concerns.

Reasonableness and the Original Position

As a device of representation, the original position emphasises that the self has to meet certain criteria of reasonableness to pursue what it considers rational. The demand this imposes on comprehensive views is that they have to acknowledge that that they have something in common. The participants to the original position have been framed, as it were, by the political imperative of conditioning co-existence and by the ethical imperative to act so as not to violate the political commonalty of sharing. Two points are important here. There is, first, the concern with defining the criteria of fairness governing the mechanisms of inclusion and exclusion in relation to society, which is an in–out type of orientation. Second, there is the concern to distinguish between exercising and abusing power, which is a limit within power that lays out the criteria for its fair exercise vis-à-vis co-existing differences, which is typically an up–down type of orientation.

The original position is a way of representing what conditions political liberty and equality. This procedure is the opposite of Habermas whose ideal speech situation requires that knowledge is free-floating in the sense of ridding itself from power, which is required for achieving epistemic and ethical validity. For Rawls, by contrast, the ethical moment is conditioned by a power to separate knowledge and self, that is, a will to ignorance with regard to one's identity and position (Rawls 1972: 145, 245). The veil of ignorance thus illustrates the contingency of the self's positioning and its claims to truth. This suspension of moral and calculative certainty is the founding political gesture conditioning public reason. The political question is to identify when or how power becomes abusive in relation to incompatible views, interests, forms of life, and so on. The limit within power between use and abuse has an ethico-political dimension, which has to do with how to comport oneself towards others and how to govern oneself and others democratically thus safeguarding the value of equal liberty.

In politics, knowledge and morality are not enough, that is, their claims to truth and the good cannot trump political concerns as this would violate the political equality of reasonably comprehensive views and hence the values of liberty and equality. To say that the principles of public reason could gain the support of an overlapping consensus means that they do not rely upon common agreement or morally binding comprehensive views. 'What binds a society's efforts into one social union', says Rawls (1972: 571), 'is the mutual recognition and acceptance of the principles of justice'. We have to accept the principles of public reason as acceptance is prior to agreeing or disagreeing. So, 'public reason does not ask us to accept the very same principles of justice, but rather to conduct our fundamental discussions in terms of what we regard as a political conception' (Rawls 1993a: 241, see also 226–227). The point is that public reason can be accepted by agonistic comprehensive views inasmuch as they recognise and accept each other (Rawls 1993a: 98; Lloyd 1994: 731). What we have here is an insistence upon the strictly political nature of the democratic ideology of orientation and justification. This is the political imperative of a democratic political society and the bottom line of being reasonable.

To approach the question of toleration in relation to reasonable pluralism indicates that it should be approached politically and not morally. It should, in other words, be dealt with from the perspective of the political symbolic order as freestanding. This is put succinctly by Laclau when he holds that 'tolerance only starts when I morally disapprove of something and, however, I accept it. The very condition of approaching the question of toleration is to start realizing that it is not an ethical question at all'. The ground of toleration is, he continues, 'the need for society to function in a way which is compatible with a certain degree of internal differentiation' (Laclau 1996a: 51). Toleration is here addressed as a political problem in a way similar to Rawls. Thus Laclau points out the difference between morally approving–disapproving of something and acceptance, which is political and prior to passing judgements on comprehensive reasoning (Rawls 1972: 527). Acceptance is the political–democratic gesture in which right–left articulates in–out and up–down orientations (external and internal limits) and which trumps moral and rational issues of respect–disrespect and agreement–disagreement, respectively.

The principle of recognising and accepting differences is a political specification of that 'certain degree of internal differentiation' which sets the limits of reasonable pluralism (Sartori 1997: 64–65; Rawls 1972: §§34–35). It is within these limits we can agree to disagree – limits which are politically contestable, as they are the means and end of public reason. This should be seen in relation to the three aspects of the function of right–left: frame, difference and centre. Their negotiable nature implies that it is necessary to discuss the limits of acceptability to be able to frame reasonable pluralism. When these limits are themselves political constructs they can have no other ground than those given by political contestations over time.

Democratic Equivalence in Relation to Anti-perfectionism

The arguments about common political concerns, relating to the co-existence of differences as well as to the mutual recognition and acceptance, imply that it is decisive for democracy that the political equality of comprehensive ways of reasoning remains open for various forms of identities and the struggles among them (Laclau 1996a: 57). This parallels the function of the modern political right–left dyad organising political orientation: the premise of parity which implies that opposition is legitimate and that opposed parties are granted the status of equal opposites in the political realm; and that 'nothing is sacred', meaning that everything is negotiable as "the markers of certainty" (Lefort 1988: 19) have been abolished. Public reasoning, sound judgement, the possibility of change through concerted action and, of course, negotiation only make sense if political equality entails openness and autonomy. What is publicly reasonable undergo changes either rapidly or slowly, which means that it is revised on an ongoing basis (Rawls 1997: 777–778). The possibility that it might be partial by partaking in abusing power is not an argument against public reason as such, because it is based on the distinction it criticises. Instead, it is an argument for the possibility and democratic necessity of negotiating its indeterminacy, which calls for keeping the empty place of power open (Lefort 1988: 17, 34) or for maintaining one public reason (Rawls 1993a: 220). Openness requires oneness in the sense given by the principle of political equivalence. This can be sustained only by anti-perfectionism that maintains public reason as freestanding in relation to comprehensive reasons and the political equality of opposites, that is, the parity of right–left. Anti-perfectionism is thus an important dimension of a democratic ideology.

Rawls's advocacy of anti-perfectionism does not imply that public reason is a neutral arbiter aiming to strike a balance between conflicting views, interests, etc., which remains unaffected by the substantive values it adjudicates. Public reason is rather an interactive political principle that triggers political conflicts when reasonable counterclaims cannot reach a solution and when public reason is confronted with, say, authoritarian comprehensive views (Burt 1994: 136). What characterises a democratic way of governing this principle is that it can only be anchored in the political symbolic order, which does not judge comprehensive views. What distinguishes democracy from every other type of political society is that inclusion–exclusion is based on the orientational and justificatory axes of democratic ideology.

Anti-perfectionism links political orientation and political justification, and gives expression to the political value of fairness, which is equivalent to balance in the terminology of right–left. Anti-perfectionism emphasises that politics is geared toward governing co-existing differences, and that this constitutes a political society in which public reason as freestanding expresses the value of the political equality of differences. The point is not that there is no place for comprehensive ways of reasoning in politics, but that public reason is open for such views on the condition that it does not to bind itself to them. Comprehensive views cannot, in other words, form the basis of public reason as this would compromise its status as freestanding by turning common concerns into a common good. The difference between the two is that the latter is a substantive norm, whereas the former is geared towards political orientation and justification that revolve around the hegemony of right–left vis-à-vis *up–down* as power and status (ruler–ruled, elite–people and high–low), *front–back* as direction (progressive–reactionary, transparency–obscurity and just–unjust) and *in–out* as membership, belonging, etc. (strict–broad citizenship, us–them and access–non-access to power).

Public Reason and the Democratic Principle of Inclusion–Exclusion

What characterises a democratic political order is that the principles governing inclusion–exclusion and use–abuse do not have to violate the principle of political equality, because it does not rely on non-political or non-negotiable assumptions. Nor does public reason rely on a trade-off between universalistic rationalism and a procedural set-up, on the one hand, and cultural relativism and normative integration, on the other.

The inclusive aspect of public reason lies in its openness to comprehensive views, whose reasonableness is conditioning it in the first place, whilst it simultaneously 'will have the capacity to shape those doctrines toward itself' usually over long stretches of time (Rawls 1995a: 145, see also 145–147; Rawls 1993a: 168, 194, 203). To claim to speak from within public reason is itself a matter of political contestations. Although this might look as if public reason is on the whole a slippery concept, it does retain an exclusive aspect. Democratic public reason has to enforce limits towards comprehensive views to maintain its defining political characteristics by excluding views if they cannot be made accessible to all on a reciprocal basis, that is, if they violate the founding principles of liberty and equality. Public reason exhibits in this respect a dogmatism of its own: that those who violate this principle must be barred access to the domain of public reason (Rawls 1993a: 64n, 151–154, 157; Žižek 1997: 34). The democratic virtue of public reason lies in its ability to include everybody as free and equal citizens, which is not possible for comprehensive reasons, because they have to reject that everybody is of equal worth in the original position and have the same potentials for political engagement. It is from within public reason the inclusive or the exclusive view can be adopted.

To adopt an inclusive view or an exclusive view depends on whether we are in a situation where somebody is excluded from public reason by being denied basic liberties. Public reason cannot accept exclusions based on, say, ethnicity, customs, religion, gender or sexuality. Any such exclusion is antithetic to the democratic principle of the liberty of equal citizenship, and hence democratic orientation and justification, because it is based on racist, religious, moral and–or sexist assumptions. In a situation like this the inclusive view could be adopted, which implies that a counterattack on these positions could be based on other comprehensive reasons (Rawls 1997: 776, 784–785). The operational matrix of public reason is a political battleground of where to draw the line between public and nonpublic, what are common concerns and what are not, and what is reasonable and what is not. It goes for both the inclusive and the exclusive views that public reason is entitled to trump comprehensive reasons as it is from within public reason that the two views can be adopted. The principle of reasonableness are laid down in the limits towards arguments and practices that attempt to exclude interests, opinions, values and ways of life on bases other than a political one. These could be those of, say, social position, ethnicity, nationality, gender, sexuality and religion. What we get is a principle of mutual political acceptance within these limits. Exclusions that are not grounded in this principle cannot be justified democratically as they violate the principle of political equality.

I have argued that a democratic ideology relies on the political symbolic order being freestanding in relation to cultural and religious symbolic orders. In other words, this order and its ability to govern common concerns can only be provided by a democratic ideology which is orientated in terms of right–left and justified in terms of public reason. The basic political value of right–left is that political authority must safeguard public reason as freestanding political judgement and decision, that is, a democratic order in which opposing parties have equal political status. Public reason as justification is based on right–left orientation, the function of which is to frame political power struggles, organise oppositional politics and seek a balance between contending forces. By stressing this orientational basis of public reason I have focussed on the distinctively political nature of Rawls's argument.

References

Bienfait, H.F. & Beek, W.E.A. (2001) Right and Left as political categories: an exercise in 'not-so-primitive' classification. *Anthropos,* 96(1).

Bobbio, N. (1996) *Left and Right* (Chicago, IL: The University of Chicago Press).

Burt, J. (1994) John Rawls and the moral vocation of liberalism. *Raritan,* 14(1), pp. 133–153.

Dyrberg, T.B. (1995) *Which Liberalism, Whose Community?* Working Papers, No. 7 (Colchester: Centre for Theoretical Studies, University of Essex).

Dyrberg, T.B. (2003) 'Right/left in the context of new political frontiers: what's radical politics today? *Journal of Language and Politics,* 2(2), pp. 333–361.

Easton, D. (1965) *A Framework for Political Analysis* (Englewood Cliffs, NJ: Prentice-Hall).

Foucault, M. (1988) The ethic of care for the self as a practice of freedom, in: J. Bernauer & D. Rasmussen, *The Final Foucault* (Cambridge, MA: The MIT Press), pp. 1–20.
Hertz, R. (1973) The pre-eminence of the right hand: a study in religious polarity, in: R. Needham (Ed.), *Right and Left: Essays in Dual Symbolic Classification* (Chicago, IL and London: University of Chicago Press), pp. 3–31.
Laclau, E. (1990) *New Reflections on the Revolution of Our Time* (London: Verso).
Laclau, E. (1996a) *Emancipation(s)* (London: Verso).
Laclau, E. (1996b) The death and resurrection of the theory of ideology. *Journal of Political Ideologies*, 1(3), pp. 201–220.
Laclau, E. & Mouffe, C. (1985) *Hegemony and Socialist Strategy* (London: Verso).
Lakoff, G. & Johnson, M. (1980) *Metaphors We Live By* (Chicago, IL and London: University of Chicago Press).
Laponce, J.A. (1972a) In search of the stable elements of the Left–Right landscape. *Comparative Politics*, 4(4), pp. 455–475.
Laponce, J.A. (1972b) The use of visual space to measure ideology, in: J.A. Laponce & P. Smoker (Eds) *Experimentation and Simulation in Political Science* (Toronto, ON: University of Toronto Press), pp. 46–58.
Laponce, J.A. (1975) Spatial archetypes and political perceptions. *The American Political Science Review*, 69(1), pp. 11–20.
Laponce, J.A. (1981) *Left and Right: The Topography of Political Perception* (Toronto, ON: University of Toronto Press).
Lefort, C. (1988) *Democracy and Political Theory* (Oxford: Blackwell).
Lloyd, S.A. (1994) Relativizing Rawls. *Chicago-Kent Law Review*, 69, pp. 709–735.
Lukes S. (1992) What is Left? *Times Literary Supplement*, 27 March.
McManus, C. (2002) *Right Hand, Left Hand* (London: Phoenix).
Nairn, T. (1973) *The Left Against Europe* (Harmondsworth: Pelican Books).
Needham, R., (Ed.) (1973) *Right and Left: Essays in Dual Symbolic Classification* (Chicago, IL and London: University of Chicago Press).
Parkin, R. (1996) *The Dark Side of Humanity* (Amsterdam: Harwood Academic Publishers).
Rawls, J. (1972) *A Theory of Justice* (Oxford: Oxford University Press).
Rawls, J. (1993a) *Political Liberalism* (New York: Columbia University Press).
Rawls, J. (1993b) The law of peoples, in: S. Shute & S. Hurley (Eds), *On Human Rights* (New York: Basic Books), pp. 41–82.
Rawls, J. (1995a) Reply to Habermas. *The Journal of Philosophy*, 42(3), pp. 132–180.
Rawls, J. (1995b) Political liberalism: religion and public reason. *Religion and Values in Public Life*, 3(4), pp. 1–11.
Rawls, J. (1997) The idea of public reason revisited. *The University of Chicago Law Review*, 64(3), pp. 765–807.
Rawls, J. (2001) *Justice as Fairness: A Restatement* (Cambridge, MA: The Belknap Press of Harvard University Press).
Sartori, G. (1997) Understanding pluralism. *Journal of Democracy*, 8(4), pp. 58–69.
Schwarzmantel, J. (1998) *The Age of Ideology* (Houndmills: Macmillan Press).
Žižek, S. (1994a) The spectre of ideology, in: S. Žižek (Ed.), *Mapping Ideology* (London: Verso), pp. 1–33.
Žižek, S. (1997) Multiculturalism, or, the cultural logic of multinational capital. *New Left Review*, 225, September/October, pp. 28–51.

Al Qaeda: Ideology and Action

JEFFREY HAYNES

> Muslim fundamentalism is at least as dangerous as communism once was. Please do not underestimate this risk ... at the conclusion of this age it is a serious threat, because it represents terrorism, religious fanaticism and exploitation of social and economic justice. (Willy Claes, Secretary General of NATO, 1995)

The US government responded to the 11 September 2001 ('9/11') attacks with an assault on both the Taliban regime and Al Qaeda – in Arabic, Al Qaeda means 'the base' – headquarters in Afghanistan.[1] Following more than two decades of constant warfare, Afghanistan was a nation in ruins, a 'failed state' with a shattered social and political structure, with numerous towns and cities reduced to rubble. According to Thürer (1999: 731), failed states, such as Afghanistan, 'are invariably the product of a collapse of the power structures providing political support for law and order, a process generally triggered and accompanied by anarchic forms of internal violence'.

These circumstances allowed Al Qaeda to set up bases in Afghanistan, with the explicit agreement of the Taliban. The circumstances of Afghanistan also highlight how failed states are always unstable states that invite external military involvement. External forces, acting alone or through the auspices of regional bodies, seek to: (1) prevent political violence spilling over to destabilise neighbouring countries, and (2) ensure that they do not become safe havens for terrorist groups, including Al Qaeda.

Once the United States had dealt with the Taliban, it turned its focus to another problematic polity: the regime of Saddam Hussein in Iraq. Alleged – but unproven – links between Saddam's regime and Al Qaeda was a stated reason for the US-led invasion in March 2003. However, despite the US efforts, the post-invasion situation in Iraq was characterised by an unsuccessful attempt to rebuild a viable state, an outcome linked to the fact that Iraq became a *cause célèbre* for numerous Islamic militants, both indigenes and foreigners. Inspired by their 'victory' over the 'godless' Russian communists in Afghanistan in 1988, hundreds of victorious *mojahedin* – many from Arab countries – had earlier unsuccessfully redirected their jihad against their own 'unIslamic' rulers before turning their attentions to the US-led invasion of Iraq.

It is difficult to be sure about the precise level of support for Al Qaeda in the Sunni Muslim world.[2] However, it does seem clear that there is a high degree of anti-US resentment among this constituency, and widespread belief that the West is opposed to Islam.[3] Such a perception is fuelled by, inter alia, President Bush's move back towards uncritical support for Israel's Sharon government and the invasion of Iraq and subsequent inability to rebuild a viable administration in the country.[4]

In March, 2003, an audio tape was handed to the Associated Press purporting to be from the leader of Al Qaeda, Osama bin Laden. He called on citizens of Arab and Muslim to rise up against their governments – if they had expressed support for the invasion of Iraq. The conflict offered a significant opportunity for Al Qaeda and its ideological allies both to foment and encourage Iraqi dissatisfaction with the invasion, as well as to try to exploit hitherto-contained political and religious competition between Sunnis and Shias.[5] Evidence for the success of Al Qaeda's strategy can be seen in the way that increasing numbers of Iraqi Sunni Muslims were apparently drawn to radical Islamic ideas after the US invasion. Pelham (2004) gives the example of a mixed Sunni-Shia town, Abu Ghaib, 10 km from Baghdad. The adult Sunni male population numbers about 20,000 people. It is estimated that about one-fifth of them, some 4,000 men, now worship at Wahhabi mosques in the town, compared to a much smaller number prior to the invasion. The imams (Muslim preachers) are now said to deliver anti-American, anti-Shia ideological messages in the mosques, a theme also pursued by influential foreign Muslim clerics (Whitaker 2004b).

Even before the war to depose Saddam in 2003, some Sunni preachers were already issuing outspoken anti-Shia denunciations. Such people were said to fear that a successful US invasion would result in Sunni submission to the Rafida or rejectionists, the Wahhabi term for Shias. Some Sunnis used the circumstances of the invasion to attack Shias, with some Sunni mosques serving as local urban bases for jihadis hiding in the hills across the Iraq–Syria border. Foreigners – including

Yemenis, Syrians and Iranians – were caught in early 2004 in several of Iraq's cities while trying to launch attacks against both the US forces and the interim Iraqi government.[6] Strikes by Islamist radicals in Iraq have both short-term tactical objectives – to impede the formation of Iraqi police and armed forces – and a longer-term strategic goal: to increase the West's sense of vulnerability by demonstrating that America's military presence is unable to protect its allies, while evidencing the religious faith of the Islamic militants.

In March 2004, a London-based and Saudi-financed magazine, *al Majalla*, ran an e-mail interview with 'an Al Qaeda leader', Abu-Muhammad al-Ablaj, who said that he had received instructions from bin Laden to direct 'the Mujahideen yearning for martyrdom' to go to Iraq. The Qatar-based Al-Jazeera satellite station, which frequently aired Al Qaeda videos, also broadcast an appeal around the same time – entitled 'Join the Convoy', supposedly featuring Abu Musab Zarkawi, a Jordanian veteran of the Afghan war, accused by the US government of coordinating the Iraqi jihad. In the broadcast, bin Laden's deputy and the chief ideologue of Al Qaeda, Dr Ayman al-Zarkawi, said: 'here is America among us. So, come take revenge on it and extinguish your thirst with its blood' (Ventzke 2004; Pelham 2004).

Over time, Iraq's resistance acquired an increasingly religious hue, issuing communiqués and daubing walls with graffiti under the name of 'Mohammed's army'. This 'army' actually appeared to be a loose coalition of cells, sporting various religious names, such as Jihadi Earthquake Brigades, Saladin Brigades and al-Mutawakkilin ('those who rely on God'). Their collective aim appeared to be to free the 'capital of the caliphate', Baghdad, from foreign, non-Muslim occupation (Ventzke 2004). Their ideological inspiration was at least in part the ideas of Al Qaeda. In the north of Iraq, a radical Sunni group, Ansar al Sunna ('the members of the Sunna'), used the Internet to claim responsibility for two suicide bombings that killed more than 100 people in the Kurdish capital, Arbil, in February 2004. Ansar distributed videos of what it claimed were attacks on British, Spanish and Canadian intelligence officers, shown with their passports and identity cards. Using a favoured tactic of Al Qaeda, the wills of Ansar's suicide bombers – detailed on its videos – warned 'the brokers of the West' that jihad would continue 'until we get back [the Jerusalem mosque of] al-Aqsa and Andalucia' [Spain].

In sum, the US-led conflicts in both Afghanistan and Iraq following 9/11 served to encourage support for Al Qaeda among disgruntled Sunni Muslims in Iraq and elsewhere in two key ways: (1) to focus discontent against the 'West', in general, and the United States in particular; and (2) to polarise often sensitive relations between Sunnis and Shias. I shall argue that both goals are in line with Al Qaeda's ideological objectives.

This article is in two sections. The first focuses – briefly – upon Al Qaeda's emergence as a global entity, and examines the contention that the terrorist threat it poses is a qualitatively new kind of menace, emanating from a particular type of violent non-state actor. Already anachronistic with respect to thermonuclear war, the 9/11 attacks emphatically underlined that geographical space is no longer a barrier to external attack on states by such actors. The second section examines Al Qaeda's ideological roots, focus and objectives.

Al Qaeda: The Emergence of a Global Entity

> On September 11, 2001 Americans were confronted by an enigma similar to that presented to the Aztecs — an enigma so baffling that even elementary questions of nomenclature posed a problem: What words or phrase should we use merely to *refer* to the events of that day? Was it a disaster? Or perhaps a tragedy? Was it a criminal act, or was it an act of war? Indeed, one awkward TV anchorman, in groping for the proper handle, fecklessly called it an accident. But eventually the collective and unconscious wisdom that governs such matters prevailed. Words failed, then fell away completely, and all that was left behind was the bleak but monumentally poignant set of numbers, 9–11. (Harris 2002)

> America's new enemies seem to have no demands. They can't be bought, bribed, or even blackmailed. They only want to strike a blow at any cost. And if a suicide hijacker or bomber really believes that by dying in his jihad (Muslim holy war) he'll go straight to heaven and Allah's loving embrace, what earthly reward could the US or anybody else possibly offer as a substitute? (Sacks 2001)

The impact of 9/11 both on the United States and internationally can be seen in four ways.

First, while political violence and terrorism issues were already important areas of concern prior to 9/11, that event provided a distinctive emphasis on international terrorism and its networks, of which Al Qaeda is the most significant, but not the sole, example (Gunaratna 2004).

Second, the 9/11 attacks were widely regarded as a profound challenge both to the US government and political analysts who had shared a hitherto apparently unshakeable belief in certain fundamental foreign policy assumptions, especially the idea that geographical isolation – such as that experienced by the United States – offers some degree of immunity from external attack.

Third, there was a profound impact on Americans' sense of security, as the quotations above from Harris and Sacks – both Americans and journalists – make plain. In short, 9/11 shattered Americans' sense of safety. The last time that the continental United States suffered anything at all comparable to the 9/11 attacks was nearly 200 years ago, in 1814. Then, the British burned down the White House. Since then, Americans have apparently lived in an atmosphere of invulnerability from foreign attack. After 11 September, that disappeared.

Fourth, the significance of 9/11 is connected to the unequal global distribution of power. Globalisation creates 'many kinds of negative externalities, including the reaction of many marginalized groups, the creation of new channels for protest, and, in particular, the facilitation of new patterns of terrorist and other kinds' of political violence' (Hurrell 2002: 189). The increasingly unequal global distribution of power – both between and within countries – may be seen to encourage both domestic and international terrorism, not only from Al Qaeda but also other radical Islamic groups, such as the Groupes Islamiques Armés and the Groupe Salafiste pour la Prédication et le Combat/Dawa wa Jihad (Volpi 2003: 125–127). This is not to imply that there this is something inherent within Islam and its belief systems that necessarily encourages and facilitates extreme political violence. It is to note that there are extremist and violent elements among Islamic groups, and that some exploit opportunities provided by domestic factors of injustice and inequality, as well as those linked to globalisation.

Al Qaeda: Ideological History and Development

For Al Qaeda, the aim of 9/11 was not simply to wreak terrible destruction but also to create a global media spectacle, a spectacular advertisement for the organisation and its militant ideological goals. The mass of 'downtrodden ordinary Sunni Muslims' was the key target audience for the highly visual spectacle of the attacks on the Twin Towers and the Pentagon. Al-Qaeda used 9/11 especially to grab the attention of such people, inviting them to make connections between the attacks on the United States itself and the multiple resentments many such people already felt against America throughout the Muslim world. Reasons for such antipathy included often single-minded US support for unrepresentative rulers in the Arab world, American-led invasions of Iraq in 1990–91 and 2003, and Israel's continuing 'harsh' treatment of the Palestinians, aided and abetted by successive US administrations. Taken together, as they often are, these issues indicate a deep degree of hatred of the United States in many parts of the Muslim world, antipathy not necessarily restricted to small numbers of religious or political radicals.

Al Qaeda was established by Osama bin Laden, a wealthy Saudi Arabian, 13 years prior to 9/11, in 1988. During the 1980s, he had helped finance, recruit, transport and train Sunni Islamic recruits for the anti-Soviet Afghan resistance. After that conflict, his intention was to bring together Arab *mojahedin* (Islamic guerrillas) encouraged by the United States to come to Afghanistan in the 1980s to fight the Soviet army, to fight a new jihad (holy war) against 'backsliding', 'non-Islamic' rulers in the Sunni Muslim Arab world. Later, the focus expanded to include the international allies of such rulers, especially the United States. In February 1998, bin Laden issued a statement under the banner of 'The World Islamic Front for Jihad Against the Jews and Crusaders'. He called on Muslims to kill not only Americans – including civilians – but also 'those who are allied with them from among the helpers of Satan' (<http://cfrterrorism.org/groups/alqaeda2.html>).

76   *Ideology Seriously*

Apart from killing Americans and their allies, Al Qaeda has four other, related goals:

- Return to a 'pure and authentic' Islam as practised by the Prophet Mohammed and his companions in seventh century Medina, in order to bring back glory and prominence to Muslims.
- Overthrow regimes Al Qaeda deems to be 'non-Islamic'.
- Expel Westerners and non-Muslims from Muslim countries – particularly the holy land of Saudi Arabia, because the West is said to have subjugated the lands of Islam, and Western individualistic values have corrupted Muslims.
- Establish a pan-Islamic Caliphate throughout the world by working with a network of like-minded Islamic militant organisations.[7]

During the 1990s, Al Qaeda expanded its capacity and network, building links with various Islamist groups, including Egypt's Islamic Jihad, whose leader, Ayman al-Zawahiri, became bin Laden's deputy in 1998. Other Islamist groups affiliated to Al Qaeda include the Islamic Jihad Movement (Eritrea), al-Itihaad al-Islamiya (Somalia), al-Gama'a al-Islamiyya (Egypt), the Islamic Movement of Uzbekistan and the Harakat ul-Mujahidin (Pakistan). Following expulsion from Afghanistan in late 2001, Al Qaeda dispersed into small, often autonomous groups in various parts of the world, a network of Sunni Islamic extremists. Al Qaeda has also developed money-making front businesses, solicited donations from like-minded supporters, especially in Saudi Arabia, and illicitly siphoned funds from donations to Muslim charitable organisations, including Islamic NGOs (Conetta 2002; Haynes 2004).

Key Tenets of Al Qaeda's Ideology

Al Qaeda's members and sympathisers are united in a belief that they are involved in a three-pronged jihad (holy war) against 'apostate' Muslims, unIslamic rulers and the West. The organisation's ideology draws on two key sources: Wahhabism – a version of the official version of Islam found in Saudi Arabia – and the ideas of an Egyptian, Sayyid Qutb. Al Qaeda's chief ideologue is bin Laden's deputy, Dr Ayman al-Zawahiri.

The roots of Wahhabism, a puritanical interpretation of Islam, are found in the ideas of Mohammad ibn Abd al-Wahhab, an eighteenth-century Sunni reformer born in Arabia. He believed that Islam had been corrupted more than a thousand years earlier, shortly after the death of the Prophet Mohammed. Al-Wahhab denounced any theology – including religious scholarship – and customs that had since developed as non-Islamic. In a religious revolution, he and his supporters took over what is now Saudi Arabia, where his ideology – known as Wahhabism – is still the dominant school of religio-political thought. Wahhabism has two central tenets: it (1) preaches against worship of 'false idols', including the mystical form of Islam known as Sufism – because Sufis worship local saints as well as God; and (2) regards Shias, Muslims who revere the descendants of Ali, the Prophet

Mohammed's son-in-law, as apostates. Wahhabism dynamically emerged from the Arabian peninsula 200 years ago, taking root among Sunni Muslims in many parts of the Middle East and elsewhere.

The second key religious and ideological thinker that informs Al Qaeda's ideology is a more recent figure, Sayyid Qutb (1906–1966). Qutb was an Egyptian, a prominent Islamist and member of the Muslim Brotherhood, the Arab world's oldest Islamist group, which advocates an Islamic state in Egypt. His thought was deeply influenced by the revolutionary radicalism of a contemporaneous Indian Islamist, Sayyid Abu'l-A'la Mawdudi (1903–1979). Qutb's ideological development fell into two distinct periods: before 1954, and from 1954 until his execution by the Egyptian government in 1966, following imprisonment and torture by the secularist government of Gamal Abdel-Nasser. Following an attempt on Nasser's life in October 1954, the government imprisoned thousands of members of the Muslim Brotherhood, including Qutb, and officially banned the organisation. During his second, radical phase, Qutb declared 'Western civilisation' the enemy of Islam; denounced leaders of Muslim nations for not following Islam closely enough; and sought to spread the belief among Sunni Muslims that it was their duty to undertake jihad to defend and purify Islam.

Bin Laden's deputy, Dr Ayman al-Zawahiri, is Al Qaeda's chief ideologue. He was the man most responsible for turning Al Qaeda into an international network after the merging of his organisation, Egyptian Islamic Jihad, with Al Qaeda in 1998. According to Montasser el-Zayat, a prominent Egyptian attorney who defends Islamic radicals and spent three years in prison with al-Zawahiri from 1981 for conspiracy to assassinate the late Egyptian president Anwar Sadat, 'he is bin Laden's brain ... the planner, the organiser and the thinker who laid the ground for the idea of an Islamic front' (<http://www.news24.com/News24/World/News/ 0,6119,2-10-1462_1500844,00.html>). Al-Zawahiri is also a key figure in promoting the use of suicide attacks. 'It is the love of death in the path of Allah, that is the weapon that will annihilate this evil empire of America', he said in an interview in 2002 (Whitaker 2004b).

Al-Zawahiri was born in June, 1951, and grew up in a family of doctors and scholars. He began his militant career in 1966, when he was arrested for belonging to the outlawed Muslim Brotherhood. He was later freed and graduated from Cairo University's medical school, earning a master's degree in surgery. Later, he was one of the founders of Islamic Jihad, which sought to overthrow the Egyptian government and replace it with an Islamic government. Having spent several years in prison, by the late 1980s he was regarded as the organisation's leader. His position was bolstered by the status he acquired by spending part of the 1980s in Afghanistan, involved with the anti-Soviet *mojahedin*. He later described the Afghan war against the USSR 'as a training ground of the utmost importance to prepare the Muslim mojahedin to wage their awaited battle against the superpower that now has sole dominance of the globe, namely, the United States' (Whitaker 2004b). After the war, he is thought to have travelled to Denmark and Switzerland, sometimes using a false passport. He also reportedly spent six months in Russian custody for alleged extremist activities in Daghestan. Over the years, al-Zawahiri has developed his ideological ideas in several books, including *The Bitter Harvest*, a critical assessment of the Muslim Brotherhood in Egypt, and *Knights Under the Prophet's Banner*, a reflection on life after the 11 September attacks, which he wrote in a cave in Afghanistan.

Following the failures of Islamist uprisings and revolutions in the Arab Middle East – most notably in Algeria and Saudi Arabia – al-Zawahiri believed that a tactical change was necessary. He is thought to have personally persuaded bin Laden to refocus Al Qaeda's attention towards the United States – and the West more generally – and to stop trying to spread revolution in the Muslim world. To this end, al-Zawahiri was the second of five signatories – bin Laden was the first – to the 1998 fatwa declaring 'jihad against Jews and Crusaders' and which 'authorised' the killing of Americans. This was a pivotal moment in the development of Al Qaeda's ideology as it gave a concrete set of goals in relation to contemporary issues which could be justified and pursued by reference to the organisation's ideological referents: Wahhabism and the ideas of Sayyid Qutb.

In sum, Al Qaeda's militant ideology has underpinned resistance to what its leaders see as the dictates of 'Western-style', that is, secular and inherently corrupting, modernisation. This is seen to bring traumatic social and economic dislocation, viz. Israel/Palestine, Iraq and Afghanistan, by undermining the stability of local Sunni Muslim cultures. Followers of Al Qaeda are urged to deal with the effects of modernisation by recourse to traditional patterns of behaviour rooted in their Islamic heritage. There is also the context provided by the fact that, throughout the Sunni Muslim world, especially among the Arab countries, Muslim traditions have for decades generally been denied or at best downplayed. This was the result of policies of various kinds of secular and secularising regimes that filled the Muslim world after the Second World War. That these countries had rulers widely believed to be 'in the pockets' of the West, while almost uniformly disappointing the developmental and political expectations of their populations, was regarded as proof of a more fundamental, holistic denial of Islam as a self-contained religious, social, political and economic system.

Al Qaeda, Orientalism and the 'Clash of Civilisations'

It is useful to examine the development of Al Qaeda's ideology in relation to the Orientalism thesis of Edward Said and the 'clash of civilisations' theory of Samuel Huntington. This will enable us to locate Al Qaeda's ideology in the context of what its cadres see as long-term, historically rooted, Western cultural, political and economic domination, involving a rejection of key 'Western' values: pluralism, liberal democracy, relativism and radical individualism.

The idea of Islam as a body of religious and social thought that is inherently atavistic and at odds with Western thought and culture is captured in the concept of Orientalism, articulated most famously by the late Edward Said in his 1978 book, *Orientalism*. Said (1978: 2) defined Orientalism as a 'style of thought based upon an ontological and epistemological distinction made between "the Orient" and (most of the time) the "Occident"'. Said claimed that many Western politicians and academics 'essentialised' both Muslims and Islam into unchanging categories, but that many of these assumptions were little more than generalisations with little or no foundation. Said cited Lord Cromer, the British governor of Egypt between 1882 and 1907, who argued that 'the Oriental generally acts, speaks and thinks in a manner exactly opposite to the European'. While Cromer claimed that 'the European' is a 'close reasoner' and a 'natural logician', he believed 'the Oriental' to be 'singularly deficient in the logical faculty' (Said 1978: 39). Although Cromer was no doubt a product of his times, there is no obvious reason to believe that his prejudiced views are entirely extinct.

A recent example of what might be called *nouveau* Orientalism is to be found in the 'clash of civilisations' theory associated with Samuel Huntington. Given that 9/11 and many subsequent terrorist outrages were undertaken by militant Muslims against western targets, then the question can be asked whether these events mark the beginning of Huntington's mooted 'civilisational' conflict between Islam and the West. It is plausible that 9/11 and subsequent US responses have made Huntington's prophecies about clashing civilisations appear far less abstract and far more plausible than when first articulated more than a decade ago.

Huntington first presented his 'clash of civilisations' in an article published in 1993, followed by a book in 1996. His main argument was that, following the end of the Cold War, a new, global clash was under way, replacing the four-decades-long conflict between liberal democracy/capitalism and communism, a new fight between the (Christian) 'West' and the (mostly Muslim, mostly Arab) 'East'. The core of Huntington's argument was that after the Cold War the 'Christian', democratic West found itself in conflict with radical Islam, a key threat to international stability. Christianity, on the other hand, was said by Huntington to be conducive to the spread of liberal democracy. In evidence, he noted the collapse of dictatorships in southern Europe and Latin America in the 1970s and 1980s, followed by the development of liberal democratic political norms (rule of law, free elections, civic rights). These events were regarded by Huntington as conclusive proof of the synergy between Christianity and liberal democracy, both key foundations of a normatively desirable global order built on liberal values. Others have also agreed that Islam is inherently undemocratic or anti-democratic. Fukuyama (1992: 236), for example, has suggested that Islamic 'fundamentalism' has a 'more than superficial resemblance to European fascism'. We can also note influential voices among American politicians, expressing opinions that play up the notion of civilisational conflict. For example, Democratic Congressman Tom Lantos stated in November, 2001, that

> unfortunately we have no option but to take on barbarism which is hell bent on destroying civilization ... You don't compromise with these people. This is not a bridge game. International terrorists have put themselves outside the bonds of protocols.[8]

Critics of Huntington's argument have noted that it is one thing to argue that various brands of political Islam have qualitatively different perspectives on liberal democracy that some forms of Christianity, but quite another to claim that Muslims *en masse* are poised to enter into a period of conflict with the West. That is, there are actually many 'Islams' and only the malevolent or misinformed would associate the terrorist attacks with an apparently representative quality of a single idea of Islam. Second, the 9/11 atrocities and subsequent bomb outrages do not appear to have been carried out by a state or group of states or at their behest, but by Al Qaeda. Despite energetic US attempts, no proof was found to link the regime of Saddam Hussein in Iraq with Al Qaeda.

Third, the idea of religious or civilisational conflict is problematic because it is actually very difficult to identify clear territorial boundaries to civilisations, and even more difficult to perceive them as acting as coherent units. Huntington's image of 'clashing civilisations' appears to focus too closely on an essentially undifferentiated category – 'a civilisation' – and as a result places insufficient emphasis on various trends, conflicts and disagreements that take place within *all* cultural traditions, whether Islam, Christianity, Judaism or whatever. The wider point is that cultures are not usefully seen as closed systems of essentialist values, *à la* Orientalism. It is actually implausible to understand the world as comprising a strictly limited number of cultures, each with their own unique core sets of beliefs. The influence of globalisation in this regard is to be noted as it leads to an expansion of channels, pressures and agents via which various norms are diffused and interact.

Finally, the image of 'clashing civilisations' ignores the fact that Al Qaeda's terrorism is aimed not only at the West or the United States: it also targets unrepresentative, corrupt and illegitimate – in short, 'un-Islamic' – governments. Since the 1970s, the general rise of Islamist groups – including Al Qaeda – can be seen as a consequence of the political and economic failures of such governments, supported by successive US administrations, rather than the result of bin Laden's influence *tout court*.

The arguments of both Said and Huntington underline that there is a deep-rooted tradition in Western thought that sees the 'Orient', including the Muslim world, as something distinct and distinctive compared to the 'Christian' West. During the centuries of Western imperialism, there were frequent debates about what rights non-Christian and non-European peoples should enjoy. In the centuries of competition and sometimes conflict between Christianity and Islam, the notion of 'holy war' emerged – that is, a special kind of conflict undertaken effectively outside any framework of shared rules and norms – and 'just war', carried out for the vindication of rights within a shared framework of values. There is also a further strand of Western thought that contends that, because of their nature, some types of states and ideological systems cannot realistically be dealt with on 'normal' terms, that is, accepted rules that govern international relations have to be set aside when dealing with them. For example, during 1980s the Reagan administration in the United States averred that there was a basic lack of give-and-take available when dealing with communist governments, which meant that it was appropriate that some basic notions of international law could be set aside in such contexts. This tradition can also be seen as manifested in the remarks of Congressman Lantos noted above.[9] It not only suggests that available options are restricted to the choice of 'to contain or to crusade', but also indicates that 'such positions clearly continue to resonate within and around the current US administration' (Hurrell 2002: 193–195).

Like certain traditions of Western thought, some aspects of Al Qaeda's ideology also have universal themes, for example, the focus on injustice and inequality. But when we ask: 'What do Al Qaeda bombers and cadres *want*?', we may be trying to apply a Western concept, underpinned by the implicit assumption that they are trying to achieve certain *finite* goals. However, the question can be posed differently: 'Why do Al Qaeda bombers *believe* that they *must* act as they do, for example, killing people apparently randomly in bomb attacks?' The answer is that they may well literally believe that they have no other *rational* choice – if they are going to defend their religion and culture against Western onslaught. Such a presumption is underpinned by the timbre of militant statements from some captured Al Qaeda terrorists that emphasise both the general and the specific. For example, Imam Samudra, the Bali bomber, perceived what he saw as a specific abomination – Bali's Western-orientated night clubs – as an integral aspect of a more general Western-directed cultural assault against *all* Muslims. This mix of specific and general concerns is a more general component of Islamic militant ideology and beliefs wherever 'Muslim terrorism' is carried out or threatened: from Kashmir to Chechnya to Kenya. For example, the day following a 1998 Al Qaeda bombing in Nairobi that killed over 200 people, the Islamic Liberation Army of the People of Kenya (ILAPK), an Al Qaeda cover organisation, issued a communiqué that included reference to both specifically Kenyan and more general concerns:

> the Americans humiliate our people, they occupy the Arabian peninsula, they extract our riches, they impose a blockade and, besides, they support the Jews of Israel, our worse enemies, who occupy the Al-Aqsa mosque ...The attack was justified because the government of Kenya recognized that the Americans had used the country's territory to fight against its Moslem neighbors, in particular Somalia. Besides, Kenya cooperated with Israel. In this country one finds the most anti-Islamic Jewish centers in all East Africa. It is from Kenya that the Americans supported the separatist war in Southern Sudan, pursued by John Garang's fighters. (ILAPK communiqué in Arabic, published in London on 11 August 1998 and quoted [in English] in Marchesin 2003: 2)

Such combinations of the specific and the general have helped to spread Al Qaeda's ideological convictions throughout the Sunni Muslim world. Al Qaeda cadres no doubt believe that they are front-line troops engaged in a battle for the survival of their society, culture, religion and way of life, undermined and attacked by an aggressive West. They believe they are fighting in self-defence in a last-ditch stand; and under such circumstances it is rational for them to justify the use of tactics – such as, apparently indiscriminate bombings – as acceptable during conditions of a no holds barred 'holy war'.

Conclusion

> We blame everything on Al-Qaeda, but what happened is more dangerous than bin Laden or Al-Qaeda ... The issue is ideology, it's not an issue of organizations ... Regardless if Osama is killed or survives the awakening has started. (Syrian president, Bashar al-Assad, quoted in Pipes 2003).

It is ironic that Al Qaeda ('the base') no longer appears to have a physical base, following its expulsion from Afghanistan. Since 2001–02, the scattering of Al Qaeda has led to claims that it has been weakened, perhaps fatally. However, these assertions appear out to be unfounded. Instead, Al Qaeda has transformed itself into a collection of regional terror groups that operate more autonomously than before, collectively informed by shared ideological convictions deriving from the ideas of al-Wahhab and Sayyid Qutb.

There is a further irony in that the war in Iraq – presented as an opportunity to do away with a brutal, obnoxious regime and, after Afghanistan, engage further with terrorism – has actually provided Al Qaeda with an excellent chance to exploit the resulting circumstances, both materially and ideologically. The US government's claim was that Saddam's Iraq was a place where terrorists gathered; it appears that it wasn't then, but it certainly is now. George Tenet, then director of the CIA, stated in early 2004 that, 'as we continue the battle against Al Qaeda, we must overcome a movement – a global movement infected by Al Qaeda's radical agenda' (<http://www.csmonitor.com/2004/0226/p03s02-usfp.html>). The inference – we can also note it in the statement of Syrian president, Bashar al-Assad, quoted at the beginning of this section – is that Al Qaeda's extremist ideology is now attracting increased support, expanding its networks among a new generation of supporters not only in Iraq but also elsewhere in the Sunni Muslim world. I have argued that such people may be regarded as often idealists who believe in the concept of global jihad as necessary to liberate the lands of Islam from Western control. Al Qaeda strategists may not have hoped to defeat or even to weaken 'America' militarily on 9/11, but to gain publicity, to reach out to further recruits; and this has been forthcoming. This amounts to a psychological victory, useful progress towards the achievement of Al Qaeda's goals: jihad against 'Christians' and 'Jews'; chase away the Americans from the holy land, Saudi Arabia; and establish the puritanical rule of Wahhabism throughout the Sunni Muslim world.

Several of these objectives have already been achieved. Some of President Bush's responses to 9/11, especially the swift war in Afghanistan, were unavoidable given the state of public opinion after the attacks. However, the unfortunate crudeness and depth of response against what many Muslims now believe is an assault not only on Al Qaeda but also on Islam itself, has done nothing either to defeat Al Qaeda or stop the spread of its ideology. President Bush quickly declared a 'crusade' both against the specific threat of bin Laden and Al Qaeda and terrorism in general. He sent the US fleet back to the Middle East, undermined the Saudi royal family, and removed US troops from the country. This led to two counterproductive outcomes: much free publicity for bin Laden and Al Qaeda, and the antagonism of many ordinary Muslims around the world because of various policies, including: 'racial profiling', draconian legislation, mass arrests, and detentions at Guantanamo Bay prison camp.

Our discussion has suggested that Al Qaeda is now as much an ideology or a set of values as a single organisation led by a single leader. It has evolved into a brand name or a franchise, ineluctably linked with the various and complex manifestations of modern Islamic militancy. It may be that this is reflected in changing patterns of Al Qaeda terrorism. For example, the Al Qaeda-inspired bombers in Madrid in March 2004 did not blow themselves up, like most of their earlier counterparts: people who saw their deaths as an essential aspect of their message ('We love death as much as you love life'). Unusually, the Madrid bombings seem to have had a short-term, instrumental purpose: withdrawal of Spanish troops from Iraq.

The Muslim militants' perception of Western belligerence is underpinned by specific factors, especially their perception of poor and declining existentialist conditions for many ordinary Muslims in the Middle East, Africa and elsewhere. Al Qaeda militants also seek explanations for the economic, military, and political failures of their countries. They work from the presumption that Islam is the perfect social system; this implies a further understanding: something or someone must be to blame for their existential problems. The rhetorical question they ask is this: 'Why are so many Muslim countries ruled by self-serving, corrupt and unrepresentative governments?' Their answer is twofold: (1) Western governments – especially that of the United States– encourage them to do so; (2) ordinary Muslims – whether passively or actively – also encourage apostate rule by failing to practise religious duties with sufficient diligence. In this context, bombs and terrorism are ways to: (1) seek to restore Muslim pride (2) weaken the power of the American 'Crusaders', and (3) facilitate the eventual return to the golden age of a thousand years ago when the Arabs lands of Islam were the world's leading power.

What can Western governments do to redress the ideological appeal of Al Qaeda, especially among the 'wretched of the earth' in the Muslim world? While the scale of the militants' aims make them very difficult to counter, there are practical policies that might help, such as, peace in Israel-Palestine, although even this unlikely event would almost certainly not end Islamic terrorism quickly; however, it would deny militant Islamists a key piece of 'evidence'. It might also help sincerely to pressurise repressive governments of Muslim countries to reform politically. However, the ultimate worry is not necessarily Al Qaeda per se but the numerous, rather diffuse militant Islamic organisations that now exist to a lesser or greater degree independently of Al Qaeda, with the ability to acquire new supporters as a result of perceived local, national and international injustices.

Notes

1. After 11 September 2001, there were many further successful Al Qaeda attacks. During 2002, a truck bomb exploded near the ancient Jewish shrine of El Ghriba on the Tunisian island of Djerba, killing 14 Germans, five Tunisians and a Frenchman. Suicide bombs followed in Karachi (26 people killed), Bali (202 people killed, 132 injured) and Mombasa, Kenya (15 dead, 40 injured). Al Qaeda was also linked to various plans that, for one reason or another, were not carried out: to (1) assassinate Pope John Paul II during his visit to Manila in late 1994, (2) kill the then-US president, Bill Clinton, during his visit to the Philippines in early 1995, (3) bomb in mid-air a dozen US trans-Pacific flights in 1995, and (4) set off a bomb at Los Angeles International Airport in 1999. The organisation also plotted, in late 1999, to carry out terrorist operations against US and Israeli tourists visiting Jordan for millennial celebrations. However, Jordanian authorities thwarted the planned attacks and later put 28 suspects on trial. In December 2001, suspected Al Qaeda associate Richard Colvin Reid attempted to ignite a shoe bomb on a transatlantic flight from Paris to Miami. Al Qaeda also attempted to shoot down an Israeli chartered plane with a surface-to-air missile as it departed Mombasa airport in November 2002.
2. Fox and Sandler (2004: 76) estimate that Al Qaeda has thousands of members and associates, with cells in up to 60 countries.
3. After 9/11, support for the United States has generally dropped in much of the Muslim world. For example, in Morocco, public opinion surveys indicated support for the US fell from 77 per cent in 2000 to 27 per cent in the spring of 2003. In Jordan, it fell from 25 per cent in 2002 to 1 per cent in May 2003. In Saudi Arabia, it fell from 63 per cent in May of 2000 to 11 per cent in October 2003 (<http://www.csmonitor.com/2004/0226/p03s02-usfp.html>).
4. Recent opinion polls indicate that around 60 per cent of Iraqis believe that their lives are better because of the downfall of Saddam and his regime.
5. Overall, Shias account for about half the population, while the Sunni Arabs, the traditional rulers of both Ottoman Iraq and of the modern state since its inception in 1920, account for around a quarter of Iraqis. Iraq's population is divided along both racial and religious lines: about 75 per cent are Arabs, 18 per cent Kurds and the remainder (7 per cent) divided among Assyrians, Turcomans, Armenians and 'Persians'. Around 90 per cent of the population is Muslim, and most of the remainder are Christians. Most Kurds are Sunnis, while the Arab Muslims belong to both Sunni and Shia sects. Overall, Shias account for about half the population, while the Sunni Arabs, the traditional rulers of both Ottoman Iraq and of the modern state since its inception in 1920, account for around a quarter of Iraqis.
6. It is important, however, to note that only a small number of non-Iraqis were captured by US forces at this time, suggesting that foreigners were not the main instigators of or participants in terrorist attacks, either against Shias or Americans. Of 9,000 prisoners, only 30 were non-Iraqis, suggesting that the Sunni Islamist movement in Iraq largely comprised indigenes (Pelham 2004).
7. In an Al Qaeda house in Afghanistan, *New York Times* reporters found a brief statement of the 'Goals and Objectives of Jihad': (1) Establishing the rule of God on earth, (2) attaining martyrdom in the cause of God, and (3) purification of the ranks of Islam from the elements of depravity (<http://cfrterrorism.org/groups/alqaeda2.html>).
8. Interview with Tom Lantos (2001), BBC Radio 4, *Today* programme, 20 November 2001, quoted in Hurrell (2002: 195).
9. Such remarks did not seem to affect Congressman Lantos's electoral popularity. In the March 2004 democratic primary in California's 12th Congressional District he gained 71.6 per cent of the votes cast. His nearest challenger acquired less than 20 per cent (19.8 per cent) (<http://www.lantos.org/>).

References

Conetta, C. (2002) Dislocating Alcyoneus: how to combat al-Qaeda and the new terrorism, Project on Defense Alternatives Briefing Memo No. 23, available at <http://www.comw.org/pda/0206dislocate.html> (accessed 24 March 2004).
Fox, J. & Sandler, S. (2004) *Bringing Religion into International Relations* (New York and Basingstoke: Palgrave Macmillan).
Fukuyama, F. (1992) *The End of History and the Last Man* (Harmondsworth: Penguin).
Gunaratna, R. (2004) Defeating Al Qaeda – the pioneering vanguard of the Islamic movements, in: R. Howard & R. Sawyer (Eds), *Defeating Terrorism. Shaping the New Security Environment* (Guilford, CT: McGraw-Hill/Dushkin), pp. 1–28.
Harris, L. (2002) Al Qaeda's fantasy ideology. *Policy Review Online*, 114, August–September, available at <http://www.policyreview.org/AUG02/harris.html>.
Haynes, J. (2004) Islamic militancy in East Africa. Paper presented at the workshop 'South-South linkages in Islam. Translocal Agents, Ideas, Lifeworlds (19th and 20th Centuries), held at the Centre for Modern Oriental Studies, Berlin, 5–6 November 2004.
Huntington, S. (1993) The clash of civilisations? *Foreign Affairs*, 72(3), pp. 22–49.
Huntington, S. (1996) *The Clash of Civilizations* (New York: Simon and Schuster).
Hurrell, A. (2002) 'There are no rules' (George W. Bush): international order after September 11. *International Relations*, 16(2), pp. 185–204.
Marchesin, P. (2003) The rise of Islamic fundamentalism in East Africa. *African Geopolitics*, available at <http://www.african-geopolitics.org/show.aspx?ArticleId=3497>.
Pelham, N. (2004) Iraq's holy warriors draw inspiration from Arab puritan of another century. *Financial Times*, 18 March.
Pipes, D. (2003) Al-Qaeda's limits. *New York Post*, 28 May.
Sacks, G. (2001) Why I miss the Cold War. *Los Angeles Daily Journal* and the *San Francisco Daily Journal*, 2 October, available at <http://www.glennsacks.com>.
Said, E. (1978) *Orientalism* (London: Penguin).
Smith, S. (2002) The end of the unipolar moment? September 11 and the future of world order. *International Relations*, 16(2), pp. 171–183.
Thürer, D. (1999) The 'failed state' and international law. *International Review of the Red Cross*, 836, pp. 731–761.
Ventzke, B. (2004) *'Banners of righteousness of the Ansar al-Sunnah mujahideen in Iraq', Video – v10, Monday, February 23, 2004* (Alexandra, VA: IntelCenter). Available at <http://www.intelcenter.com/ansar-sunna-banners-v1-0.pdf> (accessed 24 March 2004).
Volpi, F. (2003) *Islam and Democracy. The Failure of Dialogue in Algeria* (London: Pluto Press).
Whitaker, B. (2004a) Saudi call for jihad. *Guardian*, 8 November.
Whitaker, B. (2004b) Egyptian doctor who laid foundations of global Islamist offensive. *Guardian*, 20 March.

A Globalist Ideology of Post-Marxism? Hardt and Negri's *Empire*

GARY K. BROWNING

Ideology remains a central feature of the contemporary world. Political ideologies map the terrain of the political, locate politics in a wider web of meaning and impart normative direction to conduct by highlighting what is of significance and what should be done. The ubiquity of ideology in the contemporary world is occluded by a number of developments. Aspects of the contemporary world are flagged as being novel. This novelty is taken to signal an allegedly post-ideological condition. Central to the sense of the world's novelty is the notion of globalization. Adherents of the doctrine of globalization assume many standpoints but converge upon the assumption that old rules no longer apply and that preceding ideological commitments are outmoded. Politicians declaim about globalization and the novelty of the current situation in justifying wars, in reaffirming economic orthodoxies and in proclaiming that traditional socialist ideological commitments must be sacrificed due to the pragmatic requirements of economic globalization. Likewise the theory of globalization is advertised as being distinct from preceding theories, and yet its complexity, its incorporation of a range of normative standpoints and its links with preceding theories are often unacknowledged.

In this essay I argue that theories of globalization do not betoken an entirely novel post-ideological age, but that they represent complex assortments of explanation of the world, which contain implicit and explicit ideological commitments. Hardt and Negri's reading of globalization as yielding the hegemony of empire and as harbouring the prospect of global revolution is a contemporary statement of ideological radicalism, which rehearses more aspects of classic Marxist ideology than is suggested by *Empire*'s (2000) claims to theoretical novelty. Hardt and Negri are post-Marxist theorists of globalization, whose standpoint is radical in its unremitting hostility to the current dispositions of power. Just as Marx and Engels provided an ideological service in framing a highly theoretical set of doctrines for a burgeoning labour movement in the nineteenth century, so Hardt and Negri provide dense theoretical support for a burgeoning anti-capitalist movement of the present. This movement's disinclination to establish prioritised goals and hierarchical organisation is matched at an abstract level by Hardt and Negri's theoretical eschewal of specific plans and programmes on the part of the revolutionary multitude, which they envisage as infinitely plural in its composition.(For a concise account of the anti-capitalist movement's rejection of discipline and hierarchy associated with traditional Marxism see Tormey 2004: 172) Hardt and Negri's association with a distinct and contemporary ideological movement, though, does not exclude a close affinity between their standpoint and that of Marx. Held's recent *Global Covenant-The Social Democratic Alternative to the Washington Consensus* is an express continuation of social democratic ideology in new circumstances. He maintains 'a certain set of values-social democratic values-remains indispensable to a sound and feasible agenda for global change (Held 2004: xv). Likewise Hardt and Negri's break with past ideology is not clean. They are post-Marxist in that they conceive of the world in terms of an agenda and circumstances that postdate Marx, but their summative reading of history and their dialectical inter-linking of empire and multitude in framing a prospective revolution highlights a continuing affiliation to a Marxist style of theorising. In arguing this case I will draw upon Hardt and Negri's recent *Multitude-War and Democracy in the Age of Empire* (2004), where they expressly consider the possibility that their standpoint does not break with the dialectical one of their predecessors.

Explanations of globalization tend to be developed alongside the promotion of insufficiently acknowledged associated normative ideals such as emancipation from traditional or fixed values, reflexivity and cosmopolitanism (See Giddens 2002) There is nothing wrong in combining ideological commitments with explanatory analysis, but a recognition of the differing aspects of globalization and its differing dimensions that are invoked by theorists, politicians and citizens appraising the world from distinct vantage points, would militate against its reification. Increasingly, the voluminous literature on globalization shows conceptual refinement due to its incorporation of a range of criticisms and responses to criticisms, and an emerging express recognition of divergent ideological possibilities. (see Held 2004). One set of criticisms focuses on the alleged uniqueness of contemporary developments. In the light of evidence for long-standing trans-national activities, theorists of globalization now tend to be circumspect in the way they present claims for the novelty of the contemporary world. Held et al., in their discriminating conceptual and empirical study, *Global Transformations*, recognize that globalization has a history as well as a contemporary expression. Nonetheless, they maintain the novelty of the contemporary situation, by highlighting the intensity of its current phase (Held et al. 1999). They invoke empirical developments such as growth in international trade, in trans-national businesses, in regional and global political mechanisms, in trans-national communicative networks, and in international cultural discourses (Held et al. 1999). Empirical data, however, do not unambiguously indicate progressive globalization. Hirst and Thompson, in *Globalization in Question* (1996) interpret data on international trade and investment to suggest increasing regionalization rather than internationalization.

In *Global Transformations*, Held et al. also acknowledge the complexity of global developments and the differing styles and tempos of changes that occur in distinct spheres of activity. Notwithstanding their incorporation of plurality into their account, they persist in seeing this diversity as representing a set of processes that are encompassed by a single notion of globalization (Held et al. 1999). This identification of an essential underlying process of globalization underpins a reading of globalization in the contemporary era as constituting a distinctly novel form of world history. Theorists of globalization run together interpretive conceptual readings of globalization with strong causal claims and normative commitments on its behalf that tend to essentialise the notion of globalization and magnify its supposed novelty. In so doing they advertise a break with preceding theories and theorists, while holding theoretical and normative ambitions that harmonise with the classic grand narratives of modernity. Standardly, globalization is a theory that links political economy to a wider web of social relations so as to provide a comprehensive explanation of the present via wide-ranging synchronic and diachronic analyses. Its key concept, globalization is highly suggestive and captures undoubted features of the present and yet it is ambiguous and elusive. The ambition of the claims that are made by globalization theorists rehearses that of the 'global' theorising of Hegel and Marx. This shared ambition is supported by a common tendency to reduce complex phenomena to an underlying economic or systemic cause, to gloss over differences within and qualifications to an overarching theory of historical development, to undertheorise the relationship between normative and explanatory aspects of their theories and to underplay the contestability of their claims.

Affinities between contemporary globalization theory and the classic grand narratives of Hegel and Marx inform these theories, and disturb the claim of globalization theorists to present a significantly new way of conceiving of the world. In particular, this similarity between contemporary globalization theory and Hegel and Marx is evident in the continuity between Hegel and Marx's theories of the world-historical significance of the modern state and the proletariat and Hardt and Negri's identification of empire and multitude as culminating points of the historical process. Hegel begins his *Lectures on the Philosophy of History* by remarking on its global content: 'The subject of this course of Lectures is the Philosophical History of the World. And by this must be understood, not a collection of general observations respecting it, suggested by the study of its records, and proposed to be illustrated by its facts, but Universal History itself' (Hegel 1956: 12) Hegel, in establishing a comprehensive philosophical system, develops a global history that recognises the universality of the present conjuncture. The modern European world for Hegel is paradigmatic for mankind. Hegel identifies his reading of modernity to be of normative global significance; the modern state constitutes the end of the historical process. Likewise, Marx interprets capitalism as globalizing human potential. Mankind, for Marx, is social. Human beings are constituted by their social relations and capital capitalizes on this sociality by extending networks of relations across the globe as well as intensifying their operation in all aspects of the social world. The completion of this process of socialization is to be achieved by the projected world revolution of the proletariat.

The ways in which globalization may be understood as operating as a conceptual field providing an interpretive unifying framework for sets of processes and affiliated perspectives mirrors the possibilities and problems that are exhibited in the interpretive schemes of Marx and Hegel. Contemporary theorists of globalization tend to distance themselves from the preceding theories of Hegel and Marx. This rejection of intellectual forbears is not a token of increasing intellectual sophistication. While Hegel and Marx deploy sophisticated if contestable interpretive frameworks, theorists of globalization tend to undertheorize the relations between levels of analysis that are operative in their schemes. Hardt and Negri are at one with the general run of globalization theorists in highlighting the globality of the contemporary world, and in separating their theorising from the preceding modernist perspectives of Hegel and Marx.

Hardt and Negri's *Empire* is a post-Marxist globalist ideology. The work emphasises its postdating of Marxism. It underplays its shared ideological features with Marxism. Like other adherents to the thesis of globalization, Hardt and Negri exaggerate their originality and thereby underplay significant aspects of their work. In fact, like Hegel and Marx they entertain a large-scale reading of history linking past, present and future, and they see the world in teleological terms redolent of Hegel and Marx. Their claim to encompass a distinct postmodern and immanent radicalism masks their debts to dialectical and ideological predecessors. Their egalitarian emancipatory and indeterminate depiction of the multitude mirrors Marx's reading of the proletariat. The emancipatory potential of the multitude, like that of the proletariat, is shaped by preceding diachronic conditions that have opened up the global possibilities of freedom, while Hardt and Negri maintain, like Marx, that the logic of emancipation precludes determination of the course of revolutionary action. Hardt and Negri's succeeding book to *Empire*, *Multitude* (2004), acknowledges more expansively a debt to Marx's concepts and methods. Hardt and Negri admit to a 'haunting suspicion that he was already there before us' (Hardt & Negri 2004: 141) Nonetheless, they insist upon their distinctive postmodern standpoint, which breaks decisively with the dialectical heritage of Marxism and which identifies significant developments that have altered capitalist society since Marx's death.

Empire

Empire by Hardt and Negri is a significant book, and its significance lies in its promise of renewing radical and revolutionary ideology. Walker observes that 'it [*Empire*] responds to a widespread feeling that contemporary trends demand new theorisations and conceptual vocabularies, as well as far greater imagination about how we might respond to the practical challenges of our time'(Walker 2002: 338). Certainly, *Empire* assumes and subverts the language of globalization. Nonetheless, its postmodern reworking of features of the contemporary social and political landscape does not succeed in breaking from modernist ways of thinking. It advertises a purely immanent mode of reading the present, which dispenses with dialectic and teleology. Its critical globalism, however, presupposes the intertwining of its key concepts of empire and multitude, and the linking of these notions with a wider web of concepts that rehearses the dialectical paradigms of Hegel and Marx. Indeed, to recognise *Empire*'s connections with past theorising is salutary, because it alerts readers to the problems that bedevil a globalist radical ideology.

Empire is an elaborated critical engagement with the notion of globalization. Much of what it says rehearses standard features of globalization theory. These include its incorporation and eclipse of nation-state sovereignty in a wider global context, its highlighting of the prevalent decentred, de-territorializing apparatuses of rule and of the intensive socialization and mediatization of production. What distinguishes *Empire*'s theory of globalization, however, is its reversal of the ideological frameworks that standardly underpin readings of globalization. Whereas globalization standardly either is celebrated or is taken to require political reforms, Hardt and Negri reject the norms and political practices that underpin the contemporary dispositions of power. They articulate an alternative radical ideology of globalism. Walker observes *Empire*'s consonance with normative international relations theory of a preceding era: 'Ignore the term empire and large sections of the text could have been written by various "normative" theorists of the 1970s' (Walker 2002: 341). Hardt and Negri maintain the irreversibility of globalization and acknowledge its wholesale socialization of the production of life, but they project and endorse the prospective supersession of prevailing imperial power. Just as Held maintains a globalist ideology of social democracy in anticipating and supporting the development of cosmopolitan forms of democracy and social democracy, so Hardt and Negri envisage the multitude overturning imperial rule by enacting global revolution.

Empire's distinctive, ideological reading of global development, however, in which the concepts of empire and multitude are essentialised, is ultimately unconvincing. The multitude for Hardt and Negri fuses singularity with commonality due to the conditions of empire in which production is socialised on a universal, global basis. This universality is presumed to render the singularities of the revolutionary struggle immediately universal. As Negri maintains in *Alma Venus, Multitudo*, a work that is a close companion to *Empire*, 'the postmodern multitude is an ensemble of singularities whose life-tool is the brain and whose productive force consists in co-operation. In other words, if the singularities that constitute the multitude are plural, the manner in which they enter into relations is co-operative' (Negri 2000, in Negri 2003: 233–234). In *Negri on Negri*, Negri maintains that the multitude is a 'multiplicity of subjects' (Negri 2004: 111). At the same time he attributes ontological power to the multitude and declares, 'This means that the multitude embodies a mechanism that seeks to represent desire and to transform the world.'(Negri 2004, 112) Hence while the multitude is taken to exist as a plurality of independent people it is at the same time reified as an essential entity, which acts as a unified, yet mythical subject.

By the concept of empire, Hardt and Negri signpost a fundamentally new topography of power, an innovative configuration of sovereignty-a political force that is decentred and operates flexible apparatuses of rule. Empire assumes and exercises rule over hybrid identities, just as global capital maintains a smooth system of economic and cultural exchanges that incorporates industrialized, communicative, co-operative and affective labour. As Mandarini notes, 'this total subsumption (of all forms of production to capitalist relatons) expresses the material conditions grounding the claim that in Empire there is no longer an outside'(Mandarini 2003: 4). These claims about the unity and novelty of empire are paradoxical in that they are undertheorised and yet shielded from empirical discrimination by imperial rhetoric. Hardt and Negri's invocation of empirical phenomena to support their arguments in *Empire* and affiliated writings is suggestive rather than being evidentially convincing. Barkawi and Laffey comment, 'Hardt and Negri's description of an emerging political and social formation is notably threadbare' (Barkawi & Laffey 2002: 111).

Empire is the conceptual counterpart of multitude. It is endlessly plural but at the same time a unified subject. The notion of empire, like that of multitude is designed to express a pure plurality, which thereby follows Deleuze and Guattari in renouncing a dialectical reading of an entity, which combines unity and multiplicity in a structured and developmental way (Deleuze & Guattari 1988: 32). The unity amidst diversity that is characteristic of empire and its antagonist, the multitude, admits of no clear mode of discrimination, just as the positive value accorded to the multitude and the negative value associated with empire informs *Empire*'s reading of history and politics without itself receiving critical notice.

Hardt and Negri's express commitment to avoid dialectics and modernist precursors cannot disguise *Empire*'s conceptual essentialism, its contestable causal claims, its unacknowledged teleology and its unreflected normative standpoint. *Empire* is holistic in its explanatory reach but partial in its relaxed assertion of its own assumptions and terms. If *Empire*'s claims are problematic, its critique is a valuable exercise. Its developmental dichotomous conceptual reading of the present is of a piece with Marxism and affiliated ideologies. Its radical opposition to the contemporary orchestration of global power represents a distinctive normative standpoint and thereby highlights the ideological dimension of all readings of globalization. Criticism of *Empire* supersedes its specific critique of Hardt and Negri's revamping of radical ideology. *Empire*'s adherence to a combination of contestable causal, conceptual and normative terms signals the possibilities and problems associated with the frameworks of analysis that are rehearsed in more conventional ideological readings of globalization.

Post-Marxist Immanence or Dialectical Redevelopment?

Hardt and Negri highlight the originality of their perspective. They do so by contrasting the immanence of their critique to what they take to be the external teleological dialectic of Hegel and Marx. If Hegel and Marx are construed as operating by means of independently formulated logical or scientific doctrines, then Hardt and Negri aim to adhere to the immanent conditions of historical development. But Hardt and Negri's repudiation of Hegel and Marx and their claims to originality can be criticised on at least two counts. On the one hand, this repudiation plays down the immanence of Hegel and Marx's dialectical perspectives and, on the other hand, the immanence of their own advertised postmodern perspective depends crucially on a reading of history and the present in terms of a highly generalised dialectical scheme of thought. In *Multitude*, their successor to *Empire*, Hardt and Negri consider possible criticisms of their methodological standpoint. In doing so, they expressly consider the charge that they are continuing the dialectical method of Marx and Hegel. In refuting this charge, they argue unconvincingly that their explanation of terms does not assume their mutual implication. They disavow the reciprocity of the One and the Many, and that they profess a reading of identity and difference in non-dichotomous terms (Hardt & Negri 2004: 225) Their claim to be post-dialectical thinkers is compromised in that they do assume a reciprocity, for instance, between empire and multitude and Hegel and Marx are theorists sensitive to the problematic character of one-dimensional readings of conceptual relationships. Hegel in his *Logic* expressly takes the one and the many to be distinct as well as intertwined. He is careful to define identity in terms of the *unity* between identity and difference (Hegel 1976).

Hardt and Negri's failure to justify the distinctiveness of their conceptual standpoint is serious because their argument for imperial sovereignty depends not so much on the specification of new empirical political phenomena but by elaborated conceptual designation. Empire, for Hardt and Negri, is a paradigm of political power that is both systemic and hierarchical; a construction of norms and legitimacy that dominates world space (Hardt & Negri 2000: 13). The values to which it is directed and to which everything is attuned, are the promotion of order and the cessation of conflict (Hardt & Negri 2000: 38). Imperial sovereignty is decentred and operates via a deterritorialized apparatus of rule. The character of empire turns on its conceptual reflection of capital, just as, for Marx, changing state forms reflect the operational requirements of economic interests. The absolute hegemony, which empire exercises over subordinate identities, mirrors and depends upon global capital. Global capital, in turn, orders economic and cultural exchanges that incorporate industrial, communicative, co-operative and affective labour. Hardt and Negri's notion of the illimitable force of empire accords with their reading of the unremitting power of global capital. They assert, 'the increasingly intense relationship of mutual implication of all social forces that capitalism has pursued throughout its development has now been fully realized' (Hardt & Negri 2000: 25). For Hardt and Negri contemporary global capital directs universal biopower rather than controlling a delineated sphere of production.

In preceding works, Negri documented the redundancy of traditional Marxist analysis. In *Marx Beyond Marx-Lessons On The Grundrisse*, he critiqued what he took to be Marx's narrow conception of labour. He comments, 'In fact, the Marxist definition of productive labour is a reductive definition, which is linked to the socialist axiology of manual labour' (Negri 1991: 183). Negri disavows a Marxist critique, which purports to isolate value from the conditions of capitalist production. He is opposed to a standpoint, which counterposes use value to exchange value, because it assumes that the use value of labour power operates outside of the sphere of the capitalist determination of exchange value. Negri denies the validity of a non-immanent reading of contradiction. He maintains that contemporary capital subsumes all production under its network of relations. In *The Constitution of Time* Negri argues,

> Here use-value cannot appear except under the guise of exchange-value. There is no longer an external vantage point upon which use-value can depend. The overcoming of capitalism occurs on the basis of needs constructed by capitalism. But in that case, time-as-measure of value is identical to the value of labour, to time of labour as substance. (Negri 1997, in Negri 2003: 25-26).

For Negri and Hardt contemporary empire and contemporary capitalism do not allow for critical perspectives that are outside of or transcend the actual operations of global capital and imperial sovereignty.

For Hardt and Negri, capital and empire are mutually reinforcing agencies that preclude an external critical perspective. They deny a supposed critical reading of the present, which orders history and projects the future according to the dynamic of an underlying but illusory force that is insulated from the dynamics of the hierarchical system of prevailing power. They perceive the conditions of the present as precluding the ascription of an essential agency of radical change that is resistant to and independent of prevailing hegemonic forces. Negri, in *Kairos, Alma Venus, Multitudo*, underlines the pitfalls of formulating a critique, which assumes a logic that is external to the contemporary operations of power. He remarks, 'The critiques of constitutive power that play on the "instituting–instituted" opposition, whether they are of dialectical or vitalistic inspiration are false. For in postmodernity, constituent power knows nothing of that opposition, in as much as it exists in accordance with the direction that urges the common to constitute itself against the void, on the edge of time' (Negri 2000, in Negri 2003: 234). Hardt and Negri gloss resistance to global capital and imperial power as part and parcel of the process of developing and maintaining empire. They observe, 'The processes of globalization would not exist or would come to a halt if they were not continually both frustrated and driven by these explosions of the multitude that touch immediately on the highest levels of imperial power' (Hardt & Negri 2000: 59).

Hardt and Negri's concept of empire emerges out of reflection upon its conceptual, dialectical consonance with the ubiquitous, global force of capital. The advertised globality of empire renders the notion impervious to clear-cut empirical specification or criticism. Apparently recalcitrant phenomena, such as irruptions of local or regional forms of power, or forces antagonistic to generalised hegemony are redefined so that they are seen as being functionally requisite to the maintenance of empire. Nonetheless, Hardt and Negri gesture at empirical features of the contemporary world that are presumed to underscore the rhetoric of imperial sovereignty. They detect evidence for empire in an increasing reliance on global institutions such as the United Nations and a novel resort to the rhetoric of global peacekeeping and policing to justify military action (Hardt & Negri 2000: 240–260). Their resort to empirical data, though, is problematic. While the post-Cold War situation, like all historical contexts is unique, its break with preceding dualities is insufficient in itself to denote the advent of an imperial power that breaks definitively with preceding modulations of sovereignty. The recent sidelining of the United Nations by the United States and its faithful ally the United Kingdom in the war against Iraq signals that the United States of America remains an autonomous global actor. Hardt and Negri, though, by stretching their conceptual reading of empire to include unilateral operations by the United States, allow for the privileged position in empire of the United States (Hardt & Negri 2000: 37). In *Multitude* they urge that the contemporary state of war exemplifies the simultaneous prosecution of US national interests and the coordination of global, avowedly humanitarian concerns such as the promotion of human rights. In arguing for this simultaneous exercise of supra-national imperial power and of national American force, they urge, 'we should not get caught up here in the tired debates about globalization and nation-states as if the two were necessarily incompatible' (Hardt & Negri 2004: 60). To urge the complexity of contemporary sovereignty is insightful, but the devil is in the detail and a convincing exploration of this complexity would need to make pertinent distinctions about how power is being exercised in specific situations and why and how it might make sense to point to national or multi-national aspects of the exercise of power.

The notion of empire relies fundamentally upon its indeterminate and yet essentialist conceptual specification. Its meaning emerges out of its dichotomous relationship with the multitude and its symbiosis with capital. Just as Hegel and Marx employ highly abstract concepts such as value, capital, the notion and the idea to order and assimilate a range of related concepts, so empire orders and assimilates a diversity of phenomena without changing its essential form. Hardt and Negri invoke the notion of the ever-expanding American frontier to allude to the expansiveness of empire (Hardt & Negri 2000: 160–182). This metaphor of a moveable frontier captures the elasticity of their sense of empire. It trades upon, without authenticating, the tangible and mythic quality of the world encountered and constituted by American pioneers. Their analysis of the conditions of contemporary power is insightful, and suggestive without being precise. They conclude that the overall determination of the exercise of global power will have to be supra-nationalistic, given that the nature of modern warfare demands its prosecution on a networked, non-hierarchical basis to counteract the networked, global character of contemporary resistance to empire (Hardt & Negri 2004: 62). But they neither specify empirically the character of the networked opposition to empire, nor do they delineate the forms of networked international cooperation that the United States must practise in warfare. The United States practises a variety of forms of international cooperation as well as exercising a relative independence and the significance of these divergent practices is not assessed.

Hardt and Negri conceptualise the operations of empire as being linked to the unifying force of global capital. They envisage the disunities of space and time as being closed by the unifying economic operations of production and consumption, in which mediation itself becomes an aspect of a continuous economic process, the operation of universal biopower. Hardt and Negri point to the developmental and mediating role that is played by trans-national corporations and communications networks. Their account of capital and progressive global unification is closely modelled on Marx's account of the self-expansion and infinite reproductive capacity of capital (see Browning 1998; Arthur 1998). In urging the originality of their reading of empire, however, Hardt and Negri emphasise their postdating of Marx. Crucial to their designation of *Empire* as a postmodern and post-Marxist text is its highlighting of the comprehensive socialization of production in the universality of biopower in the contemporary world. They urge that a sphere of material production can no longer be separated from an immaterial social and cultural world. Mediation constantly absorbs all processes in a unifying global economy in which there is an 'informational colonization of being' (Hardt & Negri 2000: 34).

Hardt and Negri advertise the novelty of empire and their own theorising by contrasting the immateriality of their conception of production from Marx's materialism. For Hardt and Negri, the post-Marxist notion of immaterial production has profound consequences. In *Multitude* they observe that along with the emergence of immaterial labour there is a 'blurring of time divisions that we see in post-Fordist production' (Hardt & Negri 2004: 146). If production is no longer trammelled by the focus upon producing material things, then the activity of production itself is not to be encapsulated by specific designated periods of production time. Ideas, for instance, are generated at odd times, during and outside working hours. Likewise contemporary products may not be independently specifiable commodities that serve the needs of independently specifiable social consumers. Rather, they might contribute directly to the sociality of life by constituting the means and expression of communication and affective life. The joy of texting and the analytical satisfaction offered by a powerful search engine are not separable from the emotive and communicative life of the twenty-first century.

Hardt and Negri's postdating of Marxism and the specification of the originality of their own ideological radicalism are problematic. Marx's materialism and his productivism are controversial. Sympathetic and critical commentators have taken Marx to reduce the social to an underlying productive materialism (see Cohen 1978; Plamenatz 1954). Reductive readings of Marx, however, are problematic. Marx's identification of labour power as the key force production is accompanied by his recognition that the sphere of production is not to be separated conceptually from the social relations in which it operates (see Carver 1998: ch. 3; Marx 1974; Marx & Engels 1976). More generally, Hardt and Negri's conceptual map of a global economy of empire draws upon a Marxist framework of explanation, whereby the immanent logic of capitalist development, the constant exploitation of materials and labour to supply the commodities that are exchanged for money and deployed as capital, composes an endless expanding circle of transactions. The circuits of capital constitute an endless supersession of barriers to the operation of expanding circuits, in which its processes of mediation supersede material and cultural obstacles that impede an inherently globalizing process. This process consumes merely local manifestations of capital and its adversarial forms of discontent. Notwithstanding this affinity between *Empire* and classical Marxism, Hardt and Negri advertise a radical break with the preceding dialectical theories of Hegel and Marx.

A dialectical perspective that connects phenomena by way of immanent argumentative development is stigmatised by Hardt and Negri as disguising historical development as a form of teleology that presumes the external end of freedom from the outset of its analysis. They urge,

> We are not repeating the schema of an ideal teleology that justifies any passage in the name of a promised end. On the contrary, our reasoning here is based on two methodological approaches that are intended to be nondialectical and absolutely immanent: the first is *critical and deconstructive,* aiming to subvert dominant languages, revealing an alternative ontological basis that resides in the multitude; the second is *constructive and ethico-political,* seeking to lead the processes of the production of subjectivity. (Hardt & Negri 2000: 47)

The argumentative drift of Hardt and Negri is to depict empire as *sui generis* by advertising its conceptual demarcation from previous formulations of hegemony. They emphasise their distinctness from dialectical predecessors by asserting the novelty of their approach to history. They insist, 'This approach breaks methodologically with every philosophy of history insofar as it refuses any deterministic conception of historical development and any rational celebration of the result. Philosophy is not the Owl of Minerva-subjective proposition, desire and praxis that are applied to the event' (Hardt & Negri 2000: 49).

Hardt and Negri's claim over the distinctness of their standpoint is itself susceptible to dialectical critique. On the one hand, their repudiation of dialectics sits uneasily with their equal insistence on framing an immanent critique of empire. They repudiate merely external protest. 'We should be done once and for all with the search for an outside, a standpoint that imagines purity for our politics. It is better both theoretically and practically to enter the terrain of Empire' (Hardt & Negri 2000: 44). Their designation of empire, however, includes an overlapping conceptual recognition of the development of the prospective liberation of the multitude. The upshot is that by the generality of their view of history, they are committed to the very style of a teleological, dialectical reading of history, which they repudiate rhetorically. *Empire*'s teleology, which links concepts identifying past, present and future, is evidenced in the determination of Hardt and Negri to style their approach as incorporating postmodernism's supersession of modernity.

Hardt and Negri's reading of empire is informed by a highly generalised and normative interpretation of the logic of historical development. The postmodern supersedes the modern and the immateriality of biopower under conditions of new informational and communicative technologies, supersedes directly productive practices and a materialist view of labour. Likewise they style imperial sovereignty to be a form outstripping its modern subject, the nation state. The latter, in circumscribing the operation of hegemony, is as postdated as Old Europe. They observe, 'If modernity is European, postmodernity is American' (Hardt & Negri 2000: xiii). They show a sensitivity to the criticism that they are reworking rather than repudiating a dialectical style of theorising in their discussion of dialectic in *Multitude*. Here they recognise how their style of immanent critique of empire might be criticised as being an unacknowledged reworking of dialectical thinking. They urge that such a critique is misplaced because they do not merely work with the reciprocity of concepts that define the past and present, but allow for the emergence of what is distinct and different (Hardt & Negri 2004: 225)

Hardt and Negri's protestations against ascribing to them a dialectical teleological reading of history assume that Hegel and Marx did not allow for the emergence of new forms in the historical process. Hegel and Marx recognised that new social forms emerge but they identified their connections with past phenomena and with one another, just as Hardt and Negri's approach to history is dialectical in that the meaning and unfolding of new events and concepts are revealed by their inter-relations and by their relations with preceding developments. To assume that the modern is superseded neatly by the postmodern lends itself to a reading of history, in which progress is unilear and politics becomes the art of operating strategically in relation to an already identified course of events. The later Lyotard's reservations over his use of the term postmodernity reflected his own belated recognition of the susceptibility of his own discourse to the grand theorising that he sought to repudiate. (Lyotard 1992). Hardt and Negri's reliance on a teleological reading of history is evidenced by the logical and practical dependence of empire and its development upon the emancipatory potential of the multitude. The notion of the multitude, for Hardt and Negri, performs many roles. The multitude is the object of historical imperial development, and the deterritorialising mass of creative sociality responsible for, and subject to, the power of empire. Its post-national, post-industrial character distinguishes rebellion against empire from a Marxist, modernist proletarian revolution. At the same time, the emancipatory guise of the multitude provides a normative, ideological framework, which renders *Empire* more than a merely explanatory guide to the constitution of imperial power. The goal of world-wide emancipation frames an ideological interpretive scheme whereby the concepts of empire, the multitude, capital, and the postmodern form inter-secting elements of a grand narrative of historical development. Its dialectical, teleological style mirrors as much as postdates Marxism in seeing the limitations of past and present as being revealed and redeemed in a complete prospective emancipation from the fetters imposed upon social enactment in the conditions of time and space.

Hardt and Negri at times recognise how their claims to radical originality are partially subverted by their own recognition that the alternatives to empire inscribed in the global system render their analysis a more profound immanentist scheme than that achieved by Marx and Machiavelli (Hardt & Negri 2000: 65). They even conceive of their work as, perforce, following a teleological logic, in observing, 'a teleology of sorts is constructed only after the fact, post festum' (Hardt & Negri 2000: 44). This latter admission of their adoption of a teleological perspective, which is distinguished by its *post-festum* character, however, raises questions about Hardt and Negri's reading of the teleology of Hegel and Marx. For Hegel, the essence of history and the inspiration generating its study within the political community is the free activity of individuals that supersedes the merely naturalistic ties of family and tribe that develops within and promotes political cultures, which in turn recognise and celebrate it in narrative form. Given that freedom is the presupposition of history, a philosophical teleological reading of history, for Hegel, does not override the freedom of historical actors. Philosophical history is, perforce, a retrospective interpretation of how freedom has been recognised and developed in history, rather than a causal theory that can predict the future (Hegel 1956). Likewise, Marx and Engels in *The German Ideology* are at pains to distance themselves from contemporary Young Hegelians, such as Stirner, who falsify history by construing its development in *a priori* ideological terms. They make clear that their materialistic reading of history is a retrospective, *post festum* categorisation of historical development that does not foreclose on the openness of historical events (Marx & Engels 1976). *Empire*'s claim to be a novel critique of society depends crucially upon the supposed originality of its conceptual scheme. Its acknowledged *post-festum* teleological reading of history highlights its conceptual affinity with Hegel and Marx rather than marking a decisive postmodern break from dialectical predecessors.

Conclusion

Empire imagines a postmodern world, superseding previous historical forms. It is a thoroughly socialised world, which harbours global patterns of economic exploitation and imperial sovereignty. It captures aspects of the contemporary situation that are of significance, notably the complexity of contemporary sovereignty in a global world, in which the nation state is one actor amongst many. Its novelty as a post-Marxist ideology is canvassed on the basis of its mooted nondialectical, immaterial and supra-statist character. In an interview conducted for *Theory and Event* in 2000, Hardt maintains that he and Negri prefer to refer to their orientation as communist rather than Marxist because the latter is more constrictive and would derogate from the substantive criticisms that they have of Marx (see Hardt 2000).

The elasticity of the concept of empire and the conceptual resonances of the notion of the multitude, however, mirror rather than supersede classic Marxist notions of class and proletarian universality. The elasticity of the concept of empire is exhibited in its accommodation of myriad forms of resistance to and mute acquiescence in its hegemony. Empire accommodates a plurality of empirical practices.

Empire's conceptual designation of a contemporary conceptual field dominated by empire is not implausible, but the patterns whereby more specific entities such as the state and local politics are incorporated within the orbit of more general concepts revisits the conceptual world of Marx's *Grundrisse* and Hegel's *Logic* and requires the detailed elaboration of the logic of dialectical conceptual patterns that is displayed in those seminal texts. Marx's methodological credo in the *Grundrisse* interestingly specifies a method and a perception of the world, which are decidedly immaterial, and which at the same time acknowledge dialectical inter-relations between concepts. Marx conceives of the world as thoroughly social, shaped by social relations that can only be captured by concepts (Marx 1974). Hardt and Negri's insistence on the post-Marxist status of their ideological radicalism turns in part upon their postmodern immaterialism, but there is a decided continuity between their notion of postmodern immateriality and Marx's reading of the social, relational character of production. Moreover, Hardt and Negri's identification of the universality of contemporary biopower is predicated upon a general retrospective reading of historical development, which reflects the classical grand narratives of Hegel and Marx. Their identification of the universality of biopower as progressive presupposes a dialectical reading of historical concepts, whereby they are appraised normatively on a common gradational scale.

Empire is the heart of a heartless world, the sigh of oppressed biopower, which serves as a singular yet revealing mirror for the ideological dimensions of globalization theory as well as for the persistence of standard Marxist themes within speculation that advertises its post-Marxist break from its outmoded dialectical provenance. Proponents of a theory of globalization standardly urge that the contemporary world is novel due to the intensity of its global inter-connectedness, even if they differ over their ideological construals of this state of affairs. Theorists of globalization interweave explanatory accounts of globalization with differing normative perspectives on the values and forces that are seen as engendering or modifying the processes of globalization. Ohmae endorses what he takes to be the simplifying logic of global capital, while Held, McGrew and Giddens value the cosmopolitan possibilities for the renewal of the tenets of social democracy that arise out of the circumstances of globalization (see Giddens 2002; Ohmae 1989 ; Held 1995, 2004; Held et al. 1999). In contrast, Hardt and Negri endorse the revolutionary supersession of prevailing norms. They embrace the prospect of revolution to be enacted in the multitude's overturning of empire, which is to claim the entirety of the globe for the expression and development of the universality of biopower. As Passavant has observed, the impact of Hardt and Negri's *Empire* testifies to its success in framing a globalist ideology that is in tune with events such as the global impact of 9/11 and demonstrations against the war in Iraq, and with a recognition of the differential identities of diverse movements in the contemporary world (Passavant & Dean 2004).

The success of Hardt and Negri as ideologists resides in their development of a densely theoretical treatise to justify global revolution and anti-capitalism, which harmonises with the contemporary diversity of oppositional movements to capital and current configurations of power. While it purports to order and explain a range of apparently contrary empirical phenomena, though, it is actually entirely vague on how, for instance, the multitude unifies diverse movements and action. As Laclau observes, 'the unity of the multitude results from the spontaneous aggregation of a plurality of actions that do not need to be articulated between themselves' (Laclau 2004: 26). Hardt and Negri's essentialised notion of the multitude also abstracts from the empirical realities of the condition of the poor and oppressed in different parts of the world. As Bull notes, 'It is difficult to see how this analysis [*Empire*'s] comprehends the reality of powerlessness' (Bull 2003: 89).

Hardt and Negri's globalist ideology of post-Marxism purports to break with the dialectical teleological style of Hegel and Marx but their deployment of inter-related normatively charged concepts that presume a teleological reading of history. Collingwood in his economical and perceptive defence of dialectical philosophical argument in *An Essay on Philosophical Method* (1933) understood a philosophical appraisal of concepts to consist in their systematic rethinking as an ascending scale of overlapping forms, whereby the constituent concepts are retained but superseded progressively by more inclusive and intensive ones. Hence, for Collingwood, ethical concepts are to be seen as internally related to one another, so that the discharge of duty in a specific deliberated act supersedes regularian and utilitarian standpoints. Likewise, Hardt and Negri's deployment of the concepts of nation-state and empire, material production and immaterial biopower and empire and multitude represents an interweaving of normatively charged concepts that marks their enterprise as dialectical. It is neither innovatory and non-dialectical nor radically post-Marxist. Hardt and Negri's *Empire* is an ideologically charged theory of globalization, which like related but distinct large-scale theories of globalization, is linked to the classic grand narratives of modernity and should be interpreted in the light of the questions and problems that are posed by those grand schemes of thought.

References

Arthur, C.J. (1998) The infinity of capital. *Studies in Marxism*, 5, pp. 17–37.
Barkawi, T. & Laffey, M. (2002) Retrieving the imperial: *Empire* and international relations, *Millenium*, 31(1), pp. 109–127.
Browning, G.K. (1998) Infinity in Hegel and Marx, *Studies in Marxism*, 5, pp. 1–17.

Bull, M. (2003) You can't build a New Society with a Stanley knife', in: G. Balakrishnan, *Debating Empire* (London and New York: Verso, 2003), pp. 83–96.

Carver, T. (1998) *The Postmodern Marx* (Manchester: Manchester University Press).

Cohen, G.A. (1978) *Karl Marx's Theory of History: A Defence* (Oxford: Oxford University Press).

Collingwood, R.G. (1933) *An Essay on Philosophical Method* (Oxford: Oxford University Press).

Deleuze, G. & Guattari, F. (1988) *A Thousand Plateaus* (London: Athlone Press).

Giddens, A. (2002) *Runaway World* (London: Profile Books).

Hardt, M. (2000) Interview with Thomas Dumm, 'Sovereignty, Multitudes, Absolute Democracy'. *Theory and Event*, 4(3).

Hardt, M. & Negri, A. (2000) *Empire* (Cambridge, MA: Harvard University Press).

Hardt, M. & Negri, A. (2004) *Multitude – War and Democracy in the Age of Empire* (New York: Penguin).

Hegel, G.W.F. (1956) *The Philosophy of History* (London: Dover Books).

Hegel, G.W.F. (1976) *Hegel's Science of Logic* (London: George, Allen and Unwin).

Held, D. (1995) *Democracy and the Global Order: From the Modern State to Cosmopolitan Governance* (Palo Alto, CA: Stanford University Press).

Held, D. (2004) *Global Covenant-The Social Democratic Alternative to the Washington Consensus* (Polity: Cambridge).

Held, D., McGrew, A., Goldblatt, D. & Perraton, J. (1999) *Global Transformations* (Cambridge: Polity Press).

Hirst, P. & Thompson, G. (1996) *Globalization in Question* (Cambridge: Polity Press).

Laclau, E (2004) Can immanence explain social struggles?, in: P.A. Passavant & J. Dean (Eds) *Empire's New Clothes – Reading Hardt and Negri* (London and New York: Routledge).

Lyotard, J.-F. (1992) *The Postmodern Explained to Children: Correspondence 1982–1985* (London: Turnaround).

Mandarini, M. (2003) Translator's introduction, in: A. Negri, *Time for Revolution* (New York and London: Continuum).

Marx, K. (1974) *Grundrisse* (Harmondsworth: Penguin).

Marx, K. & Engels, F. (1976) *The German Ideology* (Moscow: Progress Publishers).

Negri, A. (1991) *Marx Beyond Marx – Lessons on the Grundrisse* (London: Autonomedia/Pluto).

Negri, A. (1997) The constitution of time, in: A. Negri, *Time for Revolution* (New York and London: Continuum, 2003).

Negri, A. (2000) *Kairos, Alma Venus, Multitudo*, in: A. Negri, *Time for Revolution* (New York and London: Continuum, 2003).

Negri, A. (2003) *Time for Revolution* (New York and London: Continuum).

Negri, A. (2004) *Negri on Negri*, (With Anne Dufourmantelle and translated by M.B. DeBevoise) (London and New York: Routledge).

Ohmae, K. (1989) *The Borderless World* (London: Collins).

Passavant, P.A. (2004) Introduction: postmodern republicanism, in: P.A. Passavant & J. Dean *Empire's New Clothes – Reading Hardt and Negri* (London and New York: Routledge).

Passavant, P.A. & Dean, J. (2004) *Empire's New Clothes-Reading Hardt and Negri* (London and New York: Routledge).

Plamenatz, J. (1954) *German Marxism and Russian Communism* (London: Longman).

Tormey, S. (2004) *Anti-capitalism – A Beginner's Guide* (Oxford: One World Publications).

Walker, R.B.J. (2002) On the immanence/imminence of empire, *Millenium*, 31(2), pp. 337–345.

The Intellectual as a Political Actor?
Four Models of Theory/Praxis

GAYIL TALSHIR

Introduction

A theory of ideology is usually thought of in terms of the subjects of analysis, the conceptual framework, the social actors who develop, adhere, mobilize and follow the ideology and the methodology used to decipher the set of beliefs within a certain context. An often hidden dimension of ideology is the role of the analyst himself. Still, as Bell claimed, there is an inherent relation between the intelligentsia and ideology:

> The analysis of ideology belongs properly in the discussion of the intelligentsia. One can say that what the priest is to religion, the intellectual is to ideology. (Bell 1988: 394)

In this essay, I argue that the role of the analyst is changing with respect to the political culture and the historical period in question. After setting the scene in terms of the diachronic evolution, the essay focuses on the role of the theorist of ideology within the post-Marxist school in the twentieth century. The first problem that emerges is that social theorists in the aftermath of the Second World War were reluctant to use the concept of ideology in their studies. They thus chose alternative core concepts as their focal point of social critique. The second issue is that while it could have been expected that within the same family of analytical approaches, in this case post-Marxism, there will be a shared object of ideology, and a common idea of the role of the analyst, it emerges that while all theorists turn to the analysis of discourse and a critique of the capitalist culture as a manifestation of ideology, they differ substantially in terms of the role of the analyst. I examine four major theorists, from different political cultures, as a means for developing four distinct models: E.P. Thompson, the English working-class historian turned peace activist; the Frankfurt school's idea of critical theory, and their notion of theory as practice; Michel Foucault, with the critical view on the role of academic authority within modern societies; and Richard Rorty, with his notion of humanistic intellectual. The discussion asks whether there is a place for the analysis of ideology as a scientific endeavor, with no a-priori stance vis-à-vis the intellectual as a political actor.

A Threefold Genealogy of Ideology

Many analysts of ideology focus their attention on the concept of ideology, debating whether ideology is a voluntary set of beliefs or a form of false consciousness; whether ideology is a rational, consciously held worldview or a set of emotional and irrational beliefs; whether it is a total, comprehensive and exhaustive system of values, or a partial and contradictory set of ideas; whether it necessarily conserves asymmetrical relations of power – or whether any political force will be ideological by definition; whether ideology is a *Zeitgeist* or a product of ideologues, politicians or ordinary citizens; and whether ideology is a modern phenomenon or an immanent part of human society throughout history. However, if one changes perspective, and observes the study of ideologies through the objects of ideology – the political phenomena which shape the context in which the theories are conceived – one finds that the concept 'ideology' was used to define radically different political phenomena throughout the history of the term, and that these conceptual changes correspond to the dominant political forces at play in different historical periods. Furthermore, the function of the intellectual in each context becomes distinctively different.

A historical account of the objects of ideology discloses the changing terrain of political reality since the Enlightenment. Three moments in the history of 'ideology', since the term was first used by Destutt De Tracy (1754–1836) can be identified as heuristic devices (Talshir, forthcoming). In the first ideological moment – the eighteenth and nineteenth centuries – ideology was perceived as a function of class. Thus, despite the fact that the French ideologues and Karl Marx used markedly different definitions of the term ideology, they both perceived ideology at the end of the day as a political product of social classes – liberals and proletarians respectively. While in the eighteenth century, in view of the French revolution, the free-minded liberals revolted against the ancient regime and sought the general principles of rational science – the logic of ideas – to justify their intellectual and political goals, so did Marx, in the mid-nineteenth century, analyze the rise of the working classes as the agents of social change. Ideology is thus identified with social classes. Against the Enlightenment ethos, with its trust in science and individualism, the second moment of ideology rejected liberalism in face of a greater social force. The phenomena under research in the first half of the twentieth century were nationalism, Fascism, Nazism and Communism. Ideology in the early twentieth century was often associated with totalitarian regimes. In the aftermath of the 'end of ideology' debate, the objects of ideology changed once again. Analyzing manifestos and political programmes of parties, scrutinizing the industry of culture or exposing the power-relations within social institutions and civil society, intellectuals of the last generation identified ideology with political discourse pregnant with social practices.

As for the role of the analyst, Terry Eagleton argues that 'modern European criticism was born of a struggle against absolutist state. Within the repressive regime, in the seventeenth and eighteenth centuries, the European bourgeoisie begins to carve out for itself a distinct discursive space, one of rational judgment and enlightened critique' (Eagleton 1991: 9). The intellectual and analyst, then, is a modern phenomenon; for Eagleton, his role is one of social criticism. Critique is therefore the constitutive function of the intelligentsia, and it is still his job today: 'the role of the contemporary critic, then, is a *traditional* one' (Eagleton 1991: 123). Interestingly, however, when looking at it from the perspective of the self-inscribed role, and the social function as viewed by the social thinkers themselves, a slightly different picture emerges. Thus, in each of the historical moments of the changing objects of ideology, there is a different position, a distinct self-prescribed role, for the analyst of ideology, even if they all entail a dimension of social critique. Thus, both Destutt De-Tracy and Karl Marx perceived themselves to be positivist scientists, researchers of the driving force of history, pursuing a true science. The thinkers of the twentieth century – such as Bracher, Talmon and Arendt – saw themselves as critics of totalitarian regimes. The historians of ideas were exposing the mechanisms of ideology of the oppressive reigns of our era, emphatically endorsing democratic values as a clear alternative to dictatorship. The final transformation came with the third ideological moment. In contemporary political theory, the analyst tends to perceive her social criticism as political action. By exposing the structures of power and patterns of domination, she aspires to become an agent of social change. But before addressing this issue, with the nuisances and inner-distinctions, one has to ask whether contemporary thinkers analyze ideology at all, in the aftermath of the so-called 'end of ideology'.

Ideology Under Cover?

In view of the 1960s 'end of ideology' *Zeitgeist*, it was quite hard to be engaged in the study of ideology by the late twentieth century. For one, ideology in general had very bad press from the time of its conception: Napoleon had already argued, upon his return to France in December 1812, after his military defeat by Russia, that

> it is to ideology, that obscure metaphysics, which searching after first causes, wishes to found upon them the legislation of nations, instead of adapting the laws to the knowledge of the human heart and to the lessons of history, that we are to attribute all the calamities that our beloved France has experienced. (Napoleon 1851: 401–402)

It was only a matter of time before Marxist theory, with its dominance over much of social critical thinking from the late nineteenth century, would theorize this pejorative connotation of 'ideology' in terms of false consciousness and methods of oppression and domination. With the rise of totalitarian regimes in the mid-twentieth century, ideology as a productive concept for analysis seemed to be doomed.

Second, the critical age of the rising civil society in advanced democracies coincided with the linguistic turn in philosophy. If the main thrust of the late nineteenth-century women's movements was the demand for an equal vote, the feminists of the second wave argued that equality before the law was not enough: it was social practices that had to be changed, and with them the modes of action, norms, conventions and patterns of behaviour. Complementarily, it became increasingly clear, through works by Wittgenstein, Foucault and others, that language was not transparent and that discourse was imbued with social meanings, reflected power-relations and normatively shaped people's consciousness. In a way, everything was ideological as most linguistic expressions were pregnant with social presuppositions and normative claims. Consequently, if everything is ideological then ideology becomes once again an impractical concept: the macro-ideologies are either gone or sufficiently blurred, while the micro-ideologies are scattered all over the social sphere – in the family, the neighborhood, the city, the nation and the global village. Thus, the new social forces of the late 1960s, the candidates for the bearers of a new worldview, were much more into collective action then into a revised social philosophy. The scholarly literature tended to follow suit and focus on the study of the repertoire of political means (demonstrations, sits-in, parades, alternative communities, alternative art etc.) and the formation and institutionalization of new collective bodies (NGOs, new social movements, the extra-parliamentary opposition) rather on the ideology of these agents of New Politics (Poguntke 1993; Müller-Rommel & Poguntke 1995; Buechler 2000).

The problems, naturally, were even graver for the post-Marxist schools, for three reasons. First, ideology was viewed as a tool of bourgeois domination; second, ideology was conceived as part of the superstructure, epiphenomena of the industrial forces. However, with the advent of the information society, the industry of knowledge became the leading productive trade; the demarcation of economics and philosophy was no longer helpful. Third, ideology in the Marxist sense reflected a search for truth. The critique coming from the pragmatists and the deconstructionists argued that in a sense every consciousness is a false – or biased – consciousness;

the critique should be conveyed in relation to power and domination, rather then the 'true' or 'deep' infrastructures of society.

Still, I argue that the major occupation of post-Marxists and critical thinkers in the turn of the twentieth century is with ideology. Only the term was politically incorrect. It was therefore ideology in disguise, ideology under cover. Alternative concepts were used to replace ideology, while maintaining the critical edge of analyzing ideology as a social practice. Consider, first, Gramsci's concept of hegemony in contract to ideology. First, whereas ideology, in the classic Marxist sense, was a reflection of economic interests, Gramsci saw hegemony as referring also to the cultural, political and social arena in civil society (Gramsci 1976). Second, ideology was thus relegated to the superstructure while Gramsci thought that it was the processes in the educational system and in civil society that were not less formative then the economic ones. The overarching concept for that – given the negative connotation of 'ideology' in the Marxist tradition – became hegemony (Gramsci 1976: 375–377). For Gramsci hegemony was, in Barrett's words: 'best understood as *the organisation of consent*-the processes through which subordinated forms of consciousness are constructed without recourse to violence or coercion' (Barrett 1991: 54). Gramsci maintained the critical edge in the Marxist analysis, as well as, arguably, the pervasive notion of class domination, but replaced the concept of ideology with that of hegemony; it acquired, from within a Marxist perspective, a wider role, as the structure of consent within civil society. The first reason for rejecting the concept of ideology is hence its confinement to the superstructure as a mere reflection of economic analysis.

Habermas added another dimension to the contemporary discrediting of 'ideology'. He analyzed the crisis of legitimation of the modern state, a significant part of which was the disillusionment with representative democracy and the power of the state apparatus (Habermas 1975). The identification of ideology with the party system disabled it as a critical concept. He therefore constructed the notion of communicative action (Habermas 1984). Habermas and his followers not only offered a critique, but went one step further, offering an alternative normative model of deliberative democracy. It was based on a network of communicating collective actors in civil society (Habermas 1996, 2001). Thus, deliberative democracy identifies the established political system – within which party ideology is instrumental – as part of the crisis of legitimation. It turns to civil society as an independent third realm for an alternative and legitimate democratic practice. It emphasizes communicative actions of the new collective agents in civil society as a new source of this democratic legitimacy. Still, in these new forms of communicative actions, conceptual morphologies, ideational power-struggles and patterns of norms and beliefs of different communities constitute the ideological backbone. Whether in parties or social movements, the political programmes and normative arguments entail a necessary ideological dimension.

A third example of the transformed role of ideology is that of discourse analysis. Foucault's emphasis on discourse gave rise to critical discourse analysis. For discourse analysts, the patterns of domination were to be most effectively revealed by exposing their embeddedness in everyday language. Fairclough, in *Language and Power*, explains:

> Ideologies are closely linked to power, because the nature of ideological assumptions embedded in particular conventions, and so the nature of those conventions themselves, depends on the power relations which underlie the conventions; and because they are means of legitimising existing social relations and differences of power, simply the recurrence of ordinary, familiar ways of behaving which take these relations and power differences for granted. Ideologies are closely linked to language, because using language is the commonest form of social behaviour, and the form of social behaviour where we rely most on 'common sense' assumptions. (Fairclough 1989: 2).

The critical perspective strongly relates ideology to power, and discourse studies analyze relations of domination. The emphasis moves thereby from ideology to discourse, since ideology, as previously construed, assumed that language was transparent, whereas for the discourse analyst discourse is itself a system where power relations exist and interact with reality.

Thus, critical schools of thought focused on the analysis of ideology yet disguised the concept under different names – such as hegemony, sociology of knowledge, critical theory, social discourse, communicative action. After establishing the possibility – and plausibility – that post-Marxist schools indeed address ideology, it is time to investigate the four models of theory/practice and the role of the analyst in today's society.

The Intellectual as a Social Actor: Models of Putting Theory into Practice

The challenge of redefining the role of the intellectual in the late twentieth century was of particular importance to the post-Marxist schools, as the question of theory/practice relations was a central dimension under which the New Left has emerged. The following discussion introduces four major critical thinkers, analyzing the concept of ideology and the role of the analyst in each.

E.P. Thompson – the Intellectual as a Social Actor

E.P. Thompson (1924–1993), the great English historian, a founder of 'the new social history' school and the original editor of the *New Left Review*, is one of the most intriguing and fascinating intellectuals, for whom the dilemma of pursuing an academic life vs practicing civic engagement – well beyond a philosophical dilemma – constituted a real personal choice of life. Starting as a promising materialist historian, Thompson (1963) wrote his study of the *Making of the English Working Class*, mastering a new theoretical emphasis on reconstructing past social practices, ways of life and political culture (Calhoun 1994). Just as the cleavage between top-down vs bottom-up history preoccupied him in his work as a historian, so did the cleavage within the Marxist school, in regard to Stalinism:

the first is a tradition of theology. The second is a tradition of active reason. Both can derive some licence from Marx, although the second has immeasurably the better credentials as to its lineage. I must therefore state without equivocation that I can no longer speak of a single, Marxist tradition. There are two traditions... whose final declaration of irreconcilable antagonism was delayed – as an historical event – until 1956. (Thompson 1978: 380–381)

Theory and politics are – at this stage – intertwined.

However, Thompson's anger regarding the 'religious' followers of Stalinist Communism, also gave rise to grave doubts about the relations between theory – in the academy, and practice – in the civic realm. In his essay on 'The Poverty of Theory' his rage with the intellectual pursuit of philosophy, and the unwillingness to engage with politics, marks a turning point in his own allegiances:

Enclosed within the intelligentsia's habitual elitism, the theorists disdain to enter any kind of relation with a Labour movement ... whose struggles created the institutions in which they are employed, whose labour made the chairs in which they sit, which manages to exist and reproduce itself without them, and whose defensive pressures are all that stands between them and the reasons of capitalist power. Nor have these theorists created any independent agencies of political communication and education; the only agencies created are journals in which they can converse with each other. (Thompson 1978: 383)

The disappointment with his fellow academics, charged with political inactiveness, symbolized the way Thompson would choose. Still, the final decision came not through a theoretical argument or personal discomfort, but from analysis of the events in the international scene in face of the Cold War. The reason for departing from historical pursuits and turning to activism was Thompson's analysis of the new ideology; an ideology that he defined as 'exterminism'. The poverty of theory manifested itself in all its poignancy in view of the arms race, as he explained in his essay 'Notes on Exterminism, The Last Stage of Civilization':

Comrades, we need a cogent theoretical and class analysis of the present war crisis. Yes. But to structure an analysis in a consecutive rational manner may be, at the same time, to impose a consequential rationality upon the object of analysis. What if the object is irrational? What if the events are being willed by no single causative historical logic ... but are simply the product of a messy inertia? (Thompson 1982: 43)

He thus develops a new analytical category through which to think the process which leads into human extermination: 'I know that the category we need is that of 'exterminism'(Thompson, 1982: 45). The new ideology which he proposes does not fit well with the traditional macro-ideologies, enlightened or totalitarian; it also challenged the traditional Marxian assumptions regarding ideology. There was no conscious agent, no intentional mal-doing, no rational master plan of action. Rather, it was historical inertia, driven by reactions and interactions between the two superpowers and their followers, which ignited the war, fuelling it with nuclear armament, which could have led to the end of humanity. It is this new ideology of exterminism, which left 'Zero Option', that caused Thompson to turn to political activism. Despite his former connections with the Communist Party, and his demand from his colleagues to cooperate with the Labour movement, he made another crucial choice – one between the established parties and the extra-parliamentary opposition. Thompson chose to join the peace movement and lead the Campaign for Nuclear Disarmament (CND) outside the traditional institutions.

When asked, in 1985, to talk at the New School in New York, he opened:

I feel like an impostor here, because for six years now my trade has been submerged in peace activity ... total, full-time activity. In five years I've addressed more than five hundred meetings, attended endless committees, visited as an emissary of the peace movement nineteen or twenty different countries ... I don't even have a valid ticket for the British Library or the Public Record office. As I passed the New York Public Library this morning, I felt a knife inside me – the sense of how long it was since I had been able to work among the bounty that is there. (Thompson 1995: 490–491).

Thompson's choice was one of leaving the academy and becoming a full-time peace activist.

Still, he did not think that his intellectual credentials or his position as one of the leaders of the CND lent him any superiority. In fact, the figureheads that the media chose, he thought, gave the wrong impression of a hierarchical movement with one mind and body, which he resented. The peace movement was decentralized, diverse and based on grassroots activists. He recalled the events in the aftermath of Reagan's declaration about restraining the missiles deployment in Europe: 'On Wednesday of last week President Reagan proposed what was described as a "zero option". Within minutes the telephone was ringing and I was being asked ... what I – or "the peace movement" – or the "European peace movement" thought about it ... This cannot be done ... I cannot speak for "the peace movement". I can only give an interim personal opinion' (Thompson 1982: 123). The question of the self-reflective ex-theorist was one of power-politics.

The peace movement did exert some influence over US policy, did become a significant player between the two superpowers, and did help to get the missiles out from European soil. It did not, in Thompson's mind, exterminate the logic of the irrational exterminist ideology; and he did not do it single-handedly. Still, in terms of the role of the intellectual, his personal example was clear: faced with the irrationality of historical forces, the historian has to leave the academy, as well as the attempts to construct a logical theory, and become a full-time social activist.

Max Horkheimer and Theodor Adorno – Theory as Practice?

In stark opposition to Thompson's position, so it seems, Adorno argues that the call of separation of theory and praxis often results in the adoration of practice and the prohibition of thinking; the charge that the non-active intellectuals are traitors culminates in the claim that perceives 'theory itself as a form of repression – as if praxis did not stand in a far more direct relationship to repression' (Adorno 1991: 199; Brenda 1928). The relationship between theory and praxis was a crucial question for the Frankfurt school. When Horkheimer was appointed director of the Institute for Social Research, he claimed that the institute would use methods of empirical social science to address questions of classic social philosophy and thus develop a comprehensive theoretical framework for the critical analysis of modern society (Bailey 1996: 5). For a start, they rejected the notion of ideology as a bridge between theory and praxis. Horkheimer condemned Mannheim's notion of the 'sociology of knowledge' as a substitute for ideology, arguing that Mannheim (1929) had in fact returned to an idealistic tradition (Horkeheimer 1930). However, the scholars of the Frankfurt school have generally abstained from directly studying 'ideology'; instead they offered their Critical Theory. At the centre of Horkheimer and Adorno's analysis, given the advent of advanced capitalism, was no longer the mode of production, but the manufacturing of mass culture. The transition from the industrial to advanced industrial society manifested itself in the culture of consumption and the emergence of the knowledge society. Selling images, popularizing art and the role of commercials became essential to the new dynamic of advanced capitalism (Horkheimer 1968; Adorno 1991). Their theory was critical of popular culture – which could not be seen as a mere reflection of class struggle, but captured the very heart of the consumer society. 'Ideology' was hardly used, as the very relationship between politics and economics had changed dramatically and eclipsed class analysis in advanced capitalism. Critiques of culture and consumerism were theoretically complementary to the new social order. Whereas Mannheim insisted that ideology is inherently a function of social classes, social classes as a theoretical category had to be radically transformed in order to capture the post-Second World War reality. Marcuse, for one, maintained the analysis of oppression and domination, but argued that the new social agent was composed of the Western students and intelligentsia, as well as the poor classes of the Third World (Marcuse 1967). However, Marcuse concludes his *One-Dimensional Man* by saying that 'the critical theory of society possesses no concepts which could bridge the gap between the present and its future; holding no promise and showing no success, it remains negative' (Marcuse 1964: 253). As for Horkheimer, he contended that critical theory has no obligation to social class analysis, but a general concern for the abolition of social injustice (Horkheimer 1972: 221). What, if so, is the role of the intellectual? Is critical theory devoid of politics, as the Frankfurt School scholars were often accused? (Chambers 2004).

In 'Traditional and Critical Theory' Horkheimer distinguishes between traditional science, which ignores its own activity as an expression of social action in a cultural context, and critical theory which takes that into account. Science has a function in the production process itself, and cannot be detached from it. With the emergence of advanced capitalism, the function of science within the social order also changes. It is here that the separation between theory and practice is dissolved:

> The scholarly specialist 'as' scientist regards social reality and its products as extrinsic to him, and 'as' citizen exercises his interest in them through political articles, membership in political parties or social service organizations, and participation in elections. But he does not unify these two activities ... Critical thinking, on the contrary, is motivated today by the effort to really to transcend the tension and to abolish the opposition between the individual's purposefulness, spontaneity, and rationality, and those work-process relationships on which society is built. (Horkheimer 1972: 209–210)

Whereas in traditional theory the scientist is separated from his object of study, and he acts as a citizen in the public realm, in critical theory the intellectual is a social actor, engaged with his subject of study; he is politically involved through his critical pursuit. An interesting dialectic emerges: on the one hand, the role of the intellectual becomes one of promoting humanity into self-awareness of its conditions; on the other hand, the intellectual's position has to be one of independence (Horkheimer 1972: 223). In advanced societies, the separation between the scientist and her object of research does not hold; in a self-reflective society, the rejection of the social order becomes instrumental to its transcendence:

> A consciously critical attitude, however, is part of the development of society: the construing of the course of history as a necessary product of an economic mechanism simultaneously contains both protest against this order of things, a protest generated by the order itself, and the idea of self-determination for the human race, that is the idea of a state of affairs in which man's actions no longer flow from a mechanism but from his own decision (Horkheimer 1972: 229)

Protest is embedded in the critical intellectual. It therefore emerges that despite the antipathy of Horkheimer and Adorno to the intellectual as a political practitioner, their position was one that established critical theory as a form of social action:

> The uncompromisingly critical thinker, who neither superscribes his consciousness nor permits himself to be terrorized into action, is in truth the one who does not give up ... Open thinking points beyond itself. For its part, such thinking takes a position as a figuration of praxis which is more closely related to a praxis truly involved in change than in a position of mere obedience for the sake of praxis. Beyond all specialized and particular content, thinking is actually and above all the force of resistance, alienated from resistance only with great effort. (Adorno 1991: 202).

Michel Foucault – the Intellectual as Preserver of the Social Order

In congruence with the Frankfurt school thinkers, Foucault agrees that science is embedded in a particular social reality and reflects it; in stark contrast, he contends that the role of the intellectual is more often then not to maintain, preserve and conserve the existing order, using the authority of his academic power, his control of truth as a mechanism of exclusion:

> This will to truth, like other systems of exclusion, relies on institutional support: it is both reinforced and accompanied by the whole strata of practices such as pedagogy – naturally – the book-system, publishing, libraries, such as the learned societies in the past, and laboratories today. But it is probably even more profoundly accompanied by the manner in which knowledge is employed in a society, the way it is exploited, divided and, in some ways, attributed ... Finally, I believe that this will for knowledge, thus reliant upon institutional support and distribution, tends to exercise a sort of pressure, a power of constraint upon other forms of discourse – I am speaking of our own society. (Foucault 1972: 219)

The highly educated – the psychiatrist, teacher, civil servant, warden, officer or professor – is manifesting the hidden power-relations within our society. Far from being the protestor against the existing order, he uses his knowledge authority to limit, constrain and direct other people. Thus, the intellectuals are the symbols of the power-relations in the knowledge society. Yet, Foucault distinguished between universal intellectual and specific intellectuals. The former is identified as the bearer of values, the man of letters, the jurist; the latter is rather a late development, and his model is the expert: 'for the first time, I think, the intellectual was hounded by political powers, no longer on account of a general discourse which he conducted, but because of the knowledge at his disposal' (Foucault 1984: 69). It is he who acquired powers, embedded in his scientific pursuit, and became identified with the system of rule.

Still, Foucault is not content with the universal intellectual also: 'For a long period, the "left" intellectual spoke and was acknowledged the right of speaking in the capacity of master of truth and justice ... To be an intellectual meant something like being the consciousness/conscience of us all' (Foucault 1984: 67). The problem with the intellectuals of the left, according to him, is that they operated on a system of truth and falsity. However, Foucault claims, truth isn't outside power, isn't the reward of free spirits; rather, each society has its own regime of truth, the mechanisms, institutions and systems which discipline people. 'The intellectual can operate and struggle at the general level of that regime of truth which is so essential to the structure and functioning of our society' (ibid.: 73–74).

The key to this oligarchy of knowledge is with those who decipher the codes of the structures of domination, the critical analysts: 'the critical side of the analysis deals with the system enveloping discourse; attempting to mark out and distinguish the principles of ordering, exclusion and rarity in discourse' (Foucault 1972: 234). It is here that ideology, in its reformed reference to discourse, plays a central role. Power relations are a structural part of social systems, not necessarily consciously motivated by a malevolent agent. Discourse, as the system of beliefs which is not constituted upon the true/false paradigm but on the exposition of power-relations and domination patterns, has a different twist on the study of ideology:

> The essential political problem for the intellectual is not to criticize the ideological contents supposedly linked to science, or to ensure that his own scientific practice is accompanied by a correct ideology, but that of ascertaining the possibility of constituting a new politics of truth. The problem is not changing people's consciousness – or what's in their heads – but the political, economic, institutional regime of the production of truth. (Foucault 1984: 74)

Finally, the role of the critical intellectual is one of exposing the regime of truth, in practices and in discourse. However, when the intellectual decides to go out to the streets and demonstrate, protest or bring about social change – like Foucault did in his work with and for prisoners – he has no excessive authority over his fellow-activists. His expertise and dignities remain in his study; there is no special position to the intellectual in the streets.

Thus, for Foucault there are three types of intellectuals, who do not embody a diachronic evolution, but rather different edges of the social spectrum: the specific intellectual, who – in modern society – acquires roles of a ruling elite which constitutes and preserves a certain regime of truth; the universal intellectual, the social philosopher, who seeks to be the social agent of a superior order of justice and truth: Foucault is as worried about him, for he employs categories of truth and falsity; and the critical intellectual, who helps to delineate, expose and change the hierarchies of power which take cover under the regime of truth. Still, when the critical intellectual decides to move into social action, he looses his authority and is just one among other social activists.

Richard Rorty – the Organic Intellectual

Richard Rorty shares Foucault's critique of the truth-seeking Marxist school. Rorty reiterates the two traditions – one which is devoted to finding the truth, reaching the deeper level of analysis and setting the foundation of the good society, going back to Plato; the other – critical, relativist, empirical and pragmatic – is asking rather what is useful and what can we do with this or that knowledge (Rorty 1982). The Marxist Left is found emphatically in the first category; it is therefore rejected by Rorty. In theory, then, Rorty has nothing much to do with this paper on New Left intellectuals between theory and practice; in practice, Rorty shares some of the core tenets of the Left – its critical approach, its optimism, its praxis-oriented theory and its progressivism. Rorty distinguishes between the (liberal) reformist Left and the (Marxist) New Left and places himself firmly in the former (Rorty 1998: 1–72).

What is his notion of ideology, then, and the role of the intellectual? On the face of it, ideology is a foreign word in Rorty's dictionary, for it was for too long identified with truth-seeking, coherent and consistent logical construction of the utopian good society. It is precisely this kind of intellectuals – constructors of a supposed utopian social order – that Rorty dislikes the most. However, there is no social criticism without a view of society, and there is no view from nowhere. If we reconstruct differently the contours of ideologies as the product of groups, using ideology as tools for social thought explication, which forge collective identity, and use political tools for establishing its way of social life, the pragmatist resentment may be less fervent. As for the intellectual, while pragmatism may sound like an anti-intellectual endeavour, Rorty is careful to construct the philosophical tradition in which pragmatism – going back to the pre-Socratics, the empiricists, Nietzsche, Dewey and the philosophers of language – is situated. Rorty rejects philosophy as an independent discipline, or a profession, and urges a post-philosophical culture. In this culture, the intellectual's position would be very different from the expert academics of today:

> *A fortiori,* such a culture would contain nobody called 'the Philosopher' who could explain why and how certain areas of culture enjoyed a special relation to reality. Such a culture would, doubtless, contain specialists in seeing how things hung together. But these would be people Who had no special 'problems' to solve, nor any special 'method' to apply, abided by no particular disciplinary standards, had no collective self-image as a 'profession'. They might resemble contemporary philosophy professors in being more interested in moral responsibility than in prosody, or more interested in the articulation of sentences than in that of the human body, but they might not. They would be all-purpose intellectuals who were ready to offer a view on pretty much anything, in the hope of making it hang together with everything else. (Rorty 1982: 30)

On first impression, the intellectual may be thought of as an *enfant terrible* type; however, if part of his job is to enable social views and cultural phenomena to 'hang together' one cannot do without a comprehensive, contextual theory-of-society. The intellectual thus emerges more as a synthetic intellectual (Baert 2001: 2). The intellectual, Rorty argues, who studies

> the comparative advantages and disadvantages of the various ways of talking which our race has invented ... looks, in short, much like what is sometimes called "culture criticism" ... The modern Western "culture critic" feels free to comment on anything at all. He is a prefiguration of the all-purpose intellectual of a post-Philosophical culture, the philosopher who has abandoned pretensions to Philosophy. (Rorty 1982: 32)

Thus, theory, or philosophy, comes under attack, as does the detached, aloof intellectual. In contrast, Rorty calls himself and his ilk 'humanistic intellectuals', people who try to expand their own moral imagination, and whose real social function 'is to instil doubts in the students about the students' own self-images, and about the society to which they belong' (Rorty 1999: 127). To use Gramsci's phrase, Rorty's social critic is the organic intellectual, who is connected to his community, and cares about the individual as a moral being. Yet, this seemingly apolitical function was too often accused of 'politicizing the humanities'; to both charges Rorty replies that 'we cannot take the idea of unpoliticized humanities any more seriously than our opposite numbers in the clergy can take seriously the idea of a depoliticized church' (Rorty 1999: 128). The pursuit of the intellectual, as a secular pastor, is to raise problems, contextualize, call into question and give freedom to his moral imagination, without locking it behind disciplinary doors of academic departments. This is the engaged intellectual whose way of life is part of a living, vibrant, changing community. Theory can only be an expression of lifeworld.

Conclusion: The Intellectual between Social Critic and Analyst of Ideology

This essay has addressed a very special moment in history, one in which theory became a form of action, and the social critic a political activist. The emergence of the New Left gave rise to a new facet in the theory-practice relationship, marked by a dual dialectics. On the one hand, the students, activists, protestors of the 1960s were at the same time part of the intelligentsia and agents of social change – ripe for grasping and enacting social theory; they also criticized the Old Left for being focused on theory rather than on social change, and for being too institutional – both in political parties and communist cells, but the first institution under question was the university itself. On the other hand, the intellectuals, in the era of the information society, experienced the remarkable period, in which knowledge becomes a commodity in its own right – they were, for the first time, manufacturers of real goods, producers of the artifacts most highly in demand – theory became a thing in the world, the engine of the post-industrial society; at the same time, theory was not enough: the real happening was out there, in the outskirts of the political system, in civil society. It was hard to sit inside the research institute and watch from afar. The temptation to take action, to engage, was far too great.

Thus, intellectuals of the New Left shared a critique of the post-industrial social order: condemned military and cultural imperialism, criticized the consumerist and materialist ethos, and protested against injustices concerning national, cultural, ethnic, sexual and racial minorities. They exposed relations of domination in educational, bureaucratic, institutional bodies, as in culture, art and the family. However, in the 1960s intellectuals were drawn into the alternative scene, the counterculture, as cultural heroes – Marcuse and Sartre, Arendt and de Beauvoir – were symbols of a generation. They personified the theory/praxis nexus. In view of this challenge, the New Left did not come up with a unified idea of the role of the intellectual; as we have seen, four different political actors, four different intellectuals, came up with quite distinct models. E.P. Thompson, the English historian, has desrted his intellectual pursuit, in view of the advent of the ideology of exterminism, and became the face of the peace movement. Horkheimer and Adorno resented the charge that intellectuals should obey the order of praxis; it is precisely in their critical theory that they materialize their social function and bring about social change – theory is a form of transforming praxis. Foucault rebuked the 'universal' intellectuals who sought the true principles of social critique, as he condemned the 'specific' intellectuals who – far from being social critics – were responsible for establishing and preserving the existing political order, using their knowledge expertise as a form of power. It is only the critical intellectual who can expose the power-relations embedded in social discourse and public institutions. But even he, when leaving his desk and joining the protesting crowd, loses his moral and social status and is equal to any other activist. Finally, Rorty has promoted the notion of a humanistic, organic intellectual, as part of the community in which he lives, whose main function is to pose question and promote social change.

This special moment in history had different consequences. The New Left intellectuals of the second generation – Habermas, Benhabib, Young and Fraser, to name but a few – where now developing normative blueprints for the good society which was constituted on the free hand of civil society. The principles were procedural ones, encouraging grassroots activism, communicative action and empowerment of communities. This politics of identity had a clear moral outcome: the magic of the political thinker as a social actor has exhausted itself. The communities to be empowered – Black, immigrants, cultural groups – were to develop their own ways of life, forms of communication. The theorist merely gave the philosophical foundations, be they deliberative democracy or multiculturalism – to facilitate such social practices. Within the university, new areas of study were established, devoid of disciplinary rules of theory and method, such as women's, cultural, black, homosexual and ethnic studies. The convergence of social theorists and analysts of ideology has also reached its end. In the wake from this enchanted moment of the public intellectuals, there may be a room to reconsider the new challenges of analyzing ideology today, rethinking the theory of ideology, developing the scholarly toolkit for studying the emotive, irrational, experiential, cognitive and conceptual manifestations of new collective actors in the different realms of the public sphere. The time has come to put the analysis of ideology back into work.

References

Adorno, T. (1991). *The Culture Industry* (London, Routledge).
Baert, P. (2001). Richrad Rorty's pragmatism and the social sciences. *History of Human Sciences*, 15(1), pp. 139–149.
Barrett, M. (1991) *The Politics of Truth* (Cambridge, Polity Press).
Bailey, L. (1996) *Critical Theory and the Sociology of Knowledge* (New York, Peter Lang).
Bell, D. (1960) *The End of Ideology* (Cambridge, MA: Harvard University Press).
Bell, D. (1988) *The End of Ideology* (Cambridge, MA: Harvard University Press).
Benda, J. (1928) *The Treason of the Intellectuals* (New York, Norton).
Buechler, S. (2000) *Social Movements in Advanced Capitalism* (Oxford: Oxford University Press).

Calhoun, C. (1994) E.P. Thompson and the discipline of historical context. *Social Research*, 61(2), pp. 223–244.
Chambers, S. (2004) The politics of critical theory, in: F. Rush (Ed.), *Critical Theory* (Cambridge: Cambridge University Press), pp. 219–247.
Eagleton, T. (1991) *The Function of Criticism* (London: Verso).
Fairclough, N. (1989) *Language and Power* (London, Longman).
Foucault, M. (1972) *The Archeology of Knowledge & The Discourse on Language* (New York: Pantheon Books).
Foucault, M. (1994) *The Order of Things* (New York: Vintage Books).
Gramsci, A. (1976) *Selections from the Prison Notebooks* (London: Lawrence and Wishart).
Habermas, J. (1975) *Legitimation Crisis* (Boston, MA: Beaxton).
Habermas, J. (1984) *The Theory of Communicative Action* (Boston: Beacon Press).
Habermas, J. (1996) Three normative models of democracy, in: S. Benhabib (Ed.), *Democracy and Difference* (Princeton, NJ: Princeton University Press), pp. 21–30.
Habermas, J. (2001) *Facts and Norms* (Cambridge, MA: MIT Press).
Horkheimer, M. (1930) Ein neuer Ideologiebegriff? *Archiv für Geschichte des Sozialismus und der Arbeiter-Bewegung*, 15, pp. 33–56.
Horkheimer, M. (1968) *Critical Theory* (New York: Continuum).
Horkheimer, M. (1972) *Critical Theory* (New York: Seabury).
Mannheim, K. (1929, 1955) *Ideology and Utopia* (New York: Harcourt).
Marcuse, H. (1964) *One-Dimensional Man* (Boston, Beacon Press).
Marcuse, H. (1967) *Das Ende der Utopie* (Berlin: Maikowski).
Müller-Rommel, F. & Poguntke, T. (Eds) (1995) *New Politics* (Dartmouth: Harts).
Napoleon, B. (1851) In J. Adams, *The Life and Works of John Adams* (Boston: Little & Brown).
Poguntke, T. (1993) *Alternative Politics* (Edinburgh, Edinburgh University Press).
Rabinow, P. (Ed.) (1984) *Foucault Reader* (New York, Pantheon Books).
Rorty, R. (1982) *Consequences of Pragmatism* (Minneapolis, MN, University of Minnesota Press).
Rorty, R. (1998) *Achieving Our Country* (Cambridge, MA, Harvard University Press).
Rorty, R. (1999) *Philosophy and Social Hope* (Harmonsworth, Penguin).
Talshir, G. (forthcoming) The objects of ideology: historical transformations and the changing role of the analyst, *History of Political Thought*.
Thompson, E.P. (1963) *The Making of the English Working Class* (London: Gollancz).
Thompson, E.P. (1978) *The Poverty of Theory and Other essays* (London: Merlin Press).
Thompson, E.P. (1982) *Zero Option* (London: Merlin Press).
Thompson, E.P. (1995) *Making History: Writings on History and Culture* (New York: The New Press).

(De)Contesting Ideology: The Struggle over the Meaning of the Struggle over Meaning

MATHEW HUMPHREY

Introduction

Old questions are sometimes worth reconsidering in the light of new developments. A long-standing question in social science is 'what is ideology?' Given that, whatever else it may be, ideology is a highly abstract noun, further questions regarding its identity follow: how do we recognise it? What is its form and function? What effects does it have in the social world? These questions are sufficiently perplexing (and for some the history of the concept is sufficiently tainted) for calls to be made for the abandonment of the concept altogether. For Daniel Bell (2000), of *The End of Ideology* fame, it is a concept now 'irretrievably fallen', in that it has come to refer to any political belief passionately held, and has thus lost its purchase on social explanation. For Foucault, it is at least 'difficult to make use of', partly because 'like it or not' it always stands in opposition to something called 'truth', when 'the problem' lies in understanding how 'the effects of truth are produced within discourses' (in Rabinow 1984: 60).

Despite these difficulties, any cursory glance at both the academic literature and everyday discourse shows that the concept remains stubbornly with us.[1] This is because, the claim goes, 'ideology' addresses at least one social problematic that would refuse, merely because we agreed to desist using the term, to disappear.[2] Furthermore, given its history of use and connotations, 'ideology' may have a certain utility for those trying to think about this (or these) problem(s), and we have not yet found a better language in which to express ourselves. Thus it seems that we cannot avoid the 'what is ideology?' question by abandoning the concept and finding an alternative language. If the phenomenon ideology is taken to refer to is recognised, then we will need to inquire into it, whatever we may happen to call it.

My objective in this essay, then, is to examine the nature of ideology analysis in the light of recent important developments in ideology theory. In particular I want to look at the concept of ideology as embodied in 'conceptual morphology', a form of ideology analysis developed by Michael Freeden. There are three questions here. How does the concept of ideology used in conceptual morphology 'fit' with the tradition(s) of thinking about ideology? Secondly, what does it take to be the central problematic of ideology theory? Thirdly, given the answers to the first two questions, can conceptual morphology help us to reflect more generally on the nature of ideology analysis, and its role in interpretative and explanatory social science?

The next two sections of the essay track some recent developments in ideology theory, and seek to set conceptual morphology within this context. This discussion is organised, with a certain lack of originality, around the idea that there are two traditions in ideology theory. There is no doubt that practitioners within each of these traditions see the other as both misguided and rival, and I look at the arguments for and against each tradition. Why should we prefer any one of these conceptions over any other? This takes us on to the assessment of conceptual morphology as an example of ideology theory. It clearly fits within the 'inclusive' tradition, but carries with it a distinctive understanding of what we are doing when we engage in 'ideology analysis'. Finally, I seek to use these discussions to open up a range of difficult and important questions about the role and function of ideology analysis. Is it an interpretative exercise, an explanatory one, or a normative one? Or possibly some combination of these? Are these projects sufficiently well related that it makes sense to think in terms of ideology theory as a single enterprise? Is ideology a single concept with many conceptions, or are we in fact faced with radically different classes of object, which become conflated because of the misleading apparent singularity of 'ideology theory'?

Conceptions of Ideology: Justifications and Classifications

How can a conception of ideology be justified against other conceptions? What is it that renders one conception preferable to another? Whatever the answer to this may be, it is clear that we cannot resolve the question merely through stipulation. The assertion that ideology *is* 'x' is (as we shall see from an example given below) simply and massively question-begging. In dealing with an abstract noun referring to a thought process (or form of belief, or condition of consciousness) which may (or may not) be grounded in material reality, theorists of ideology have little in the way of observable referent to point to. There is of course established usage, but with ideology that is precisely the problem. 'Established usage' is so variant and contradictory (see for example the list in Eagleton 1991: 1–2) that no shared account could ever be reconstructed. The insistence that ideology 'is' one thing rather than another appears, under these circumstances, as little more than an attempt to impose definitional fiat.

There is a more promising avenue, however, and that is to settle on a conception of ideology not by stipulation, or historical usage, but rather from what it is we might be trying to explain or understand through its usage. The thought here is that our conception of ideology should not be arbitrary (see Seliger 1976), and the question then becomes one of discerning the dimension along which accounts of ideology might be considered (usefully) non-arbitrary. The interpretative or explanatory power of the concept in relation to puzzling social phenomena would appear to be the most promising approach here. This does not of course make the problem of discerning the appropriate usage of ideology easy, the question of what needs explanation and why is, as we shall see, no less contested than the account of ideology itself. Nor, on many views of ideology, do the questions we pose lack ideological motivation. It does however offer a plausible way into thinking about the problem and it is where we find the most interesting accounts (in the sense of their non-arbitrariness) of why we should prefer one conception over another. In these arguments conceptions of ideology tend to fall into either one of two categories, referred to variously as 'restrictive vs inclusive'; 'critical vs neutral', or 'evaluative vs non-evaluative'. All of these binaries are problematic, but for the purposes of exposition I will divide them into 'restrictive' and 'inclusive' conceptions.

Caution is required here not least because within both of these categories there is considerable internal differentiation, and an argument in support of one version of the restrictive or inclusive conception would not necessarily favour another version in the same category. A justification for thinking about ideology as false beliefs about social phenomena may not work as a justification for thinking about ideology as masking the operation of a socially dominant power, for example. Furthermore there may be overlap between the two approaches which become difficult to discern precisely because of the dichotomous approach (for example how an interpretative understanding may also have some explanatory power). As with many such dichotomies, then, that between 'restrictive' and 'inclusive' conceptions of ideology is in some ways misleading and will doubtless conceal as well as reveal. I would nonetheless defend it as a heuristically useful device.

The 'Inclusive' Theory of Ideology

Arguments for an 'inclusive' view of ideology divide, as one might expect, between attacks on the inadequacies on the more restrictive definitions, and positive arguments for more inclusive accounts. Three claims stand out in the literature, and these concern epistemology, class (and other forms of) domination, and the scope of the object of ideology.

Epistemology

This refers to a well-rehearsed reason for abandoning the 'critical' conception of ideology, which seeks to portray ideological thought as suffering from a false claim to true knowledge. It looks back to one of the ways in which Marx and Engels discuss ideology in *The German Ideology*. As Slavoj Žižek asks, rhetorically, 'does not the critique of ideology involve a privileged place, somehow exempted from the turmoils of social life...? Is not the claim that we can accede to this place the most obvious case of ideology?' (Žižek 1994: 3). As we shall see later, Žižek goes on to defend a specific Lacanian usage of the concept, but the questions he asks at the outset are those frequently employed now against this particular Marxist conception. Claims to epistemological privilege in this guise, as allowing us to reveal the 'true' nature of social reality as against the partial and one-sided view of others appear naïve and misguided, the 'most obvious case of ideology'. Foucault abandoned the use of the concept of ideology for much the same reason, it is inherently connected, in his view, to an unsustainable claim to epistemological advantage (in Rabinow 1984: 60).

The decisive step forward here, on the view of some defenders of an inclusive paradigm, was made by Karl Mannheim in his *Ideology and Utopia*. He turns the light of Marxism back on itself, in order to show that it is as much a function of the world from which it emanates as any other body of social thought. It is no less an ideology than any other worldview adhered to by a social group. One does not have to believe in the success of Mannheim's overall project in the sociology of knowledge to believe that in this, at least, he was correct. 'Karl Mannheim's contribution into the inquiry into ideology was ... decisive both in heightening awareness of its epistemological pitfalls, and in rescuing ideology from some of the dead ends of Marxist analysis' (Freeden 1996: 26). Similarly, Seliger notes that Mannheim 'used ideology not only inclusively, but also neutrally ... Ideology represents the outlook associated with a given historical or social situation ... Mannheim insisted that the socialist-communist claim to be free of such a limited outlook and hence free of any 'ideological taint' was untenable' (1976: 80).

Class Domination

Another version of the restrictive conception of ideology ties it to class domination.[3] This dimension is quite separate from that of epistemological falsity, in that one does not have to take a position on the latter in order to believe that ideological ideas (or forms of consciousness) are those that serve class domination.[4] As with all versions of the restrictive view, this understanding is questioned not only by those who employ a more inclusive conception, but also by those who prefer an alternative restrictive conception.

We can begin here with an example of how stipulative conceptions do nothing to help resolve the problem of how best to conceptualise and employ the concept of ideology. Zeus Leonardo, discussing John B. Thompson's preferred account of ideology, claims that his 'negative theory of ideology appears incomplete. Despite its thoroughness, it fails to explain how ideology may not serve the interests of domination, but rather resists and contests it' (Leonardo 2003: 205). But this assumes that we somehow 'know' that ideology is something that can apply both to systems of ideas that support domination and to those that resist it. As we shall see below Thompson explicitly restricts his account of ideology to ideas that serve the interests of domination, and he justifies this through an account of puzzling social phenomena that this version of ideology might help us explain. To accuse him of not seeing that 'ideology' can explain other social phenomena if it used differently is to perform what one might call the 'stipulative error', in that of course a different conception of ideology will cover different phenomena. This does nothing, however, to answer the question of why we should prefer Leonardo's conception to Thompson's. We have to start from an examination of what Thompson is seeking to explain, not from the conception of ideology that only emerges from that inquiry.

So the appropriate question for the student of ideology is whether Thompson's project of social explanation is the appropriate one. Should ideology be used if and only if we are seeking to explain how 'meaning serves, in particular circumstances, to establish and maintain relations of power which are systematically asymmetrical i.e. relations of domination' (Thompson 1990: 6). Thompson's own arguments for that view will be considered in the next section. The view against is articulated by Balkin, who argues that Thompson's conception of ideology is 'underinclusive'. Not, note, merely because he does not understand what ideology 'really' refers to, he is free to delimit the scope of his study, but because a 'large portion' of the social phenomena we should be interested in studying in a theory of ideology will be missed. In particular the 'domination' view of ideology risks 'sentimentalizing the attitudes and interests of other groups, in particular subordinated groups' (Balkin 1998: 114). Subordinated groups can hold beliefs about each other that result in unjust practices (for example, black anti-Korean beliefs in the United States) and in order to bring such phenomena within our purview we require a broader, less Marx-inspired conception of ideology than Thompson uses. On this view Balkin's own restrictive conception, whereby ideological phenomena are those that 'help create or sustain unjust social relations' is to be preferred because it includes phenomena that should be of interest to students of ideology, but which Thompson's account excludes (Balkin 1998: 104). These unjust social relations are not *necessarily* relations of domination.

The more comprehensive rejection of this approach just takes Balkin's complaint about Thompson further, suggesting that there are no good reasons to restrict the application of ideology to those ideas that are in the service of injustice any more than there are good reasons for stopping at class domination. Balkin notes that the very notion of 'domination' is itself subject to ideological dispute, but, as he accepts, this insight applies also to his own account of injustice. The inclusive view of ideology[5] extends this insight, and holds all views about domination, injustice, illusory social beliefs and so on to themselves be categories open to ideological contestation. The Mannheimian turn against Marxism is given broad domain, and all forms of political discourse are recuperated back into an interpretative framework. The very notion that ideology is something to be uncovered and ultimately destroyed takes its place amongst the canons of ideological belief, resting as it does on a number of assumptions and presuppositions about the nature of reality and its relationship with human thought processes.

The Scope of Ideology

The rejection of these two Marxist elements of ideology theory, epistemological illusion and the service of class domination, leads to an argument regarding the scope of ideology, particularly when the epistemological realism of Marx gives way to more constructivist views. For Freeden the hermeneutic and linguistic 'turn' in our understanding of political thought led to a 'focus on constructed and invented realities as necessary forms of both reproducing knowledge and understanding' (Freeden 2001: 5). Once all 'reality' is understood as inherently mediated in this way, then the old epistemological divide breaks down, and we are 'no longer able to rely on the Marxist usages of ideology, irrelevant as they appeared to the understanding of Western political thought manifestations' (Freeden 2001: 5). Martin Seliger's defence of an 'inclusive' conception of ideology rests upon a claim that ideology cannot be consigned wholesale to the realm of distortion. This is because 'it can be shown that politics cannot be reduced to arguments over technicalities' (1976: 17) – merely the administration of things. Disagreements over policies and priorities will always have a normative dimension, a 'moral texture' as Seliger calls it, and a more useful account of ideology will help us understand these disagreements. In moving away from Marxism, theorists of ideology have to delimit the scope of their enquiries in other ways (all conceptions of ideology are 'restrictive' in this sense). Freeden, for example, argues that ideology analysis can allow us to understand and navigate our way through the complex universe of political thinking. How do political thinkers manage the inevitable indeterminacy and inconsistencies of political thought? How do they attempt to 'close down' meaning and instantiate their preferred interpretation of the world? How does political thought relate to political action? What role does emotion play in the development of political thinking? These are the kinds of questions that Freeden's own theory of ideology seeks to help us understand, as we shall see. Here, clearly, the scope of ideological thought is far broader than on a Marxian conception, becoming a synonym for 'political thought', viewed from a particular perspective. This breadth is not necessarily a problem, after all the thought that everything on Earth is atomic matter does not make the job of classifying that matter into a periodic table an unhelpful endeavour – quite the opposite. Similarly, the interpretative task of classifying and analysing the various forms that ideology can take may well enhance our understanding of political thought.

The 'Restrictive' Conception of Ideology

Restrictive conceptions of ideology in the contemporary literature take a number of forms, each seeking to focus on what is seen as a particular problematic social phenomenon. Three versions are readily identifiable in the literature: ideology as beliefs (or reasons for holding beliefs) that are, in some sense, illusory or false; ideas that serve the interests of a dominant and oppressive power, or which cause injustice; and the Lacan-inspired notion of ideology as that which seeks to achieve the impossible task of representing the world in its self-transparency. Some of these elements can be found combined in the same account, such as the view that false beliefs must also serve an unjust social order for them to 'count' as ideological.

Ideology as Falsehood

As we have seen, a standard criticism of 'ideology as false belief' (or consciousness) is that it seems to imply the possibility of a 'view from nowhere' of truly objective knowledge about the social world, and this itself seems to be 'ideology *par excellence*'. Given this problem of the apparent claim to epistemological privilege, how is this conception defended by its current adherents? For Michael Rosen, 'false consciousness' is a necessary condition for ideology (the subsequent condition being that these ideas also serve to sustain a particular social order). Note that it is the consciousness that is false, not necessarily the ideas, which may be true but be held for reasons that have nothing to do with their truth. Tommie Shelby also articulates this conception of ideology: to hold a belief in false consciousness is to be deceived about one's motives for holding it – noncognitive motives operate 'behind one's back'. It does not follow from this that the beliefs in question are illusory (see Rosen 2000: 393–395; Shelby 2003: 170). What ideologies have in common is that through their illusions they cause people to fail to see that they are implicated in social relations of oppression (Shelby 2003: 176).

Take, for example, the belief that the 'talented' could not be induced to work hard without receiving an unequally large financial reward. The claim that this belief is ideological is not (necessarily) to say that the belief is empirically false, but rather concerns the holder's reasons for asserting this belief. It may be that the holder of this belief is someone whose abilities are rewarded in the labour market already at above average. It may be that the belief is true only under a contingent set of social and economic arrangements, but the holder is unable to think beyond this set. It may be that the holder believes that her below average share of earnings if justified by her 'lack of talent', when in fact it exists for other reasons, and so on. In any of these events it is not necessary to show, empirically, that the claim is false, but rather to question the motivation for believing something to be the case.[6]

On this understanding of illusory belief one epistemological problem is avoided, it is not necessary to pass judgement on beliefs per se as true or untrue. There is, however, the potential problem that this form of argument merely pushes back the epistemological problem one stage. We are not now (necessarily) arguing for the falsity of the belief, but we are seeking to make a judgement about the reasons for holding such a belief, and these have to be identifiable independently of the view of the belief holder. Thus there still appears to exist, potentially, a demand for an 'objective' perspective that allows the ideology analyst to decree that an agent holds a belief for noncognitive reasons. Does this still demand an epistemologically realist position?

For Rosen, the realist/anti-realist debate is not what is at issue here. The question is one of whether we are able to distinguish between propositions, and anti-realists do not deny that this is possible, they deny rather that there are particular sorts of reasons that can be successfully alluded to in order to justify a preference for one proposition over another. Once that set of 'realist' reasons have been excluded, there are still a range of justifications for the preference of one proposition over another that can be called upon, and that, for Rosen, is enough for the theory of ideology to be able to make a plausible claim that someone holds a belief for a noncognitive reason. We make judgements about whether certain beliefs are true of false, or held for particular reasons, and we are then under an obligation to justify that judgement (see Rosen 2000: 398).

The ultimate problem with this way of thinking about ideology, for Rosen, lies in its causal account of false consciousness, which contains an implicit and unargued-for functionalism. 'It is simply not clear that societies *do*, as a rule, produce the consciousness required for their preservation' (Rosen 2000: 399), and there is no good evidence for believing that 'consciousness is systematically determined by society in such a way as to correspond to society's need for self-determination' (Rosen 2000: 400). He goes on to suggest that a functionalist assumption of this sort exists in the work of Althusser, Habermas and Foucault. The Marxist tradition of ideology theory has no grounding explanation, of the sort that neo-Darwinists have for functional changes in species-genotypes, in order to justify a functionalist account.

Is it possible to retain the restrictive conception whilst moving away from a functionalist causal account of ideology? It is certainly possible to focus on the apparent social *effects* of certain types of belief, without claiming to identify any causal mechanisms that brings these beliefs into existence (at the obvious risk, however, of making the restrictions of the restrictive conception appear increasingly arbitrary). J.B. Thompson, for example, focuses on beliefs that have the effect of causing or entrenching forms of social domination – systematically asymmetric relationships of power. This, as Balkin notes in relation to Thompson, is not a functional explanation because the focus is on the effect of ideology (serving domination) without making the further claim that these beliefs come about *because* they serve this purpose. The causal mechanism is left unspecified, thus it could be just as likely that oppositional beliefs will come into existence. The reason that these latter would not be ideological would simply be that they do not reinforce dominant power relations.

As seen, for Balkin himself Thompson's account is underinclusive, as dominated groups may commit unjust acts against each other without furthering systematic asymmetries of power, and the concept of 'ideology' should stretch to cover these as well. If this reconception is to be more than merely stipulative, clearly Balkin needs to offer a justification as to why this is the case. The claim that Thompson's conception is 'too simplistic to describe a large number of ideological phenomena' would indeed be merely stipulative. The more pertinent justification comes when Balkin accepts that Thompson is free to delimit the concept as he sees fit, but that 'the danger is that a large portion of what most people would consider ideological phenomena will be missed' (Balkin 1998: 113). Of course Thompson is equally free to suggest that most people would simply be wrong, in that case. For Balkin however, Thompson's conception's 'limitation may have significant ideological effects on the analyst's own thought about ideology and social conditions' (1998: 113). Thompson's view is seen as ossifying a Marxist model of society, in which there are two classes and an ideology that justifies the subordination of one class by the other, but this model of dominated and dominator threatens to become ideological itself in that it obscures the complexity of social issues (Balkin 1998: 116). Furthermore the very concept of domination employed to distinguish the ideological from the non-ideological is itself an object of ideological disputation (Balkin 1998: 118).

Whilst this may be true, it does nothing to demonstrate why Balkin's version of ideology is preferable, as any notion of justice that he chooses to employ in order to differentiate the ideological from the non-ideological will of course be no less subject to ideological dispute. A view of ideology as injustice is no less likely to confer 'ideological effects' upon the thinking of the analyst than a concept of ideology of domination is. It thus has to be the part of Balkin's argument that commences from problems requiring explanation wherein lies some promise of justifiably extending the scope of ideological inquiry. His point here is that some groups, who appear 'dominated' on any measure of income, wealth, and life chances can hold beliefs that lead to their behaving unjustly towards other groups in society, who may or may not also be dominated groups. His main examples are anti-Semitism and anti-Korean prejudice in America's black community. This argument at least takes Balkin's conception beyond the stipulative, it calls for an inquiry into why groups who may not do well out of the existing politico-economic relations hold beliefs which turn them against each other rather than against the existing political system.

The Lacanian understanding of ideology is that it 'can, and should be retained as a potentially fruitful political category with considerable analytical and critical value' (Glynos 2001: 191). However, at least vis-à-vis the Marxist tradition this requires a fundamental reshaping of the notion of 'ideological misrecognition', which, rather than referring to illusion or unwitting complicity in oppressive social structures, revolves around the apparent elimination of contingency. Ideology seeks the complete closure and apparent mastery of the social world; ideologies offer us a picture of the world complete. Thus, on this view, it is 'rendering contingency *visible*, therefore, [that] grounds the process of ideological critique' (Glynos 2001: 191). Revealing the 'Real', as constitutive lack, becomes the task of the critic of ideology on this view.

Although this Lacan-inspired conception sees ideology is inherently related to a form of distortion, and is thus 'restricted' in my sense, it also sees ideology as an ineliminable aspect of social communication, and thus contains elements of both the restrictive and inclusive accounts. This combination of both distortion and permanence is most clearly articulated by Laclau, for whom the very idea of 'objective meaning' is itself a form of misrepresentation. The ideological effect consists in the belief that a particular social arrangement can bring about the self-transparency of society (as, for example, communism was expected to). This form of distortion is however 'constitutive' of our discursive practices, and thus the thought of an 'end of ideology' is an impossible dream (Laclau 1996).

Justifications for the Restrictive Conception

Some of the justifications for the various versions of the restrictive conception have been touched upon, but it is worth giving these underlying reasons explicit treatment, as the case for thinking restrictively about ideology rests with them. These justifications generally consist in accounts of social phenomena that are, *prime facie*, puzzling, and which should, it is argued, fall within the purview of a theory of ideology. Inevitably the claim that 'this is something that a theorist of ideology should be interested in' draws on the history of the use of the concept, even if it seeks to extend it in new ways. These are claims of plausibility, rather than attempts at 'objective' judgements about the rights and wrongs of the use of the concept.

For Rosen, there is a genuine puzzle as to why people *appear* to accede to their own oppression – 'those who are maltreated – oppressed, exploited, even enslaved – do not always reject that treatment.' This is what requires explanation, and although, in that explanation, the 'theory of ideology [in its Marxisant forms] is fundamentally unsatisfactory' it is nonetheless an 'ineliminably critical concept' (Rosen 2000: 393). The functionalist shortcomings of Marxist ideology theory do nothing to alter the fact that there remains a puzzle regarding people's apparent cooperation in their own servitude that requires an explanation.

Shelby also believes that the concept should be retained for a theory that seeks to explain why people hold beliefs that contribute to their own oppression, in this case, as with Rosen, beliefs held on noncognitive grounds that have this effect. He holds out hope, where Rosen does not, that a theory of ideology can be equal to this task. The epistemological requirements of a theory of ideology are 'modest'. The theory does not require, pace the argument rehearsed by Žižek, that the theorist occupy some Archimedean point outside of social space in order to offer an 'objective' critique of ideological thinking, but rather a 'rejection of global relativism and subjectivism about knowledge claims' (Shelby 2003: 168). Ideology critique must be able, as Gramsci held, to take us beyond common sense, and there is nothing unusual in seeking deeper explanations of social phenomena than those provided by first appearances. The question is the extent to which such explanations can be justified. Balkin concurs with this view, there is nothing to ideology critique that involves it standing 'above other forms of knowledge creation or acquisition', if anything, it is marked out by its 'utter ordinariness' as a field of social inquiry (Balkin 1998: 134). For Balkin as we have seen, the restrictive conception helps us to understand why people hold beliefs that lead to 'oppression or injustice.' Thompson also holds that we need to explain why people hold beliefs that appear to entail their voluntary servitude, but that we do not have to assume that these beliefs are in any way 'illusory' (see next section). Thus with Thompson we have a restrictive conception that does away with the main epistemological problematic, whether its aspirations be modest or not, and which concentrates instead on the effects that certain beliefs have with regard to those who hold them.

The Argument against Inclusive Conceptions

Inevitably, arguments from those who support a restrictive conception of ideology against more inclusive conceptions will tend to mirror the arguments for the inclusive conception. Nonetheless it is worth asking why defenders of restrictive conceptions do not see more inclusive conceptions as *encompassing* their own concerns rather than working against them. The very notion, from Seliger, of an 'inclusive' conception seems to suggest a version of 'ideology' that incorporates more restrictive conceptions whilst also moving beyond them.

There are three arguments here: one is that defenders of inclusive conceptions are mistaken in their belief that restrictive conceptions are misguided, therefore there is no need to move 'from' a restrictive conception 'to' an inclusive one. A second would be to suggest that this language of restrictive and inclusive conceptions is misleading. The 'neutral' (to use another term favoured by some) conception, far from being more inclusive, is merely restrictive in different ways, and rather than moving beyond the restrictive conception, neutral conceptions take our attention away form the important social phenomena that called for a critical conception of ideology in the first place. The third argument concerns the relationship between the ideology analyst and the world that she studies. On this view ideology critique is far from being a neutral academic activity, it is, and should be, a *intervention* into the political realm intended to liberate people from beliefs that cause damage to themselves. This activity becomes impossible on the inclusive account of ideology.

To give brief examples of each of these arguments, in Thompson's discussion of Seliger, he notes that Seliger takes issue with a particular version of the Marx and Engels' thesis on ideology, that which opposes ideology to truth. This however, is not the only (and for Thompson certainly not the most important) use of ideology in Marx and Engels' work. Amongst the various conceptions of ideology Thompson finds at work in Marx and Engels, Thompson focuses on what he calls the 'latent' conception of the link between ideology and domination. This conception is not dependent upon revelation of epistemological falsehood and so is not vulnerable to Seliger's critique of that understanding. Whatever the merits or demerits of the latent conception, Seliger does nothing to undermine its validity as an appropriately restricted conception.

The second argument is, largely, the converse of the argument for restrictive conceptions – given that they will focus our attention on particular social problems, more general conception will distract our attention from these. The danger then is that we will overlook the 'cluster of problems' that Thompson seeks to call to our attention. Similarly, Balkin argues that 'neutral' conceptions, whilst appearing to embody 'detached objectivity' or the 'fairness and openness of liberal enquiry' cannot in fact sustain any claim to neutrality for long, as 'perfectly' neutral conceptions would 'make it impossible for the analyst to explain how particular beliefs lead to oppression or injustice' (1998: 124). Thus as with Thompson attention is distracted in the neutral conception from the important problems that it should address, but not simply because they are overlooked, but rather because this approach makes the question *impossible to ask*, as 'oppression and injustice are themselves contested terms between competing ideologies' (1998: 124).

As an example of the third stand of argument, Tommie Shelby suggests that 'we' should oppose ideologies not only because they peddle illusions but also because of the oppressive social consequences of their widespread acceptance. Ideology critique has to have '*some* potential to contribute to the subversion of structures of hegemonic power', otherwise it is hard to see why progressives should bother engaging with it (Shelby 2003: 175). Those seeking to retain and employ the critical conception see themselves within a broader tradition of critical theory, and the 'unmasking' moment of ideology critique as inherently part of the political struggle against oppression or injustice (see also Talshir 2005).

Conceptual Morphology as an Inclusive Conception

Having considered these general arguments with regard to rival conceptions of ideology, I want to consider how an important recent development in ideology theory, the conceptual morphology associated with Michael Freeden, fares when tested against some of these considerations. What sort of conception of ideology is it, and what are its strengths and weaknesses when considered against the background of the contemporary literature in ideology theory?

The contrasts between different conceptions of ideology are mapped out in various ways in the literature, usually through a dichotomised relation between the preferred and the rejected conceptions. Thus Seliger favoured his 'inclusive' conception over the 'restrictive' one; Thompson divides between 'descriptive' and 'evaluative' and also between 'neutral' and 'critical'; his preferred conception being both evaluative and critical. Balkin (1998) employs a threefold division between 'pejorative' (Marxisant), 'neutral', and his own preferred 'ambivalent' conception for which he retains the notion of 'critical'. On this understanding 'critical' is not used in the sense of 'capable of unmasking distortions and oppression', but rather in being reflexive and self-aware. Shelby (2003) distinguishes 'evaluative' and 'non-evaluative' conceptions, of which the former (including his own) are also inherently 'critical'. For Rosen ideology is an 'inherently critical' concept and 'looser' definitions are 'useless' in terms of explanatory social science (Rosen 2000: 395).

There is no doubt that conceptual morphology is both an 'inclusive' and 'neutral' conception of ideology on the above understandings. These terms are of course relative, and it is not the case that 'everything is ideological' on the morphological view, much depends upon context. Nonetheless, it does not seek to restrict ideology either to cases of illusory belief nor to those beliefs that cause or sustain relations of injustice, exploitation or domination. This would appear also to render it 'non-evaluative' as well, in that it does not engage in the task of uncovering these falsehoods and relations of domination, and thus the ideology analyst engaged in a conceptual-morphological study is not seeking to make a liberating political intervention, but is rather engaged in a scholarly activity which has the intention of revealing the ideological structure of political thinking. (So much for intentions, in terms of effects little can be said, as much depends upon the consumption of the activity of analysis as well as the production. It may be that the very process of mapping a system of belief conceptually undermines or enhances its normative appeal).

Conceptual morphology is a complex approach to the study of ideology and difficult to summarize succinctly. However, the activity the analyst using this approach is engaged in is that of seeking out the conceptual structures that are present in political thinking, in order to clarify the nature of (and to some extent classify, although this is problematic) political thought. This in turn is fleshed out by analysing not merely where certain concepts are placed within an ideological framework, but also, crucially, examining how these concepts are 'decontested' (given definite content) within particular ideological traditions. Such an analyst is as engaged with popular forms of political thought as manifested in pamphlets, party manifestoes and newspapers as he is with sophisticated works of political philosophy. The analyst seeks continuities and differences, both diachronically and synchronically. Ideological forms are not presupposed but emerge through careful empirical analysis of thought instantiations. Self-descriptions (as liberal, conservative etc.) are taken seriously but set against historical traditions of such self-definition to test for similarity and difference. From the range of political concepts in use, certain patterns of persistence emerge that allow us to talk of different 'families' of political thought, as core concepts appear relatively stable and persistent through time. Thus we can identify schools of liberal, socialist and conservative thought for example, although the conceptual boundaries are always fluid and any individual thinker is likely to bear resemblances to more than one family. Conceptual morphology is intended to aid our understanding of political thought by providing us with a mental map through the conceptual pathways that can be and are taken, allowing us to identify certain forms of thought as likely members of one family rather than another.

The charges that might be levelled against this conception of ideology, given the account of the literature that we have examined, is that it

(1) distracts us from important social problems that an adequate theory of ideology should be seeking to explain; and

132   *Ideology Seriously*

(2) prevents the ideology analyst from undertaking her responsibility to make a liberating intervention by unmasking hidden forms of oppression. Ideology analysis has little point absent this function.

Is there any reason, inherent to conceptual morphology, to expect that the problems referred to by defenders of the critical conception of ideology to appear on its radar screen? And if they do not, is that something that should be of concern to putative students of ideology? These problems were (i) that people can hold illusory beliefs, or hold some belief in a condition of false consciousness, and/or (ii) that with or without (i), people can hold beliefs that, unwittingly, serve to place them under or sustain oppressive or unjust socio-economic relations. On none of the approaches considered here was (i) considered a sufficient condition for ideology, but either (i) and (ii) together, or (ii) alone, were. Balkin's previously cited complaint about 'neutral' conceptions generally will, *inter alia*, apply to conceptual morphology, namely that it serves to: 'make it impossible for the analyst to explain how particular beliefs lead to oppression or injustice, for oppression and injustice are themselves contested terms between competing ideologies' (Balkin 1998: 124).

We need to distinguish between intent and outcome here, although the two are of course connected. Given the agenda laid out above, it does not seem to be part of the intent of the analyst using conceptual morphology to reveal injustice and oppression, but (i) is this because, as Thompson suggests, inclusive conceptions direct our attention elsewhere, and if so, should this be a concern? And (ii) does it entail the outcome that the conceptual morphologist *could not*, sensibly, given her presuppositions and starting point, seek out instances of oppression and injustice even if she wanted to, which appears to be Balkin's suggestion? Or could conceptual morphology claim to be a 'genuinely' inclusive conception of ideology in that it can encompass the concerns of Thompson and Balkin but go beyond them as well?

With reference to the first suggestion it has to be said that conceptual morphology leads us to examine the structure of *beliefs* about such matters as justice, oppression and domination, rather than to make evaluative judgements about them. The conceptual morphologist is interested in how political concepts have been and are used rather than in making evaluative judgements about these beliefs vis-à-vis a model of what oppressive and unoppressive social relationships might consist in. It has to be true that the intellectual agenda of conceptual morphology does not point people towards the social phenomena that Rosen, Thompson and Balkin think they identify. The latter question really comes down to whether conceptual morphology leaves any 'space' for normative commitment on the part of its practitioner. I think the answer to the latter question is also 'no', and this is so because of the disjuncture between the objectives and methods of conceptual morphology and critical approaches to ideology.

Consider the following extract on American neo-conservatism from Freeden's *magnum opus* on conceptual morphology, *Ideology and Political Theory*:

The importance of an attachment to a traditional liberal past – by now concealing a conservative view of organic change which recognised the 'conservative predispositions of the people' – was bonded by Kristol to a resistance to the gnostic antinomianism of the 'French-Continental Enlightenment'. Adjacent concepts were drafted in to secure the new intellectual structure: a Friedmanite market economy as an engine of social growth, the Hayekian notion of a spontaneous social order, and a Straussian search for pre-capitalist values as a moral anchor, establishing the priority of politics over economics ... Although in his earlier writings Kristol seemed to go out of his way to deny a natural conservative order, he also extolled the attractions of subscribing to a 'prevailing social philosophy' and reiterated the allure of authority and leadership. Those principles are regularly employed by conservatives to lend justification to, and to seek a legitimated stability in, a non-volitional social order, one not based on wills expressed in national participatory democracy. In other works Kristol belied his conservatism by frequently slipping into the language of conservative discourse. (Freeden 1996: 407)

It is worth quoting this at length, both to get a sense of the morphological approach in action and because it is an apposite passage. It is the latter for two reasons, firstly, the discourse of conservatism and neo-conservatism is one that is likely to be taken to be pre-eminently 'ideological' on the critical approach. Secondly, its references to concealment and belied beliefs suggest that there is some element of masking going on here, so if conceptual morphology does have the capacity to incorporate the critical agenda, we might hope to find some evidence of that in this passage.

The passage offers an interpretation of Irving Kristol's brand of American neo-conservatism which supports Freeden's contention that a central element of conservatism is the positing of an extra-human, 'non-volitional' social order. The element of concealment appears when an attachment to an apparently 'liberal' past is used as a vehicle for a conservative perspective on social change. An organic view of social development has become attached to a 'liberal' version of history. In the second case, Kristol 'belies' his conservative beliefs in his 'frequent' slippages into conservative discourse, despite having explicitly, in earlier works, denied the notion of a 'natural' order of the sort conservatives tend to endorse.

There are a number of elements to note in this use of the language of concealed beliefs. Firstly, there in nothing to suggest that Kristol is engaged in a process of deliberate deceit here for strategic reasons. He is not playing the part of conservative wolf wrapped in a woollen fleece of liberalism. Rather, conceptual elements of conservatism and liberalism come together in his thought. Although these may remain in some tension with each other, there is nothing unusual in this cross-pollination between different ideological families, and the potential tension may well not be sufficiently severe to render the thought edifice unstable. There is concealment here, but not deceit.

The second point is more important in our context, in that this concealment is not one that can be exposed in order to reveal a 'true' relationship of oppression or domination, nor is any epistemological illusion about the true nature of the world shattered by the revelation of concealment. There is a 'truth' revealed here, but it is not that one. The truth for the morphological analyst lies in digging beneath the surface of a discourse and revealing the 'true' ideational architecture that underpins it. This is the interpretative project, the interpretation of Kristol as a member of the family of conservatives, rather than a liberal, is to be preferred because, despite some superficial similarities with liberal discourse, there are core conservative decontestations at work in Kristol's work. This is revealed when the apparent attachment to a 'traditional liberal past' is shown to entail a large conservative assumption. This tells us something important about the relationship between American neo-conservatism of the sort Kristol claims to represent, and liberalism on the one hand and traditional forms of conservatism on the other. The main task of conceptual morphology is not, however, the pigeon-holing of thinkers into ideological traditions, but rather to offer an insightful understanding of their political thought.

The 'truth' that is revealed, then, in this process of uncovering concealed assumptions, is a truth about the nature and conceptual architecture of political thought within certain traditions or in respect of particular thinkers, it is not a wider truth claim regarding the state of the world or uncovering masks of empirical instances of oppression, domination, or injustice. Indeed as Balkin suggests, discourses about oppression or injustice become part of the object of analysis for the conceptual morphologist. Morphological analysis can, nonetheless, be viewed as a 'critical' enterprise in the sense that it seeks to dig beneath the surface manifestations of political thought in order to reveal the underlying conceptual structure.

Does this restriction prevent, to turn to our second question, the analyst using this method from making an intervention into political life through the process of uncovering discourses that mask relations of domination? This is something about inclusive conceptions that frustrates Shelby, as we have seen (Shelby 2003: 175). I believe it has to follow from the answer to the first question that the answer to this question is also negative. Strictly qua conceptual morphologist, it has to be true that the analyst is not in a position to make the sort of intervention that critical theory is interested in. Conceptual morphology just is not that kind of exercise, and in order to make that kind of intervention the analyst must, as it were, remove his morphological spectacles and argue in different terms. Thompson's claim has to be true, the way in which we conceptualise ideology directly affects the kind of questions we ask of the social and political world. If we believe that what is important is the unmasking of meaning in the service of domination, then conceptual morphology does not fit the bill, it does not, and is not designed to, supply the traction required for normative criticism.

The implication of this does not follow, however, if we take the implication to be Rosen's claim that inclusive conceptions of ideology such as that used in conceptual morphology are obviously 'useless' for explanatory social science. In the field of explanatory social science this in part is dependent upon the thorny question of the perceived relationship between ideas and action. For those of us who believe that ideas matter, and indeed that the dichotomy between action and ideas needs to be questioned (for example in the way that conceptions of interests are themselves formed though filtered perceptions of how institutions operate), then a plausible interpretation, backed with empirical detail, of how politicians framed their activities in terms of their beliefs may well have power in social science explanation; there is, at the very least, certainly not anything obvious about the alleged 'uselessness' of this approach.

Two Concepts? Or One Concept, Many Conceptions?

The first lesson to draw from this survey is the truth of the claim, made by both Thompson and Balkin, that the way in which we structure our analytical tool-kit will at least partially determine the questions that we can ask about social phenomena. The tools available to the analyst using conceptual morphology enable him to offer an interpretation of the conceptual architecture of political thought, to map out priorities and relationships, and determine different decontestations of political concepts. It does not, however, lend itself to the task of uncovering hidden relationships of domination, nor epistemological falsehoods. One important reason for this is that the crucial assumption of the essential contestability of concepts in conceptual morphology militates against any notion of 'true' political beliefs, whether or not that notion of truth rests on epistemological realism or not.

To suggest, however, that an analytical tool-kit cannot perform a task for which it was not designed does not in and of itself constitute a criticism, merely an observation. The criticism would only follow if either it was inadequate for the task for which it *was* designed (which nothing herein gives us reason to suppose), or if that task itself was somehow misguided. It is the latter thought that is directed by supporters of restrictive conceptions of ideology towards those who hold to more inclusive conceptions. In this regard one merely has to hold that conceptual maps of political thought are useful in orientating our understanding, and providing insight into the nature of political thinking, which is itself a political phenomenon, to reject the accusation of inadequacy. As long as conceptual morphology is capable of doing the job it is designed for, it has utility to the student of politics.

The error embodied in the accusation is the supposition that 'ideology' must always and everywhere involve the unmasking of illusion and/or domination. There is no reason to suppose that such an abstract noun must be restricted in this way. If our criteria for usage is usefulness in social inquiry, 'inclusive' ascriptions have their place. However, this is not to say that the task of ideology critique as set forth by Thompson et al is unimportant, or that inclusive conceptions are somehow adequate to this particular task. The notion of an 'inclusive conception' of ideology is misleading if it appears to suggest that such conceptions can perform the role of the critical conception and more besides. Inclusive conceptions such as conceptual morphology offer insufficient traction for this kind of critical endeavour, so if we believe this form of social inquiry is important, we just do require a contrasting conception of ideology (if we use a conception of ideology at all here) in order to undertake this task. We require a different analytical tool-kit, one of the sort offered to us by Thompson or Balkin.

Does this entail that what we have here are, ultimately, not merely differing conceptions of a single concept but, rather, two different concepts going under the same name? Are we dealing with different classes of object here, or different interpretations of the same class of objects? How could we tell? We need to ask what the important features of the concept(ion)s of ideology are, and the extent to which these are shared or unique to each. This will offer us some sense of how to think about the relationship between these two different projects. Balkin's four criteria of ideology are useful here, in that they give us a framework for thinking about what we are doing when we engage in ideology analysis. Each of these features is capable of being instantiated in radically different ways. What follows is inevitably aggregating across internal complexities and thus schematic.

Balkin's four features are: (1) The object of study; (2) The mode of explanation; (3) the interpretative stance; (4) The problem of self-reference.

On (1) the common elements is that both approaches take as their object political thought, broadly defined, and, crucially, the struggle and conflict over the meaning of concepts and speech acts. As Eagleton (1991: 9) notes, 'have you put the cat out yet?' is not an intrinsically ideological statement. It can be one, however, if there is also an underlying, unspoken content such as: 'have you put the cat out yet; or are you being your usual shiftless proletarian self and not bothered?' It would then be a statement constituting a part of the process of class domination that Thompson is interested in. All forms of communication are potential grist to the mill for this form of ideology study.

That all forms of communication are possible subjects of scrutiny is also true for the conceptual morphologist. Any text has the possibility to reveal the underlying conceptual architecture of the political thought that it expresses, and the analysis is by no means confined to 'scholarly' political publications. On (1) then, there appears to be common ground between the two approaches.

On (2) we are concerned with what ideology is defined in terms of – for example its causes, its social function or social effects, its content or some combination of these. Here the two approaches seem to clearly diverge. For the critical approach, ideology is studied according to its causes and/or its effects and/or its content. Specifically the critical analyst is interested in what causes people to hold illusory ideas or ideas for noncognitive reasons or ideas that contribute to their own servitude. The effects studied may be similar (e.g. contributing to one's own subjection) but eschew the notion of explaining causation. The content will be of interest in terms of assessing the precise ideas that apparently carry out these social functions, but the interest in content is secondary – we are only interested in the content of these ideas because they have these particular effects.

For conceptual morphology, the focus is on content, but more directly. The interest of the analyst here is in mapping out that content and providing an account of the conceptual architecture of a system of beliefs. The focus is not on what causes these beliefs to be the ones subscribed to, nor directly on the effects these beliefs have in the social world, although the conceptual analysis may provide raw material for such a study.

On (3) there are clear differences which have been covered in the main text of this paper. On the critical, pejorative view ideology is something to be destroyed. It contributes to forms of oppression, injustice or domination, whether or not it also involves a process of cognitive misrecognition, and is thus a social bad. Its suppression will usher in a future in which social relations are grasped more clearly. For the analyst employing conceptual morphology the expectation is that ideology is with us always, and to envisage a world without ideology is to envisage a world without political thought. The Lacanian conception of ideology is interesting here in that it straddles both views. It does see ideology as a form of distortion, but this distortion is both constitutive of social communication and ineliminable, and the belief that it could be eradicated is itself an example of ideology.

For (4) we face the potential problem that the analysis of ideology may itself be an ideological manoeuvre. This is a potential problem on both approaches but the problem operates in a different way in each. We have already seen the argument rehearsed by Žižek, in which the critical interpretation is seen to require a position somehow outside of social space in order to posit a 'true' social reality in contradistinction to its ideological representation. The 'view from nowhere' here is a view of the social world somehow uncluttered by the mediations of language. It is also quite feasible to complain that conceptual morphology presupposes some neutral ground that it is impossible to occupy. This would however not refer to the prospect of an uncluttered view of social reality, but rather to the view that it is possible to characterise systems of political thought without occupying one of those positions, at least when one is acting as an analyst rather than as a citizen. That is to say the interpretation of socialist political thought, for example, given to us through conceptual morphology, is not taken to be 'socialism from a liberal perspective', but rather 'socialism from an analytical perspective'. This understanding might be challenged if, for example, conceptual morphology is believed to embody some fundamental liberal philosophical beliefs about, say, the manner in which individuals or groups engage with and come to hold their political beliefs.[7] Freeden acknowledges that the morphological approach is underpinned by liberal epistemology, although not liberal ideology.[8] It remains an open question (one which I do not have the space to deal with here) whether this distinction between liberal epistemology and liberal politics can be sustained to the extent sufficient for conceptual morphology to insulate itself from 'ideological' liberal demands.

What this brief analysis demonstrates, I believe, is that the disparities between the critical approach to, and the inclusive conception of, ideology are so great that it may be more fruitful to consider them as two separate concepts (rather than different conceptions of the same concept) and accept that they are engaged in radically different exercises. Here I make use of the concept/conception distinction as used by H.L.A Hart and John Rawls. On this view, even when people have different conceptions of justice, they nonetheless agree on the need for 'a characteristic set of principles for assigning basic rights and duties and ... the proper distribution of the benefits and burdens of social cooperation' (Rawls 1999: 5). They have, that is, a common understanding of what justice demands in the abstract, and they flesh out their understandings of how to fulfil these demands in different ways according to the conception of justice with which they operate. Between the critical and inclusive conceptions of ideology it is difficult to discern any such common ground, other than that they both concern themselves with political thought, which could hardly suffice alone. It is all too easy to be seduced by the common nomenclature into believing that, because both of these approaches concern themselves with the nature of 'ideology' they are both investigating the same phenomenon. A common heritage, however, does not result in a common contemporary project. Mannheim's turning of Marxism back on itself was a decisive moment in the bifurcation of the study of ideology along very different paths. The study of ideological illusion and the operation of meaning in the service of domination are so fundamentally different to the mapping of conceptual architecture that it is difficult, and perhaps misguided, to try to think of them in terms of a single project or theory. Even though they have the same broad referent in that they study political ideas, they diverge in terms of their mode of explanation, their interpretative stance, and the manifestation of their problem of self-reference. Whilst it is true that the critical project can always be recuperated back within the interpretative one, such that we can ask what it means for someone to believe they are 'unmasking' coded political language, it is also the case that the interpretative project can be captured by the critical one as well. This is the case when the non-evaluative approach to ideology is criticised for removing attention from important social phenomena; it is itself then seen as being guilty of a form of masking. Neither of these recuperative strategies demonstrates that we are dealing with a single concept here.

Michael Freeden is aware of this possible categorisation of ideology in terms of two distinct concepts, but is resistant to it. 'Surely the end of total and false systems was entirely separate from the semantic and cultural recapturing of diverse patterns of social meaning and communication across societies? This 'two concepts of ideology' view is to a large extent misleading' (Freeden 2001: 5–6). This is because; although there has been a 'veritable explosion in the usages of ideology', there is still, within the field of ideology theory, a common agenda of 'accounting for and assessing the political thinking that aims to direct – or simply directs – the public activities of a society' (Freeden 2001: 6). I think both of these claims are true, there has been such an explosion, and there is this common agenda. It still, however, can also be the case that firstly this diversity of usage is captured within two broad categories of evaluative and non-evaluative conceptions; and secondly that within this common agenda such is the disjunction in meaning between the two traditions in terms of *what it is* to 'account' and 'assess' that what we have on our hands is two radically different projects, and two concepts of ideology; i.e. two classes of objects that are mutually exclusive but also collectively exhaustive of the conceptions of ideology that are in common currency.

Conclusion

This essay has looked at the criticisms of, and defences available to, two broad approaches to ideology theory, the restrictive and the inclusive. It has then examined one inclusive approach, conceptual morphology, in detail as an important new development in ideology theory. I have argued that what this assessment shows is the truth of Thompson's claim about the relationship between the nature of the analyst's 'tool-kit' and the range of social phenomena that then come within her purview. This non-evaluative conception is not suitable for carrying out evaluative work, but given the purpose for which it was developed this should come as no surprise. The question then becomes one of assessing the validity of the evaluative and non-evaluative projects. The two projects are, however, so radically different that it appears to make little sense to attempt to criticise one in light of the terms of reference of the other. It may instead be more profitable to accept that there are two concepts of ideology at work here, each with radically different but worthwhile objectives. There may be a common project in the most general terms of analysis of political thought, but in terms of mode of explanation, interpretative stance and the problem of self reference, we are faced with divergent projects. Far from being 'misleading', this conclusion opens up the space for an appreciation of both the merits and problems entailed in both approaches and allows us to think about the nature of ideology, in both these manifestations, more clearly.

Notes

1. In, for example, news items. To take one case the BBC recently reported on the looming 'ideological battle' over the world's water; see ⟨http://news.bbc.co.uk/1/hi/sci/tech/2861095.stm⟩.
2. For example the social and political problems raised by Thompson, Shelby and Balkin, all of which are discussed below.
3. See for example the work of John B. Thompson.
4. One may, of course, believe that in order to qualify as ideological beliefs have to both be false and serve the interests of class domination, such that either becomes a necessary but not sufficient condition. The connection is not, however, logically necessary.
5. This is an example of where this terminology can be misleading. *All* conceptions of ideology are restrictive in some sense, even it that is merely a restriction of 'ideological' ideas to those that seek to have some sway over public policy outcomes.
6. The holder of such a belief is also likely to lack empirical grounds for it, and in some cases of moral certitude empirical grounds may not anyway be available.
7. As, to take a parallel example, Valerie Kerruish holds that contemporary jurisprudence is liberal ideology (Kerruish 1991; see also Goldsworthy 1993).
8. See Freeden 2005.

References

Balkin, J.M. (1998) *Cultural Software: a Theory of Ideology* (New Haven, CT: Yale University Press).
Bell, D. (2000) *The End of Ideology: On the Exhaustion of Political Ideas in the Fifties* (Cambridge, MA: Harvard University Press).

Eagleton, T. (1991) *Ideology: An Introduction* (London: Verso).
Freeden, M. (1996) *Ideologies and Political Theory: a Conceptual Approach* (Oxford: Oxford University Press).
Freeden, M. (2001) Political ideologies in substance and method: appraising a transformation, in: M. Freeden (Ed.), *Reassessing Political Ideologies: The Durability of Dissent* (London: Routledge).
Freeden, M. (2005)Confronting the chimera of a 'post-ideological' age. *CRISPP* 8(2), pp. 247–262 (this volume).
Goldsworthy, J. (1993) Is jurisprudence liberal ideology? *Oxford Journal of Legal Studies*, 13(4), pp. 548–570.
Glynos, J. (2001) The grip of ideology: a Lacanian approach to the theory of ideology. *Journal of Political Ideologies*, 6(2), pp. 191–214.
Kerruish, V. (1991) *Jurisprudence as Ideology* (London: Routledge).
Laclau, E. (1996) The death and resurrection of the theory of ideology. *Journal of Political Ideologies*, 1(3), pp. 201–220.
Leonardo, Z. (2003) Discourse and critique: outlines of a post-structural theory of ideology. *Journal of Education Policy*, 18(2), pp. 203–214.
Mannheim, K. (1936) *Ideology and Utopia: an Introduction to the Sociology of Knowledge* (London: Routledge & Kegan Paul).
Rabinow, P. (1984) *The Foucault Reader* (Harmondsworth: Penguin).
Rawls, J. (1999) *A Theory of Justice: Revised Edition* (Oxford: Oxford University Press).
Rosen, M. (1996) *On Voluntary Servitude: False Consciousness and the Theory of Ideology* (Cambridge: Polity Press).
Rosen, M. (2000) On voluntary servitude and the theory of ideology. *Constellations*, 7(4), pp. 393–407.
Seliger, M (1976) *Ideology and Politics* (London: Allen & Unwin).
Shelby, T. (2003) Ideology, racism, and critical social theory. *The Philosophical Forum*, 34(2), pp. 153–188.
Talshir, G. (2005) The intellectual as political actor? Four models of theory/praxis. *CRISPP*, 8(2), pp. 209–224 (this volume).
Thompson, J.B. (1984) *Studies in the Theory of Ideology* (Cambridge: Polity Press).
Thompson, J.B. (1990) *Ideology and Modern Culture: Critical Social Theory in the Era of Mass Communication* (Cambridge: Polity Press)
Žižek, S. (1994) *Mapping Ideology* (London: Verso).

Confronting the Chimera of a 'Post-ideological' Age

MICHAEL FREEDEN

Is there nowhere for students of ideology to escape, not even when on holiday? A paragraph in a recent flight magazine of Iberia Airlines begins with the following popular perception: 'At the dawn of the 21st century with ideologies in decline and a future that looks laden with pragmatism' (*Iberia Magazine*, October 2002). The end of ideology prophets are back on the streets or, in this case, in the skies, peddling their dichotomy between thinking and doing or, more accurately, between a stifling idealism and trial-and-error expediency. So where do ideologies stand at the beginning of the twenty-first century, and where does their investigation stand? In what sense is this *not* a post-ideological age, and why could we argue that post-ideological ages are an impossibility in exactly the same way that post-political ages would be? How can we bring home the point that ideologies are not visions of alternative worlds, be they alluring or terrifying, but conceptualizations of the political worlds we already inhabit, even when critical of those worlds? And how can we sufficiently emphasize that sentient and reasoning human beings always possess a conceptualization of the political world, at whatever level of sophistication? An unideological person is simply one who has sadly passed away.

The Persistence of 'Endism' as the Product of Misrecognition

The persistence of the 'end of ideology' thesis can no longer be dismissed as an oddity of the mid-twentieth century, or the later twentieth century – even though it is an oddity. There is something far more fundamental lurking behind it, something epistemological, something psychological. What makes people afraid of ideologies? Is it the worry that ideologies will infringe their autonomy, that ideologies aren't transparent, that ideologies manipulate them so that they – and in particular others – do things that they would not have done if they were moral rational entities, whatever that may be? Is it a dread of the herd when in the grip of a powerful emotional vision or hallucination? Is it the frightening closure of time and space that so many ideologies impose on politics that puts paid to our illusions of an open world in which we, as individuals and as societies, can achieve anything we want if we put our minds to it? Or, conversely, the embarrassment of conceding that we are prey to intellectual, cultural and religious fashions that we have unthinkingly adopted from those who socialize us? Or is it simply the fear of ideas: the resentment of those who cannot easily abstract from reality and maintain distance between themselves and events, against those who can? The anxiety about mind control, and the assumption that theory always fails to engage with praxis?

That said, it seems obvious enough that we are facing an ideological turn, that something is happening to the ideologies that permeate our political habitats, and that a corresponding turn in the scholarly study of ideologies is therefore necessary. But I want to contend that this is only one way of approaching the problem. It may well be that the reverse holds, that we are experiencing a turn in *analyzing* ideologies that can open our eyes to what ideologies are, where we find them, and how to identify them. Throughout most of the twentieth century, we have ingested ideologies as fairly fixed and unambiguous traditions. They have come to us nicely packaged, bearing labels such as conservatism, socialism or nationalism. Political philosophers have exacerbated this sharply defined view by modelling them as ideal types and co-opting them for philosophical purposes – that has, for instance, been the fate of liberalism in the late twentieth century, contrasted artificially and incorrectly with constructs such as communitarianism, and insultingly disempowered through pretences that it is neutral; indeed, neutered by the attempted removal of its emotional force and its value-preferences. In addition, the Marxist tradition of analyzing ideology has left a remarkable – and to some extent, pernicious – hold on scholarly imaginations. In its monolithic and cardboard cut-out perception of ideologies as dissimulative it has incorporated the view that ideologies are good for one thing only – ideology-critique that will burst the balloon of hot air that has distorted our capacity to see the social world clearly. In the early stages of that tradition, to discover or uncover an ideology was the necessary step towards annihilating it, rather than exploring it. Even though later Marxist scholars came to terms with the permanence of ideology, they found it difficult to abandon their lack of interest in its internal variations. And the experience the twentieth century had with totalitarian ideologies of the right and the left has further presented ideologies as all-or-nothing systems expanding into all available personal space, while suppressing the values and practices that proper political systems should produce.

Yet the more we move away in time from the early and mid-twentieth century, the more Fascism, Nazism, and Stalinist communism appear as ideological aberrations, as exceptions to the norm concerning what ideologies are. Indeed, even their reputation for being extreme and ostensibly closed and dogmatic does not always pass muster when those ideologies are subjected to more minute scrutiny, for they too evinced dissent, movement and variations. Nevertheless, it is quite common practice to refer to 'ideologized politics', as if non-ideological politics was either the existing norm or a far more desirable state of affairs. But perhaps the most striking fact about the way we handle contemporary ideologies is that so few academics are engaged in developing new methodologies aimed at responding to the changes that ideologies have been undergoing. There is much research into the measurement of attitudes and opinions. There is a well-established line of argument that singles out political parties or even political movements as the sole loci of ideological activity. There is also a buoyant industry among poststructuralists and post-Marxists who continue in the grand tradition of unmasking the illusions that ideologies foster and in spelling out the modes through which they construct our comprehensions of the world. And there is a broader area of discourse and cultural studies alert to problems of interpretation and to the consumption of language, but only loosely focused on political thought and expression. All this is well and good, but it is by no means all of the story and perhaps not the main story. For, given that ideologies are undergoing considerable modification and adopt mutating forms, how do we identify those changes? What questions must we ask in order to elicit useful information? What are we failing to identify? How can we best relate the study of ideologies to the study of politics more generally?

To begin with, we need to brush aside two competing views. The one is that ideologies have – for the second time, oddly enough, within 50 years – ceased to be. The other is that one ideology, liberalism, has come to prevail over all others. The first, millenarian, view suffers from a weakness in the conceptualization of ideologies that makes all ideologies, except for doctrinaire and highly coherent ones, invisible. That of course helpfully supports the aspirations of most ideologies to attain 'natural' status, and thus plays into their hands. Committed ideologues should heartily welcome the 'end of ideology' myth – it makes their work so much easier by perpetuating an illusion under which they can continue to proselytize.

The second view suffers from a teleological perspective and from a belief in end states displayed more typically through utopias, not ideologies. If liberalism is indeed victorious, the undisputed champion of the world, then it is that rarest of things, an achieved utopia. There are two methods through which one may claim that utopias are achievable. One of them is indeed to be found *within* the broad family of liberalisms, but it is the province of philosophical liberalism alone. Philosophical liberals wholeheartedly believe in a rational convergence of members of a society on an agreed ethical point, which they usually consider to be coterminous with liberalism – a liberalism in which freedom, justice and fairness predominate. That convergence is a result either of deliberation or of the rational appeal to unencumbered intuitions, in which ground rules are fixed for once and for all and removed from the political agenda.

The other genre of 'practical' utopianism, Marxism, posits a contingent universalism, the consequence of the spread of a point of view, perhaps even a social truth, through space, vanquishing ideological resistance en route, until it finally conquers the globe. The apparent victory of liberalism at the end of the twentieth century has, if at all, to belong to this second category of universalism through struggle (not through 'snap your fingers' logical necessity), for the first category does not even offer a glimmer of hope for political practitioners, describing itself as occupying a neutral political ground. A neutral political ground is a contradiction in terms. It is an area outside politics, inasmuch as politics is concerned with power, persuasion, the management of diversity, the mobilization of support, and with attempts to implement particular political visions. To claim to be neutral towards any or all of these is an abstract form of the denial of social life. That type of utopianism is located outside space and time. As a thought-experiment it may intrigue philosophers or literary craftsmen and women. But the illusion it promotes has nothing to do with the world of politics.

The fact is that, just as in the 1950s and 1960s, new ideological positions have emerged exactly where their impossibility has been announced, thus nullifying the case for the second kind of utopianism. The end of the Soviet Empire saw the resurrection of political ideologies that came out of a deep freeze, especially forms of nationalism of the centre and of the right, fortified – as this volume attests – by admixtures of populism. And a few years later, the continued presence of political Islam was noticed, not because it had not already existed for quite a while, but because it began to intrude on the space of that *soi-disant* dominant liberalism in the West, and because the revived interest in religion caused individuals to ask new questions about the relationship between religion and politics. The presence of extra-Western ideologies is still in an embryonic state of study, as is the two-way street of mutual influence between West and non-West – take for example the far-Asian conjunctions of technological globalism and time-honoured localism.

The issue, however, is not simply that of the multiplication of new ideologies. The problem principally relates to ideological misrecognition, misrecognition fostered by inadequate theorizing and buttressed by the predominance of myths concerning the nature of political beliefs and what they contain. Thus, if our theories of ideology were largely modelled on our experiences of totalitarianism, it is unsurprising that the passing of totalitarianism was equated with the passing of ideology (Bell 1962). That such a view was itself the product of a deeply-held ideological position is also beyond doubt: a world apparently bifurcated between reason and unreason, between extremism and moderation, between freedom and oppression. It is all the more telling that this was the view of American scholars who had just emerged from a home-made mini-totalitarianism in the shape of McCarthyism, and whose society is once again host to similar cultural constructs.

Liberalism as a Template for Identifying Ideologies: From Pluralism to Fragmentation

Ironically, if liberalism is now misrecognized as the dominant ideology (though one might anyhow ask, which of the many sub-sets of liberalism is dominant?), its paradoxical impact on the world of ideologies has been to reduce its own dominance. A century ago, liberalism was accused of fostering an imperialism the aim of which was to mould the world in its image, and of promoting an elitism that sought to impose hierarchies of conduct, taste and values on all cultures. Sixty years ago, however, liberalism was accused of a tolerance and a relativism that permitted extreme ideologies and their regimes to gain ascendance (Hallowell 1946; Freeden 2005: 28–30). Notwithstanding, over the past 20 years the built-in pluralism of liberalism, its espousal of diversity, has been expressed in a predilection for multiculturalism and the legitimization of manifold viewpoints. Because multiculturalism reflects the liberal partiality for individual diversity, but writ large and projected on groups, its popularity as a research category proffers fertile ground for ideological analysis. For we must recall that groups, and groups alone, are the carriers of ideologies, as Marx, Mannheim and their successors knew. The structural conclusion to be derived from liberal group-pluralism seems to be a world of manifold ideologies, one in which a permanent population of ideologies exists side by side. That puts paid to Gramsci's notion of a monolithic hegemony, a very unsubtle tool already when it was coined. It has also contested the Rawlsian project of a free-floating 'political' (what a misnomer!) liberalism.

I want to argue that it is the battle over liberalism, and how to interpret it, that offers clues to different ways of conceptualizing and investigating ideologies. The issue at stake is not the nature of liberalism as an ideology, but the methodological epistemology that liberalism imparts to our conceptualization of ideologies. On the surface, a creed so wedded to individualism would appear to be a poor tool through which to appreciate ideologies as social phenomena. But, again, even on that surface, liberalism has increasingly come to terms with the importance of groups and with the social nature of individuals. That aside, there are two aspects, methodologically speaking, of the impact of liberalism on current approaches to ideology.

The one aspect is that the pluralist wing of liberalism encourages choice and reassessment. As Mill already made clear, truth is temporary and its forms are constantly open to revision:

> The beliefs which we have most warrant for have no safeguard to rest on, but a standing invitation to the whole world to prove them unfounded ... if the lists are kept open, we may hope that if there be a better truth, it will be found when

the human mind is capable of receiving it, and in the meantime we may rely on having attained such approach to truth as is possible in our own day. (Mill 1910: 83)

Translated into the terms of ideology research, that openness undermines closed conceptions of ideology that claim epistemological certainty, as well as theories positing the inevitability of clear-cut dominant ideologies. It also challenges the opposition between truth and ideology, at the very least by introducing a limitless trajectory of time that applies to both and that, in hermeneutical terms, offers continuously changing horizons of interpretation. A social world of ideological diversity is built into liberal individualism and pluralism; in its excessive modes individualism has coalesced with atomistic conceptions of society, but even in its more moderate manifestations, individualism endorses variety – a central theme in the writings of Wilhelm von Humboldt (Humboldt, 1969). Variety and divergence in their turn ensure the impermanence of human conduct and thought. Historically, however, that was partially balanced and countered by a strong evolutionary current in twentieth century liberal thought. The normality of individual development – riding on an enlightenment view of *Bildung* and of progress – was harnessed to a parallel view of social development. It assumed that the future was controllable by human reason, not random and not even multi-faceted. The evolutionary path of human and social development, though non-teleological in liberal fashion, was clearly towards greater cooperation and the application of collective, democratically controlled, intelligence. Only one optimistically-anticipated future beckoned, even if its features never attained perfection. Even here, though, liberalism's strong internal holism would have dismissed the more recent rupture between a political and a comprehensive liberalism.

Mainstream twentieth-century liberalism, then, contributed to the legitimization of a state of affairs in which scholars as well as ordinary participants can assert that a society containing one ideology is either pathologically suppressed or 'pre-liberal' and 'pre-pluralist' on an imputed evolutionary scale, whereas a society containing *many* ideologies is normal. That was a vital shift away from seeing a society with one, indeed any, ideology as pathological and a society with *none* as normal. However, within the liberal family a hard-fought contest has been taking place between those for whom liberalism is an ideology of humanism, of individual growth, flourishing and mutual aid, and between those – predominantly in the United States and in some Eastern European countries – for whom liberalism is an ideology of capitalist free enterprise (see e.g. Hanley 1999: 163–189). The second view of liberalism is of course eagerly adopted by its detractors as well: after all, it makes it much easier to present liberalism in an unsympathetic light and it minimizes the overlap humanist liberalism displays with other progressive ideologies.

Here is the second methodological aspect of the impact of applying liberalism, broadly defined, to the conceptualization of ideologies. Significantly, it has been provided through a very different variant of liberalism. Recent self-proclaimed proponents of liberalism have eroded the thicker twentieth-century mainstream notions of liberalism. They have done so by conceptually redefining the adjacent liberal concept of choice and reducing it to acts undertaken by maximizing consumers rather than to acts undertaken by reflective reasoners. Ostensibly, that option had been available in the liberal arsenal for a very long time, but what is new is that those models of choice are fashioned not through emulating the exploits of entrepreneurs and captains of industry equipped with a vision and sense of purpose, but through popular experiences of supermarket consumption patterns. As a consequence they have contributed significantly to the ephemerality and unpredictability of our awareness of our own choices. They have also invited us to use our shopping trolleys to mix and match, to employ – on a more positive note – our imaginations to create new combinations out of existing materials and – on a less positive note – other people's imaginations to accomplish the very same. All this has resulted in a mottled landscape of colours and shapes in which the future is less 'knowable'. Pluralism is thus converted into fragmentation, and fragmentation exposes the underlying indeterminacy that all ideologies try to reduce. The old enlightenment assumption that a holistic harmony will hold variety together is by now hardly available to students of politics.

In other words, the hidden potential of ideological contestability – conventionally overridden by the tendency of ideologies to impose certainty on political language through decontesting devices – is now becoming more evident in political discourse. There are of course occasional lapses into the language of assurance – one of which was inspired by the approaching millennium, which provided its own short-lived iconography of an inviting and exciting future – but experimentation and fluidity are once again the order of the day. European polities, for instance, have been experimenting with countless versions of 'safe' or 'respectable' nationalism and populism, with the integration of green perspectives into former mainstream ideological positions, and with public-private enterprises that endeavour to recreate the balance between welfare and efficiency that has been at the centre of social-democratic domestic politics for much of the twentieth century.

Put in these terms, liberalism can be costly in terms of the attributes of ideology. Some of the main features of an ideology are to mobilize support for political decisions and systems, as well as to map the political world in a clear and communicable manner. In its more clouded moments, however, liberalism can encourage sitting on fences, uncertainty, unreflective spontaneity, or a whole range of equally plausible solutions. The legitimization of policies then becomes rather more complex. While political philosophers, especially but not exclusively of the Anglo-American variety, wish to see the burden of understanding and of choice transferred to the reflective and participatory individual, that burden is one that many people do not wish to take on, and cannot shoulder. The alternative is to bow to the numerical and power preponderance of certain groups or even, more amorphously, of certain fashions. Then the problem of competing understandings becomes inescapable, and the relativization of truths – the very issue on which liberalism has been frequently berated – re-emerges.

148 *Ideology Seriously*

These conceptual indeterminacies are of course the normal properties of ideologies, because of the essential and the effective contestability on which conceptual meaning is grounded (Freeden 2003: 3–11 and 225), but that does signal the impermanence as well as the non-doctrinaire nature of much contemporary political thinking. And when reflective choice is conflated with market choice, and ideologies are seen as political goods with little intrinsic and much instrumental worth, the fragility of their existence appears to become even more salient.

Fragmentation and the Slackening of Political and Cultural Constraints

Fragmentation, however, is not merely the consequence of flippant consumerism. Another of its causes lies in the fact that mass democratization, as Gramsci already pointed out, brought about a change in the social distribution of ideological producers (Gramsci 1971: 327–240). Intellectual elites began to relinquish control over a relatively tight ideological structure, and 'grass-roots' ideologies, though existent in the past, found new ways of influencing the map of mainstream, state-recognized, ideological positions. This has a number of facets. First, the mass media – those crucial disseminators of ideology – have become far more oriented towards so-called mass political cultures, both reflecting and shaping commonly held views, and often exploiting the marginalization of some groups in order to sell newspapers with populist and nationalist prejudices. Of course, the media monopolies work against rather than with democratization, but equally, monopoly liberalism is that version of liberalism the furthest removed from democracy and one of the principal targets of humanist liberalism. Second, political activism has been more keenly reflected in the ideological positions that became publicly salient, and the evanescence of many such activist movements has quickened the pace of perceived ideological change. Thus, the form in which ideologies are now most likely to be noticed in the West is that of the new, and not so new, social movements, specifically targeted programmatically in the fashion of pressure groups, and often cobbled together from an eclectic range of beliefs. They are also to be identified among horizontal social networks, operating outside, or cutting across, more conventional political institutions. Third, the dumbing down of political language has both disguised ideologies – hitherto marketed in terms more familiar to the elitist language of political theory or the high culture of the serious weeklies – and has enriched the linguistic and communicative forms in which they appear. Ideologies are increasingly presented in 'fast-food' easily consumable format, with a very limited shelf-life, once again reinforcing the loose mix and match configurations of ideas that many ideologies have adopted, but this time not on the grounds of economic consumption but of relative linguistic and semantic lawlessness.

All that means that the ideological field, at present, is particularly challenging to the researcher. Some of it appears in old clothing: types of conservatism, of nationalism, of aggressive populism have been around for a while in recognizable forms. Socialism has shrunk and is seriously ill, so we are told, though social democratic ideologies have survived by opening their boundaries to the kind of economic and managerial content that would have been decisively and derisively excluded a couple of decades ago. Moreover, it would be premature to predict the demise of socialism, as its conceptual frameworks satisfy political and ideological needs – concerning redistribution, the recognition of human identity, and the group nature of human organization – that will simply not wither away. Witness the current resurrection of some of the social democratic forms in France and in Spain, however local the circumstances may be. On the other hand, what I have elsewhere termed 'thin' ideologies – ideologies that lack a comprehensive set of plans for political action (Freeden 1996: 485–487) – seem to be thriving, perhaps another facet of the intellectual simplification and more modest and impatient features of contemporary ideologies.

The notion of a 'post-ideological' age is itself a masking device – a screen constructed by a motley coalition of different groupings: by those who are intent on waving goodbye to macro-ideologies that might attain a life of their own and thus threaten agency-rich conceptions of human initiative and control; by those who wish stealthily to move into that ostensible vacuum in order to set up their own anti-utopian – yet at the same time unattainable – vision of hegemony; as well as by those who still adhere to a strong anti-intellectualism in which ideas are marginal epiphenomena. Perhaps we just aren't looking carefully enough; perhaps we aren't tuned in to observing the fleeting and fragile manifestations of current ideologies; perhaps, even, their ephemerality reflects a confused and anxious flight from the traditionally constraining patterns of language and custom, at least on the surface. While ideologies possess the crucial function of decontesting essentially contested meanings, that feature is always a struggle against linguistic indeterminacy that can only temporarily succeed. Battles may be won, but the war for assigning precise meaning to political language is doomed to be lost, much as ideologies loudly proclaim the opposite, and much as politics – with its urgent need to make decisions – cannot take place unless some of those individual battles are victorious.

For ideologies exist in an elaborate relationship with time. The tendency of textbooks on ideology to present them as static articles of belief and as stable compounds complements almost exactly, if unintentionally, the abstract ahistoricity of philosophical models. On the other hand, we cannot go along entirely with the hermeneutic view of the 'authorless text' subject to boundless readings by individual readers. One of the most intriguing aspects of ideology as 'text' is that it is constantly being *re-written*, not just reread, because its producers inherit that creative task from generation to generation, even from month to month, as the life span of ideology-formulating groups extends beyond that of their individual members. Even when we do factor time into the equation, the inclination is to see time as disruptive, as a challenge to the quiescence, the harmony and the balance ideal-type politics is supposed to engender.

But what if we were to conceive of ideological change, dynamics and malleability as normal, and ideological stasis as an anomalous blip in modern societies that are continuously subject to rapid transformation – a blip caused perhaps by totalitarian control over time, or a product of inadequate observation and analysis on the part of the scholar? Could the path-dependency ostensibly manufactured by a tradition turn out on closer inspection to be a continuous process of path-creation? The school of conceptual history has focused to some extent on paradigmatic shifts, on what Koselleck has termed a *Sattelzeit*, and the monumental work presenting the nineteenth century as such a bridging period is the *Geschichtliche Grundbegriffe* (Brunner et al. 1972–1996). Although such sudden shifts have occurred from time to time, those grand events cannot come to terms with the everyday fluidity of ideological morphology. Here Wittgenstein's analogy with a thread comes in handy, for it can draw attention to the unceasing microchanges that ideologies undergo, and the parallel requirement for ideology scholarship to develop micro-tools to detect them. Indeed, we are far too bedazzled by the grandness of some ideological edifices to notice the mundanity of most others. And while mundane does not make the headlines, it is the very substance of political analysis. For most of the time we experience the ordinary, and it is the ordinary ideological maps that, because of their low visibility, require particular awareness and decoding.

On the other hand, fragmentation exists only potentially within the world of ideologies. The patterns are there, even if we need to increase our shutter speed to capture them. Change is never entirely random. The world of ideologies is less centrifugal than the presence of fragmentation may allow because of the patterns that ideologies adopt, and because what we often get are offshoots of past and existing ideational configurations, adapted deliberately or, more often, unconsciously to new contingencies, new theories and new fashions. And while the multiplicity of ideologies might suggest fragmentation, each ideology on its own is a necessary attempt at the stabilization of a fluid set of relationships among political concepts and ideas. The world of ideologies is both a continual series of challenges to the inertia of established ideological macro-families and, conversely, an endeavour to curb artificially the relentless process of amorphous change that political ideas undergo. And when boundaries are very much on the political agenda once again: boundaries against mass migration to Europe, boundaries against the spread of terror and its political hosts, boundaries against the economic instability brought about by the very success of the welfare state with its concomitant climate of citizens' high expectations – ideological systems relapse into oversimplifications such as the 'clash of civilizations' or the 'third way' and retreat into their own confines, however transient.

If liberalism encourages ideological pluralism, the retreat from socialism – let alone communism – has encouraged a backlash against ideology itself. Here it is precisely the inevitable group nature of ideology that is the problem. For if theories such as socialism, in which groups play central roles, are in the decline at the expense of burgeoning new forms of individual entrepreneurship and of the resurrection of leadership and 'steering' roles in politics, it is not surprising that their accompanying epistemology, in which group products are salient, withers away as well. Nevertheless, ideologies are, and will continue to be, created by groups. As social scientists we cannot be taken in by extreme individualism and close our eyes to the patterned interaction of human beings; nor can we assume that such group conduct must always tend towards unstable and extreme manifestations as in some current forms of populism and anarchism. We need to re-identify the groups from which ideologies emerge and that serve to sustain them.

In Pursuit of Ideologies and How to Behave when We Find Them

Preparing conceptual and research agenda for the scholarly study of ideology, and of concrete ideologies, may involve a number of moves. First, we need to jettison the anthropomorphization of groups, as if they had a homogeneous structure, let alone a fixed personality, that is amenable to the formation of dogma. We could take a couple of leaves out of Dahl's and Lipset's pioneering work between the 1950s and 1970s, in which groups underwent continuous processes of recombination, and in which social relationships were fluctuating and re-aggregated (Dahl 1971; Lipset, 1959). If groups – the producers and carriers of ideology – mutate constantly, it may be assumed that their ideational creations will do likewise, and that ideological aggregations within a society will be open to frequent reconfiguration. That has some significant consequences for contemporary political thought. In particular, the recent popularization of Carl Schmitt's distinction between friend and enemy, also proffered by postmodernists as the notion of the 'Other', relies precisely on the kind of stark dichotomization that more sophisticated theories eschew. While that dichotomization may be vaguely true of elementary nationalism as well, one of the central features of conservatism, to the contrary, is to be found in the construction of *multiple* 'others' against which the conservative profile reacts sequentially in mirror-image style, emphasizing in turn its own legalism, traditionalism, anti-egalitarianism, individualism, or tribalism. Conservative ideology hence contains a range of substantive conceptual arrangements united loosely in a specific grammar of reaction (Freeden 1996: 317–383).

Second, the process of cultural decentralization opens up various loci of ideological production. These existed before, but social insensitivity towards them meant that they were overlooked or trivialized. Now, however, increased efficiency of communication, more widespread education, as well as the attention paid to local cultures, present ideologies in complex societies as actual competitions over the public ear and eye, even if not all contestants are able to claim equal significance. Instead of up-down structures, horizontal sites can make themselves heard through the power of the purse, through iconic cultural status, through diligent campaigning, or through the news-value of the unusual or the bizarre.

Third, ideologies are undergoing a process of delocalization. I prefer that term to 'globalization' not only because there exist competing forms of globalizing but because it pinpoints one of the more important features of contemporary ideologies: they have become detached from the contexts in which they originally made sense. While globalization is often seen as a manifestation of the power of the globalizing agents, ideological delocalization represents a weakening of structural and conceptual stability. The familiar is normally stronger than the distant, particularly because the gap between the intentions of the producers and the understandings of the consumers is more easily bridgeable. It may be the case that ideologies now appear to travel easily and lightly, and that globalization offers them speed and marketability. Yet seemingly similar patterns across space turn out on inspection to be something entirely different. Conventional labels such as liberal, conservative and even fascist have been casualties of dilution, confusion and misappropriation. In extreme cases, they do not operate as signifiers for an ideology at all, but merely as name-tags to arouse a single association and knee-jerk responses, as do sound-bites. In a re-run of 1950s millenarianism, a new kind of end of ideology appears to be back, in that all we appear to hear about are artificially manufactured responses to focus-group concerns that are as ephemeral as yesterday's newspaper. That appearance is of course misleading. But in a broader sense delocalization increases the variety of members of a particular ideological family often to stretching point; the question is whether some of those members are usurpers or bringing a new gene pool to the family. And a related question is, if there still are local ideologies, what are the features that distinguish them as local?

Fourth, after a period of increasing democratization, at least on the superficial level of mass adoption and mass support, ideologies seem to be undergoing a process of contraction in support, of 'de-massification'. Even recent 'populisms' may need to have their popularity carefully scrutinized. In part this contraction is related to the revulsion in the West against totalizing ideologies; in part to the alternative cultural claims on members of affluent societies at the expense of political involvement, be those religious or, more likely, connected to the world of entertainment; in part to the current decline in 'inspirational' ideologies that offer clear visions of the future – itself due to a disillusionment with the promise of future trajectories. But, mainly, ideologies have become subject to marketing rules in a novel manner. In the past it was assumed that ideologies were just there, as part of the political landscape. Conservative ideologies in particular were seen as natural growths, but even progressive ideologies were regarded as the products and reflections of evolving social forces that either developed as a facet of human rationality or were subject to deterministic laws. Now the Weberian notion of disenchantment needs to be applied to ideologies as well. The impact of advertising raises the possibility that one can construct, market and even purchase an ideology. Ideologies thus become instrumental to the service of short-term political and economic ends, not general belief systems to which the world of politics has to adapt. And once ideologies are seen as manufactured artificially, we may not be far away from the development of designer ideologies, available on tap through specialist think-tanks ready to cater to a range of political situations that require immediate ideological underpinning.

Curiously enough, a similar conclusion can be drawn from post-structuralist theory in its insistence on the social construction of beliefs, but only to the extent that it is prepared to entertain a salient role for human agency and the possibility of deliberately fashioned ideologies, a role that in many of its manifestations it is reluctant to adopt. But all this does not mean that as analysts of ideology we must conclude that all meanings and constructions are equally valid. An olive branch may

The Chimera of a 'Post-ideological' Age   153

be held out to political philosophers and ethicists by showing them that the kind of cultural and moral validations in which they engage can be more carefully assessed once we know what fields of meaning and of value the various conceptual configurations – of which ideologies are constituted – can produce. We need to know what our purchases will look like when we bring them back home and how to avoid tripping over them.

The fragility of particular ideological arrangements must not be confused with the fragility of ideology in general. The de-dogmatizing of ideologies is a de facto recognition of their internal malleability, and a means of protecting them from the breakable brittleness of more rigid ideological structures. Ideologies that adapt to the natural suppleness of language and meaning, while maintaining some continuity as well as a principled vision that can inspire support, are far more likely to flourish in cultures not based on mass movements or on hierarchically maintained belief systems. By contrast, in cultures where mass conduct is strongly regulated through cultural and religious norms, ideologies based on traditional mores and views of repetitious or cyclical history will be internalized with little reflection.

This raises the issue of the boundaries between a political ideology and other cultural belief systems. One of the most significant features of Western ideologies is their differentiation from other belief systems. This aspect of intellectual division of labour has seen the emergence of a set of thought practices specifically aimed at the mobilization of political support and at control over public decision-making. Of course, ideologies are only quasi-autonomous in that respect, and will rely heavily on cultural constructs, fashions and conventions that have resonance in other spheres – the physical imagery of a country, the habits of interaction, milestones of history, quirks of personality, iconic landmarks of literature. But they have partly disentangled themselves from religious faiths, from myths and from social and psychological dispositions. The recent rise of the political salience of religion challenges that quasi-autonomy. This leads, among others, to the difficulty of dealing with ostensible hybrids such as political Islam – itself subject in the West to the kind of undiscerning monolithic treatment that is nourished on older, doctrinaire, conceptions of ideology. Although it is clear that different versions of political Islam display variable degrees of undergirding by religious precepts, the type of questions still asked, for instance 'is there an Islamic economics?' (Pfeifer 1997: 154–165) demand comparison with European phenomena such as Christian democracy as well as with non-European phenomena such as American neo-conservatism, precisely in order to ascertain the level of differentiation of their pool of ideas and signifiers from religious discursive patterns.

So how and where do we find ideologies in the twenty-first century? Here again some confusion reigns. Historians may write about the ideology of beer-brewing when they really mean the *ideas* that a particular practice incorporates. Not every set of ideas is an ideology, though it may be a segment of one. Political scientists frequently refer to over-ideologized politics, when they mean to indicate that a set of political aims and justifications has become detached from the policies and activities undertaken under its aegis. Post-structuralists point to specific ways of articulating perceptions of reality as being at the heart of the ideological domain, but their focus is on perception and misperception and on the formation of illusions and their critique. More complicated is what counts as an ideological statement or text. Discourse analysis permits any sentence to be regarded as a carrier of ideological import. That is generally plausible, though discourse and ideology are not one and the same thing. Discourse is both broader than ideology – any communicative act counts as discourse, not only those with significant political content – and narrower than ideology, because its analysis may underplay the social and historical contexts in which language is used and the special public role that political concepts and substantive arguments play in ideological structure.

However, since words in the field of ideology are the signifiers of political concepts, the slippage of meanings, deliberate or unintentional, that a word carries may serve as a highly significant indicator of a broader ideological shift (Laclau 1996: 209–215). When John Major, then British prime minister, introduced the notion of a citizens' charter to refer to meagre financial compensation for individuals when public services failed them, he was capitalizing on the political gravitas of the two words, with their foundational constitutional implication. Effectively, however, citizens were transformed through this 'charter' into clients or customers, and the state into a provider. The 'contract' between the state and its citizens had been commercialized. Word combinations may also accrue meaning through historically contingent circumstances. The phrase 'national socialism' can no longer be co-opted as an indication of a sub-species of socialism – its 'innocence' has been irredeemably corrupted – although it would be less cumbersome than Stalin's 'socialism in one country'. Certain words, as cultural historians and anthropologists know, burn out and have to be substituted. If according to Althusser naming (interpellation) is a defining feature of ideology (Althusser 1984: 48–49), so is re-naming. The admixture of linguistic and conceptual indeterminacy ensures that the naming game is something analysts of ideology will always have to master.

Many containers of ideological subject-matter offer ideologies a deliberate or unintentional free ride through the internet, television, the cinema, posters, logos, and public spectacles such as military marches, celebrations of independence or labour days. Some of these are new, some well-established, but they all reflect the increasing awareness we have of non-verbalized ideological dissemination, for which discourse analysis is, again, inadequate. A host of cultural artefacts now serves as conveyor of multiple messages, some of which are plainly ideological, in the sense of rallying support for, or opposition to, areas of public policy. But granted that slogans are not on their own ideologies, are catch-phrases or logos sufficiently intricate to attract our attention as analysts of ideology? Of course they are, and in two senses – as pocket-maps for people in a hurry, who only need the main street through town; and as a fast mobilizer of political support from citizens, who otherwise would ignore deliberately targeted ideological messages. On the other hand, these snippets cannot live up to the general function of a political ideology as a vehicle through which complex public policy is shaped. Traffic lights may signify the authority of the state in regulating public conduct, and a Coca Cola sign may symbolize the global economic reach of the giant multinationals, but they are just tiny windows into intricate and interwoven social practices and the ideological understandings they contain. We cannot just go away and announce smugly, with our prejudices comfortably reinforced, in the first case, 'the state is all-powerful!', and in the second case 'capitalism reigns supreme!'. Techniques and styles of argumentation, fragments of discourse, are all important clues but no substitute for the detail and complexity of ideological maps that advanced societies need in order to navigate. The big packages will not become redundant because in highly-differentiated societies the human imagination requires a vast pool of interpretative and policy options.

Another issue that deserves careful treatment is the confusion between an ideological system and certain historical themes in political thought. One example of this is republicanism – a topic that contemporary political philosophers in conjunction with early modern historians have identified as permeating a range of political positions. For some, this is a significant point in the tradition of political thinking when civic liberty and a civic spirit were formed and embodied embryonic notions of public participation and accountability (Skinner 1998). For others, it is a modelling device for a conception of liberty as non-domination (Pettit 1997). But republicanism is not easily comprehended as an ideology. It is a set of conceptions and dispositions that was not perceived as a coherent, let alone collectively-held, set of political beliefs. At best, it intersected with what could be seen as ideologies, that is, with languages competing over the control of public policy, languages such as liberalism, nationalism and quasi-socialist discourse. At worst, it is a post-factum academic construct, a paradigmatic aid intended to tease out seminal changes in public behaviour unknown to, or barely surmised by, their practitioners.

But then, how do we distinguish between the social constructs and discoveries that we as scholars produce or unearth and ideologies as popular social self-understandings? Sometimes a re-reading and re-labelling can turn out to be instructive. Perhaps welfarism serves as such an instance more than republicanism. The early twentieth-century development of welfare state thinking has been the site of attempts at appropriation both by socialist and by liberal ideologies. It is however much more instructive to see it as occupying a space that overlaps with both the traditional ideologies but that shares insufficient features with either. The possessiveness of political parties over a major policy field (was the welfare state the achievement of Liberals, Labour or Social-Democrats?) has distorted the emergence of a new point of view, a new set of ideological beliefs. Those were consciously held by large groups of people who were to some extent misled by the paucity of available conceptual frameworks with which to appreciate what they were doing. But the ideology of the welfare state was nameless at the time, and retrospectively recognizing it and naming it can make sense of a real-world ideology.

All this is part of the excitement of working with ideologies. The subject-matter at our disposal offers virtually infinite possibilities for research and analysis. Thus, for example, the micro-analysis of ideologies permits both strong comparative juxtapositions and allows the analyst to explore conceptual aggregations and configurations at any level of magnification. That means that we can either adopt existing and conventional ideological structures or families and subject them to investigative scrutiny, or decide on larger, smaller and cross-cutting constellations, as befits our research purposes. The experimentation here is not only that of the ideological innovator but that of the researcher who chooses on which morphological sample to focus, a decision that itself produces new insights. That is indeed a critical study of ideology, in the non-Marxist sense of ideology-critique: the ability to use the investigation of ideology as a critical tool for interpreting institutions, practices and social thought-patterns all at once. Concurrently, more traditional macro-analysis needs to continue inasmuch as individuals' perceptions of ideological wholes such as liberalism or fascism – however simplified those labels may be – play a vital part in accounting for their conduct; and inasmuch as ideological wholes share a host of functions such as legitimization or social integration/alienation. Students of ideology should not be too quick to abandon research into the conventional ideological macro-families just because some new ones are grabbing the headlines.

Crucially, studying ideology cannot be disentangled from studying politics: ideologies are not optional extras or 'externalities' but rather the codes that organize all political practices – the DNA of praxis. Moreover, ideologies are both socially inherited and malleable – to push the analogy further, they may be genetically modified, for good or for evil, to improve current practices or enable new ones. Ultimately, the analysis of ideologies has to be brought back to the very mainstream of politics. How that could ever have been otherwise now seems incomprehensible.

References

Althusser, L. (1984) *Essays on Ideology* (London: Verso).
Bell, D. (1962) *The End of Ideology* (New York: Collier).
Brunner, O., Conze, W. and Koselleck, R. (Eds) (1972–1996) *Geschichtliche Grundbegriffe*, 8 vols. (Stuttgart: Klett-Cotta).
Dahl, R. (1971) *Polyarchy* (New Haven, CT: Yale University Press).
Freeden, M. (2003) Editorial: Essential contestability and effective contestability. *Journal of Political Ideologies*, 9, pp. 3–11, 225.
Freeden, M. (1996) *Ideologies and Political Theory: A Conceptual Approach* (Oxford: Clarendon Press).
Freeden, M. (2005) *Liberal Languages: Ideological Imaginations and Twentieth Century Progressive Thought* (Princeton, NJ: Princeton University Press).
Gramsci, A. (1971) *Selections from Prison Notebooks* (London: Lawrence and Wishart).
Hallowell, J. (1946) *The Decline of Liberalism as an Ideology* (London: Kegan Paul).
Hanley, S. (1999) The new right in the new Europe? Unravelling the ideology of 'Czech Thatcherism'. *Journal of Political Ideologies*, 4, pp. 163–189.
Humboldt, W. von (1969) *The Limits of State Action* (Cambridge: Cambridge University Press).
Laclau, E. (1996) The death and resurrection of the theory of ideology. *Journal of Political Ideologies*, 1, pp. 201–220.
Lipset, S.M. (1959) *Political Man* (London; Heinemann).
Mill, J.S. (1910) *On Liberty* (London: Dent).
Pettit, P. (1997) *Republicanism: A Theory of Freedom and Government* (Oxford: Oxford University Press).
Pfeifer, K. (1997) Is there an Islamic economics?, in: J. Beinin and J. Stork (Eds), *Political Islam* (Berkeley and Los Angeles, CA: University of California Press).
Skinner, Q. (1998) *Liberty before Liberalism* (Cambridge: Cambridge University Press).

INDEX

Al-Ablaj, Abu-Muhammad 73
absolutism 105
accountability 26, 32, 155
Adorno, Theodor 111–12, 117
advertising 152
Afghanistan 71–3, 75–8, 82
Africa 81, 83
agriculture 29
Algeria 78
Ali 76
Allies 51
Althusser, L. 126, 154
America *see* United States
American Revolution 21, 56
Americanization 6
Amsterdam Treaty 58
analyst role 103–4
anarchism 41, 71, 151
Ansar al Sunna 73
antagonism 39–54
anti-capitalism 88, 101
anti-Fascism 40, 50–2
anti-globalization movement 2, 25, 33–4
anti-perfectionism 67–8
anti-Semitism 127
apathy 13
apostates 76–7, 83
Al-Aqsa mosque 81
Arabs 4, 16, 72, 75, 78–9, 83
Arendt, Hannah 105, 116
aristocracy 31
Al-Assad, Bashar 82
assimilation 28, 32
Associated Press 72
Australia 19, 23–4, 27–8, 32, 34
Austria 28
authoritarianism 44, 49, 51–2, 67

Bali 81
Balkin, J.M. 123, 126–30, 132, 134–6
bankers 31
Barrett, M. 107

Beauvoir, Simone de 116
Bedeschi, Giuseppe 40–1
Bell, Daniel 3–4, 6, 103, 119
Benhabib, Seyla 12, 117
Berlin Wall 4
Berlusconi, Silvio 43
Betz, Hans-George 22
big business 23, 25, 31–2
Black movement 3
Blair, Tony 15
Bobbio, Norberto 20–1, 25–6, 43
Bossi, Umberto 43
bourgeoisie 105–6
Bracher, Karl Dietrich 1, 3, 105
Britain *see* United Kingdom
Browning, Gary K. 16, 87–102
Bull, M. 101
bureaucracy 27, 29–31, 33, 116
Bush, George W. 7, 28, 72, 82–3
Byrberg, Torben Bech 16

Cairo University 77
Caliphate 76
Campaign for Nuclear Disarmament (CND) 110
Canada 23–4, 28
Canovan, Margaret 20, 30
capitalism 4, 10–11, 20, 24
    decontesting 133
    populism 29, 32–3
    post-ideology debate 146, 155
    post-Marxism 88, 90–1, 94, 97
    Al Qaeda 79
    theory/praxis models 104, 109, 111–12
Carocci, Giampiero 43
cartel parties 2, 5–6
Cassirer, E. 40
catch-phrases 154
Catholicism 40, 42, 49
Central Intelligence Agency (CIA) 82
centre 61, 67
Chechnya 81

Christianity 4, 6, 42, 51, 79–80, 82, 153
churches 42
cinema 13
citizenship 27, 31, 34, 60, 63, 65, 68–9, 154
civil religion 41–2, 44, 51–2
civil rights movement 3, 29, 34
Claes, Willy 71
clash of civilizations 78–82, 150
class conflict 29, 39, 46, 52
    decontesting 122–4, 127, 136
    post-Marxism 100
    public reason 57, 60, 63
    theory/praxis models 104–5, 107, 109, 111
classifications 120–1, 124, 131
Clinton, Bill 4, 7
coalitions 43
Cold War 9, 39, 42–3, 79, 95, 109
collective actors 11–12, 16
Collingwood, R.G. 101
colonialism 56
commercialization 154
Committees for National Liberation 51
communications 12–14, 96, 98
Communism 1, 3, 41–3, 49
    decontesting 122
    post-ideology debate 143, 150
    post-Marxism 100
    poststructuralism 51
    Al Qaeda 71–2, 79, 81
    theory/praxis models 105, 109, 116
Communist Party 110
conceptual morphology 120, 130–9
conscience 113
consensus 44, 88
conservatism 6–7, 11, 16, 23
    decontesting 131, 133–4
    populism 27–8
    post-ideology debate 142, 148, 151–2
    poststructuralism 48
conspiracy theory 26
constraints 148–51
consumerism 6, 17, 23–4, 31, 96, 111, 116, 147–8, 152
Continental philosophy 47
Coole, D. 47
cooperatives 32–4
corporatism 29, 31–3, 96

Critical Theory 104, 111–12, 117, 130, 134
Croce, Benedetto 41
Cromer, Lord 79
culture wars 34
Czechoslovakia 9

Daghestan 78
Dahl, R. 151
D'Azeglio, Massimo 41
De Felice, Franco 52
De Tracy, Destutt 104–5
deconstruction 52, 97, 106
deliberative democracy 12–13
delocalization 151–2
demand overload 23, 34
democracy 1–14, 16–17, 19–26
    decontesting 133
    ideology 55–70
    populism 29, 31–2, 34–5
    post-ideology debate 146, 148, 152–3
    post-Marxism 88, 100
    poststructuralism 40, 42–3, 47, 49
    Al-Qaeda 78–80
    theory/praxis models 106–7, 117
Denmark 58, 77
deregulation 24
designer ideology 152
Dewey, John 115
dialectics 88, 90–1, 93–5, 97–101, 112, 116
dictatorship 1, 50–1, 79, 105
difference 61, 67
Dillon, Michael 40
discourse 8–10, 12–13, 16
    decontesting 120, 124, 133–4
    populism 22, 25, 33, 35
    post-ideology debate 143, 147, 153–5
    post-Marxism 89, 98
    poststructuralism 44–8, 51–2
    public reason 59
    theory/praxis models 104–8, 113–14, 117
disenchantment 152
dislocation 47
domination 122–7, 129, 132, 134–8, 145–6, 155
dualism 63
Dyrberg, Torben Bech 55–70

Eagleton, Terry 105, 136
Eastern Europe 43, 146
Easton, D. 64
ecology 11
economics 3–7, 10–11, 13–14
    decontesting 125, 127, 132–3
    populism 20, 23, 27–9, 32–3
    post-ideology debate 148, 150, 152–4
    post-Marxism 87–9, 94, 96–7, 99
    public reason 56, 60, 63
    Al Qaeda 71, 78, 80, 83
    theory/praxis models 106–7, 111–12, 114
economy 133
education 7, 23–4, 107, 109, 113, 116, 151
Egypt 76–9
elections 5–7, 13, 28
elites 1, 19, 21–3, 26
    populism 28–35
    post-ideology debate 145, 148
    poststructuralism 42–3
    public reason 57, 60, 68
    theory/praxis models 109, 114
Empire 87–102
empiricism 47, 115
end of ideology 2–9, 105, 119, 141–56
endism 2–9, 105, 119, 141–56
Engels, Friedrich 88, 99, 122, 129
English Civil War 30
Enlightenment 104–5, 133, 146–7
entrepreneurs 30–1, 147, 150
environmentalism 11, 24, 33
epistemology 17, 47, 122
    decontesting 124–5, 128–9, 134–5, 137
    post-ideology debate 142, 145–6, 150
equality 21, 26–30, 34–5, 50–1
Eritrea 76
essentialism 44
ethics 65–6, 97, 101, 144, 153
ethnicity 69
Euro-sceptics 58
Europe 2, 4–6, 19–20, 22–4
    populism 27, 32
    post-ideology debate 147, 150, 153
    post-Marxism 90, 98
    poststructuralism 47
    Al Qaeda 79–80
    theory/praxis models 105, 110

European Community (EC) 58
European Union (EU) 10, 22, 43
evolution 146, 152
exchange value 94
exclusion 31, 44, 46–8
experts 113, 115
exterminism 109–10, 116

failed states 71–2
Fairclough, N. 108
false consciousness 14, 104, 106, 125–6, 132
Fascism 1, 11, 16, 22
    post-ideology debate 143, 152, 156
    poststructuralism 40–2, 49–52
    Al Qaeda 79
    theory/praxis models 105
feminism 11, 106
First World War 27
Foucault, Michel 8–9, 104, 106–7, 113–14, 117, 119, 122, 126
fragmentation 145–51
frame 61, 67, 69
France 106, 149
franchise 27, 34
Frankfurt school 104, 112–13
Fraser, - 117
free market 4, 31
Freeden, Michael 11, 16–17, 20–1, 30, 48, 120, 124, 130, 133, 137–8, 141–56
freedom 26–7, 33–4, 47
French Revolution 5, 56, 104–5
Friedman, Milton 133
front-back 56–7, 60, 62–3, 68
Fukuyama, Francis 2, 4, 10, 79
functionalism 126, 128
fundamentalism 2, 4, 14, 56, 71, 79

Garang, John 81
gender 63, 69
Gentile, Emilio 41–2
Germany 3
Giddens, Anthony 15, 100
Gingrich, Newt 28
globalization 2, 4, 6, 9–10
    populism 19–20, 25, 34
    post-ideology debate 14, 151–2
    post-Marxism 87–9, 95, 97, 100–1
    Al Qaeda 75, 80

Gramsci, Antonio 41, 44–5, 107, 116, 128, 145, 148
grand narratives 39, 41, 89, 99–101
green movement 11
Guantanamo Bay 83
Gundle, S. 51

Habermas, Jürgen 13, 66, 107, 117, 126
Hardt, M. 17, 87–102
Harris, L. 74
Hart, H.L.A. 137
Hayek, Friedrich 133
Haynes, Jeffrey 16, 71–86
Hayward, Jack 23
Hegel, G.W.F. 47, 89–90, 93, 95, 98–101
Hegelianism 47, 99
hegemony 6, 10, 16, 41
    decontesting 130
    post-ideology debate 149
    post-Marxism 88, 94–5, 97–8, 100
    poststructuralism 44–5, 47–8, 50–2
    public reason 56, 60–3, 68
    theory/praxis models 107–8
Heidegger, M. 47
Held, D. 88–9, 100
hierarchy 31, 56–8, 88
    post-ideology debate 145, 153
    post-Marxism 93–4, 96
    theory/praxis models 110, 114
Hirst, P. 89
history 1–4, 8–10, 14, 25, 40–1, 44, 52
Hofstader, Richard 26
Horkheimer, Max 111–12, 117
humanism 41
Humboldt, Wilhelm von 146
Humphrey, Mathew 17, 119–40
Huntingdon, Samuel 78–80

identification 56–61
identity formation 44–7, 49, 51–2
ideology
    antagonism 39–54
    categorizations 135–8
    challenges 9–16
    conceptions 120–1
    contesting 119–40
    democratic 55–70
    designer 152
    end of 2–9, 105, 119, 141–56
    falsehood 125–8
    genealogy 104–5
    globalist 87–102
    identifying 145–8
    inclusive 121–4, 129–35, 139
    phoenix 1–18
    problem 40–4
    pursuing 151–6
    Al Qaeda 71–86
    restrictive 125–9, 139
    rethinking 48–50
    scope 124
    under cover 105–8
imams 72
immaterial production 96, 100–1
immigration 28, 32, 50
imperialism 3, 6, 10, 16–17
    post-ideology debate 145
    post-Marxism 93, 95, 98–9
    poststructuralism 46
    Al Qaeda 80
    theory/praxis models 116
in-out 56–8, 60–3, 65–6, 68
inclusion-exclusion 68–9
incompleteness 41–2, 49
individualism 105, 145–6, 150–1
industrialization 106, 111
inertia 109–10
information society 7, 106
Institute for Social Research 112
Intel 10
intellectuals 103–17
International Monetary Fund (IMF) 10
Internet 4, 12, 14, 73
interpellation 154
invisible power 26
Iran 73
Iraq 10, 72–3, 75, 78, 80, 82–3, 95, 101
Islam 2, 4, 16, 72–3, 75–80, 83, 144, 153
Islamic Jihad 77
Israel 72, 75, 78, 81, 83
Italy 3, 16, 39–54

Japan 3
Al-Jazeera 73
Jordan 73
Judaism 80, 82

justice 63–4, 66, 71, 113–14
    decontesting 125, 127, 132, 134, 137–8
    post-ideology debate 144
justification 55–6, 58, 62–4, 66, 68–9, 120–1

Kashmir 81
Kenya 81
knowledge society 111, 113
Koselleck, - 150
Kristol, Irving 133–4
Kurds 10, 73

labour 24, 29, 31, 88, 94, 96–7, 109–10, 125, 154
Lacan, Jacques 47, 122, 125, 127–8, 137
Laclau, Ernesto 29, 40, 44–8, 58, 66, 101, 128
Bin Laden, Osama 72–3, 75–8, 80, 82–3
language 108, 115, 120, 129, 133, 137–8, 143, 147–9, 153–5
Lantos, Tom 79, 81
Laponce, J.A. 58
Latin America 79
Laycock, David 16, 19–38
leadership 133, 150
Left 1–2, 4–7, 9, 14, 16
    populism 20, 22, 25, 27, 29–35
    post-ideology debate 143
    poststructuralism 39, 43–4, 50–1
    public reason 55–70
    theory/praxis models 113–14, 116
Leonardo, Zeus 123
Lepre, Aurelio 42, 50
Levellers 31
Leviathan 33
liberalism 2, 4–5, 8, 11
    decontesting 131, 133–4, 137
    political 55–70
    populism 21–2, 27, 29, 32–3
    post-ideology debate 143–8, 150, 152, 155–6
    poststructuralism 40–1, 48, 50–2
    Al Qaeda 78–80
    role 13, 17
    theory/praxis models 104–5, 114
libertarianism 28
linguistic philosophy 106, 115, 124
Lipset, S.M. 151

logos 154
London School of Economics (LSE) 15
Lyotard, J-F. 98

McCarthyism 3, 145
MacDonalds 10
McGrew, A. 100
Machiavelli, N. 99
Mair, Peter 6
Major, John 154
manifestos 5, 10, 14, 105, 131
Mannheim, Karl 10, 111, 122, 124, 138, 145
Marcuse, Herbert 111, 116
Martin, James 16, 39–54
Marx, Karl 8, 15, 88–91, 93, 95–101, 104–5, 109, 122, 124, 129, 145
Marxism 14, 16–17, 22, 41
    decontesting 122, 124, 126–7, 130, 138
    post-ideology debate 142–4, 156
    post-Marxism 88
    poststructuralism 44, 46–7
    theory/praxis models 106–9, 114
material world 45–6, 50
materialism 96–7, 99, 101, 108, 116
Mawdudi, Sayyid Abu'l-A'la 77
Mazzini, Giuseppe 41
media 1, 6, 12–13, 24, 33–4, 43, 75, 110, 148
metaphysics 106
middle class 7
Middle East 16, 77–8, 83
military 51, 72–3, 82–3, 95, 116, 154
Mill, John Stuart 145–6
mind control 142
misrecognition 142–5
modernism 2, 8, 14
Mohammed, Prophet 76–7
mojahedin 72–3, 75, 77
monarchism 51, 56
money 97
monism 56
monopolies 148
morality 63, 66, 69, 116–17, 133, 142, 153
Mouffe, Chantal 40, 44–8, 50
moveable frontiers 96
Mujahideen *see mojahedin*
multiculturalism 27–8, 32, 34, 117, 145
multinational corporations 10, 155
Muslim Brotherhood 77–8

Muslims 71–3, 75–83
Mussolini, Benito 43, 50

nanny state 33
Napoleon 106
Nasser, Gamal Abdel 77
national subjects 41–2, 49–50
nationalism 20, 32, 34–5, 43
    post-ideology debate 142, 144, 147–8, 151, 155
    theory/praxis models 105
Nazism 1, 3, 51, 105, 143
negative exclusion 44–7
negativity 47–8, 52
Negri, A. 17, 87–102
neo-conservatism 21, 132–4, 153
neo-Darwinism 126
neo-liberalism 4, 6–7, 10
New Labour 15
New Left 6–7, 114, 116–17
New Politics 2, 106
New Right 19, 23–4, 27–8, 32–4
new social history 108
new social movements 2, 6, 11, 98, 106, 148
New Zealand 19, 28
Nietzsche, Friedrich 115
North America 19–20, 23, 27, 32–3
novelty 87–9, 96–7, 99–100
Nozick, Robert 24

objectivism 56
Occident 79
Ohmae, K. 100
oligarchy 113
ontology 40, 44, 47, 97
opinion polls 6
Organization for Economic Cooperation and Development (OECD) 25
Orientalism 78–82
orientation 55–62, 65–9
Other 46, 151

Pakistan 76
Palestinians 75, 78, 83
paradigm shifts 150
parapolitical systems 64–5
parties 2, 4–8, 12, 19
    populism 22–4, 28–30, 33–4

post-ideology debate 155
poststructuralism 42–3, 51
theory/praxis models 107, 112
Passavant, P.A. 101
Pavone, Claudio 52
peace movement 104, 110, 117
peacekeeping 95
pedagogy 113
Pelham, N. 72
people 30–3, 35, 43
philosophy 14–15, 47, 63–4
    decontesting 131, 133, 137
    post-ideology debate 142, 144, 147, 149, 153, 155
    post-Marxism 90, 97, 99, 101
    theory/praxis models 106, 108–9, 112, 114–15, 117
Plato 114
pluralism 12, 17, 22, 24
    populism 29, 33–4
    post-ideology debate 145–8, 150
    public reason 56, 58, 60, 62–3, 66–7
Al Qaeda 78
politics 1–8, 12, 33–5
    actors 103–17
    capital 64
    economy 25–6, 29, 31, 89
    philosophy 15, 17, 43, 47
    poststructuralism 39–42, 44–6, 48–50, 52
    science 6, 15, 23, 44
populism 16, 19–38, 43, 49, 144, 147–8, 151–2
positivism 47, 105
post-Fordism 96
post-ideology 2, 17, 39, 141–56
post-Marxism 46, 87–102, 104, 106–8, 143
postmodernism 2, 8–9, 90–1, 93–4, 96, 98–100, 151
poststructuralism 9, 16, 39–54, 143, 152–3
power relations 9, 15, 25–6
    decontesting 123, 126
    post-ideology debate 144, 147
    post-Marxism 88, 93–6, 98, 100–1
    public reason 67–9
    Al Qaeda 71, 75
    theory/praxis models 104–8, 113–14, 117

pre-Socratics 115
private sphere 5, 63
production 96, 112
proletariat 90, 99–100, 104, 136
psychology 142, 153
public goods 27
public reason 16, 55–70
public sphere 5, 7, 9, 12–13, 16, 24, 27, 34
Al Qaeda 4, 10, 16, 71–86

Qutb, Sayyid 76–8, 82

race 63, 69
radicalism 3, 6–7, 11
Rafida 72
Rawls, John 16, 55, 62–9, 137, 145
Reagan, Ronald 28, 80, 110
reason, public 55–70
referenda 29
regime change 49
regionalism 40, 50
regionalization 89
religion 4, 11, 13–14, 16
    post-ideology debate 142, 144, 152–3
    poststructuralism 41–2, 44, 51–2
    public reason 55–6, 62–3, 69
    Al Qaeda 71–3, 76–8, 80–1, 83
    theory/praxis models 109
representation 21–31, 33
republicans 4, 6–7, 28, 32, 155
Resistance 51–2
Right 1, 4–5, 7, 9
    populism 19–20, 22–31, 33–5
    post-ideology debate 14, 16, 143–4
    poststructuralism 39, 43–4, 50
    public reason 55–70
Risorgimento 41
Rorty, Richard 104, 114–17
Rosen, Michael 125–6, 128, 130, 132, 134
Rousseau, Jean-Jacques 21
Royalists 31
Russia 72, 77, 106

Sacks, G. 74
Sadat, Anwar 77
Saddam Hussein 72, 80, 82
Said, Edward 78–80

Salvadori, M.L. 42, 44
Samudra, Imam 81
Sartre, Jean-Paul 116
Saudi Arabia 73, 75–6, 78, 82–3
Saussure, Ferdinand de 45
Scandinavia 28
Schattscheneider, E.E. 4–5
Schmitt, Carl 151
science 8, 15, 17, 105, 111–14
Scoppla, Pietro 42
Second World War 3, 78, 104, 111
secularization 78
Seliger, M. 122, 124, 129–30
semantics 46, 48
September 11 2001 4, 71, 73–5, 78–80, 82, 101
sexuality 28, 30, 68
Sharon, Ariel 72
Shelby, Tommie 125, 128, 130, 134
Shias 10, 72–3, 76
signification 45, 47, 50, 154
single currency 58
slavery 46
Smith, Anna Marie 45
Smith, Gordon 5
social actors 108–16
social chapter 10
social democracy 25, 27, 29–30, 33–4, 147–8, 155
socialism 3, 11, 15, 29–30
    decontesting 122, 131, 137
    post-ideology debate 142, 148–50, 154–5
    post-Marxism 87, 94
    poststructuralism 40–1, 48, 50–1
    public reason 55
socialization 90, 96, 99, 142
sociology of knowledge 108, 111, 122
Somalia 76, 81
Sony 10
sovereignty 19–38
Soviet Union 9, 75, 77, 144
Spain 3, 83, 149
Spaventa, Bertrando 41
special interests 27–8, 31–4
Stalin, Josef 154
Stalinism 108–9, 143
state 5–7, 9–11, 13, 21–2

populism 24, 26–9, 31–4
post-Marxism 98, 100–1
poststructuralism 39–40, 42–3, 50–1
Stirner, - 99
Strauss, Leo 133
subsidies 24
Sudan 81
Sufism 76
Sunnis 10, 72–3, 75–8, 81–2
superstructure 44–5, 106–7
surveillance 26
Switzerland 77
symbolic world 45, 47, 51
syndicalism 41, 43
Syria 72–3, 82

Taggart, Paul 20, 22
Taliban 71–2
Talmon, - 105
Talshir, Gayil 1–18, 103–18
Tangentopoli scandals 42
taxation 23–4, 27–8, 30–2, 34
technology 12–13, 26
teleology 90, 93, 97–9, 101, 143, 146
television 13
Tenet, George 82
terrorism 46, 71–5, 79–83, 150
Thatcher, Margaret 6, 28
theory/praxis models 103–17, 142
thin ideology 11, 149
think-tanks 31, 34, 152
Third Way 4, 6, 15, 50, 150
Third World 111
Thompson, E.P. 104, 108–10, 112, 116
Thompson, G. 89
Thompson, John B. 123, 126–7, 129–30, 132, 135–6, 139
Thürer, D. 71
toleration 66
Toqueville, Alexis de 21
totalitarianism 1, 3, 9, 14, 16, 50–1, 105–6, 109, 143–5, 149
trade 89
trade unions 6, 42
trans-national corporations 96
transparency 26
tribalism 151
truth 8, 21, 42, 113–15, 117

decontesting 119–20, 122, 125, 130, 134–5, 137
post-ideology debate 145–6

United Kingdom (UK) 15, 27–8, 59, 95, 147, 154
United Nations (UN) 95
United States (US) 3–4, 7
decontesting 123, 127, 132–4
populism 23–4, 27–8, 34
post-ideology debate 145–7, 153
post-Marxism 95–6
Al Qaeda 71–5, 77, 79–83
theory/praxis models 110
universalism 144
universities 7, 116–17
up-down 56–7, 60–3, 65–6, 68, 151
Urbinati, Nadia 22, 25
Us-Them 46, 68
use value 94
USSR *see* Soviet Union
utopias 42, 115, 122, 143–4, 149
Uzbekistan 76

values 88, 100, 113, 145, 153
Vietnam War 3
violence 71–2, 74–5
voters 1, 5–6, 24, 27, 60

Al-Wahhab, Mohammad ibn Abd 76, 82

Wahhabis 72, 76–8, 82
Walzer, Michael 29
wars 87, 96, 101, 109–10
Weber, Max 152
welfare state 4, 6–7, 20, 24–5, 27–8, 30–1, 33, 35, 150, 155
Wenman, M. 47
Wittgenstein, Ludwig 106, 150
Wolin, Sheldon 21, 31
women's movements 106
working class 104–5, 108
World Bank 10
World Social Forum 10

xenophobia 19–20, 32

Yemen 73
Young, - 117

Young Hegelians 99
Yugoslavia 9

Zarkawi, Abu Musab 73

Al-Zawahiri, Dr Ayman 73, 76–8
El-Zayat, Montasser 77
Zeitgeist 104–5
Žižek, Slavoj 122, 128, 137

CPSIA information can be obtained
at www.ICGtesting.com
Printed in the USA
BVOW04*1130270217
477125BV00005B/26/P

9 780415 366786